Buckskin Boys

Buckskin Boys

A History of the Buckskin Council, 1919–2004
Boy Scouts of America

W. JOSEPH WYATT

Pictorial Histories Publishing Company, Inc.
Charleston, West Virginia

LIBRARY OF CONGRESS CONTROL NO. 2004113987

ISBN: 1-57510-114-9

First Printing: October 2004

BOOK & COVER DESIGN Arrow Graphics, Missoula, Montana
PRINTED BY Jostens Printing, Visalia, Califorina

PUBLISHED BY
Pictorial Histories Publishing Company, Inc.
1125 Central Avenue, Charleston, WV 25302
PHONE (304) 342-1848, FAX (304) 343-0594
wvbooks@verizon.net

CONTENTS

Scoutmaster Bill Wyatt at New Orleans, July 1953, en route to the National Jamboree at Irvine Ranch, California.

Fifteen-year-old Joe Wyatt on the Adahi Trail, April 21, 1963. He's flanked by Jim Cottrell (left) and Jay Cottrell (right).

FOREWORD

WHEN MY FATHER, William H. "Bill" Wyatt, died on January 14, 2000, I was aware that he had been developing a manuscript outline and collecting photographs and other memorabilia for a history of the Buckskin Boy Scout Council of West Virginia. I found the materials he had collected, his outline and even the start-ups of several sections that he had written by hand on several yellow legal pads.

After I reviewed his material, it seemed only natural that the project be completed. As I worked to develop the history book he had started, I drew heavily on an earlier memoir written by the first Buckskin Council executive, M.H.F. Kinsey. Kinsey served the Charleston Area/Buckskin Boy Scout Council longer than anyone since, more than 25 years. Kinsey's memoir, written in 1948, detailed numerous events from the time he became the first scout executive in 1919 until his retirement in 1946. Thus, I owe a debt of gratitude to the late Mr. Kinsey. Much of the material in this council history was shamelessly borrowed from Kinsey's memoir.

There are many other people to thank as well. Chief among these is Stan Cohen of Pictorial Histories. Cohen was himself an Explorer Scout in Charleston and attended the 1953 National Jamboree in California. Ironically, that local area troop was led in part by my father. Cohen's publishing house, Pictorial Histories, has published several hundred books, many of them history related. Thus, Stan Cohen was a logical choice when it came to completing this book.

Two others who provided great help by reviewing several drafts of the book's manuscript and by searching out information on dozens of present and past scout troops are Robert Skinner and John Howell. Skinner also patiently helped me photograph numerous items shown in the book. Their help made the book much richer.

Others who contributed greatly to this book by providing photos, clippings, anecdotes, brochures, and other memorabilia include Russ Bennett, Chris Blankenship, Walter Caldwell, James Chandler, Judy Cooper, Clarence E. Dillon, James Dubee, Donald Ellis, David Emanuel, Ramona Erwin, Edward Hacala, Jan Hacker, Jeff Hall, Juanita Hanna, Newt Harmon, Dale Harwood, Susan Hayslett, Edgar Johnson, David Kelly, Ed Lewis, Mrs. Elena G. Lilly, Ann Meredith, Barbara Mitchell, Colvin Morgan, Chris Parsley, Roger Rasmussen, James Rice, Mrs. Kenneth Robbins, Carlton Starr, Ruth Stigall, Howard Swint, Leonard Taylor, Virginia Thompson, Benjamin Toliver, Jr., Andy Waddell, Elvin Wickline, Robert Wilson, Douglas Witten, and Stan Wyatt.

Additional thanks go to Debra Basham of the WV State Cultural Center who located several photos that appear in the book, to Buckskin Council Scout Executive Stan Willey who helped in numerous ways, and always did so quickly and completely, whenever I needed it. Thanks also to other council office staff who are pictured elsewhere in this book and to Barbara Wyant (who typed the manuscript). Thanks to family members Barbara Wyatt, Gerry Wyatt, Betsy Wyatt Douce and Tom Douce (who proofread the manuscript). Special thanks go to Dr. Michele Schiavone of Marshall University who did the excellent edit of the manuscript.

I would be surprised if there were not omissions in this book. My greatest concern is that I will have neglected to mention or feature a longtime contributor to Buckskin Scouting, or a pack, troop or post that should have been given ample space, but wasn't. I regret such omissions very much, for they have given their time, energy, creativity and other resources to advance the lives of Buckskin Council youth. They deserve our love and thanks.

In order to minimize such omissions I did the following: I twice placed announcements in the *Courier*, the Council's monthly newsletter, in which I sought photos, clippings, anecdotes and the like for this book; I gave interviews in which I requested materials from the public and which resulted in several articles about the project in the Charleston newspapers over the past two years; press releases requesting information were sent to all daily and weekly newspapers in the council (whether they all were actually published I don't know); requests for relevant information were sent to a dozen or more longtime scouters outside the Charleston-metro area, where material was more difficult to come by. They, in turn, were asked to pass my request along to others in their areas. All of these efforts were productive to some extent.

I hope you enjoy this book. And if my father is looking down at the finished product, I trust he will approve.

—W. Joseph Wyatt, 2004

A Note on the Council's Headquarters

Since 1978 the Buckskin Councils' headquarters has been located in Daniel Boone Park on Rt. 60 East, about one mile east of the State Capitol in Charleston.

The first office was established in 1919 in the downtown Masonic Building. By 1935 it had moved to Room 205 of the Public Library Building (the old State Capitol Annex) just east of the Lee Street triangle. Soon it was relocated to Room 215 of Charleston's Professional Building.

By 1963 the council headquarters had again been moved, this time to 1514 Kanawha Blvd. E. By 1967 the office had moved again, to nearby 1414 Kanawha Blvd. E. By 1977 the office was to be found at 1319 Quarrier Street prior to settling the following year in its present location at Daniel Boone Park. The office was re-dedicated as the William H. Wyatt Scout Service Center in July 2000.

Shots of the Buckskin Council headquarters, located in Daniel Boone Park.

INTRODUCTION

WHEN WILLIAM D. BOYCE, a Chicago publisher, stopped in London, England on a business trip, he did not know at the time that he would be inspired to organize the Boy Scouts of America. Losing his bearings in a heavy London fog, he was approached by a young boy with a lantern. The boy offered to guide him to his destination. When Boyce wanted to pay him, the boy said that he was a Scout and did not take money for a good turn.

The boy later led Mr. Boyce to a British scout office nearby. Boyce began to study the British scouting materials that he obtained there and listened as people gave accounts of their scouting activities.

He came to believe that this would be a good thing for American boys. Boyce became determined to start scouting in America and, on February 8, 1910, he filed papers incorporating the Boy Scouts of America in Washington, D.C.

Interestingly, a few scout troops were already in existence in the United States, mainly organized through the YMCA, so Boyce was persuaded that the existing troops could be of great help in getting the Boy Scouts established. Later, boys' groups such as Ernest Thompson Seton's Woodcraft Indians and Dan Beard's Sons of Daniel Boone and others came together to form the Boy Scouts of America as it is known today.

In the latter part of 1910 James C. West was hired as the first national Boy Scout Executive, a post he held for 42 years.

It is not known which community or communities had the very first scout troops in the United States. Several have made the claim. But it is known that by early 1910 dozens of troops had been established.

In addition to the YMCA, other troops grew out of Sunday school classes, school groups, and other organizations. Most of the troops took their programs from a book by the founder of scouting—Lord Baden-Powell's *Scouting for Boys*, as at that time the Boy Scout movement in the United States was yet to become well recognized.

Over the next ten years numerous scout councils grew up throughout the country. One such council was the Charleston Area Council, later known as the Buckskin Council.

EARLY BOY SCOUT REGISTRATION CARDS WERE TRI-FOLD AND FEATURED INTERESTING ARTWORK.

Badges and a neckerchief from Stan Cohen's personal collection.

A Note from the Publisher

I first met Bill Wyatt when I signed up, thanks to my parents' generosity, for the 1953 Scout Jamboree at Irvine Ranch, California. I was a member of Explorer Post II in Charleston at the time. Bill was our troop's scoutmaster for the jamboree and he appointed me as the troop's quartermaster. For a 15-year-old kid from West Virginia the trip to California was the greatest experience of my life up to that time. Bill was a great scoutmaster. It wasn't until almost 40 years later that I again became associated with him. By this time he was the scout emeritus of the Buckskin Council and founder and chief push for the wonderful scout museum.

I had moved west and was in the book publishing business and had encouraged Bill to finish his book on the history of the council. Unfortunately he died before writing the book, but it is a great credit to his son, Joe, to have finished the project. It is with great pleasure that I have had the opportunity to publish this book as a tribute to my old friend, Bill Wyatt.

This book will bring back memories to the old-timers and I hope will inform the present and future generations of scouts with a sense of their council's history. So sit back and enjoy a bit of scouting and area history.

—Stan Cohen, September 2004

Cohen's troop at the Charleston train station just before boarding a C&O train for the 1953 Scout Jamboree at Irvine Ranch, California. Front, left to right: Walter Witchey, Stan Cohen, Bill Miller. Back, left to right: Ted McClure, John Young, Larry Berman, and Walter Walker.

THE BUCKSKIN COUNCIL
THE BOY SCOUTS OF AMERICA
OHIO
WEST VIRGINIA
KENTUCKY
VIRGINIA
PUTNAM
PIONEER
KANAWHA
MOUNTAIN RIFLE
SCOUT SERVICE CENTER
CAMP CHIEF LOGAN
BRAXTON
CLAY
WEBSTER
NICHOLAS
WILDERNESS
POCAHONTAS
BOONE
FAYETTE
GREENBRIER
SENECA
BUCKSKIN SCOUT RESERVATION
LOGAN
RALEIGH
MINGO
CHIEF CORNSTALK
SUMMERS
MONROE
WYOMING
PIKE
CAMP MINTER
MCDOWELL
MERCER
GILES
MOUNTAIN DOMINION
TAZEWELL
BLAND
CAMP ROLAND

CHAPTER ONE

Organization & Early Activities

Before Buckskin's Formal Organization, 1910-1918 Charles P. Guice

CHARLES P. GUICE, AGE 35, IN FULL UNIFORM, 1917.

Even before the first full-time council executive, M.H.F. Kinsey, there was Charles P. Guice. Guice spent a lifetime working with young people, serving as a scoutmaster for various Boy Scout troops, and as camping director for several scout camps. He was also a teacher and principal in southern West Virginia schools for 40 years.

Guice was born July 21, 1882, in Fayette, Missouri. He attended schools in Meridian, Mississippi and Vanderbilt University in Nashville, Tennessee.

It was in 1908 that he began teaching in Harrison County, West Virginia, schools. He came to St. Albans in 1912 after serving as principal of Barrackville High School in Marion County, West Virginia. At St. Albans he was principal of the high school and was the first superintendent of the St. Albans School System from 1913 to 1920, with the exception of one year he spent serving in World War I.

Guice was coach of the first football team in St. Albans High School history. He later instituted football at Duval High School in Griffithsville, Lincoln County, where he served as principal from 1921 to 1923. From 1924 to 1926 he was principal at Matewan High School

Charles P. Guice chats with a young camper on an outing at Droop Mountain Battlefield State Park in 1930.

In this 1931 photo Guice was 49 years of age.

Guice in 1938.

age of 51. In those days there was no age limit on when an individual could attain the Eagle Scout rank. In fact, it was quite common for grown men to receive the award until mid-century when the age limit was set at 18 for receiving the Eagle badge.

It is thought that Guice was probably the first man to be commissioned as a scout master in the State of West Virginia. He received that commission on December 10, 1910, just seven months after the Boy Scout movement was organized in America. At that time he was serving as supervisor of Fairmont District Schools in Marion County. He organized Troop 1 in Barrackville in 1910, with 18 scouts. The following summer he conducted the first Boy Scout camp in West Virginia.

In July, 1913, Guice became the first superintendent of schools in the city of St. Albans. Legend has it that a scout named Edgar Delaney of St. Albans was in Charleston for some sort of celebration and Guice noticed the boy, who was in uniform, as he stood on the steps of the old Capitol building. As they chatted, Delaney said he was from St. Albans. Guice said to the boy that he would form a troop there. It was thereafter that he organized Troop 3 in that town, a troop which developed into one of the best scouting units in the country.

His leadership attracted national attention and he was commissioned by the National Council of Boy Scouts as Special Field Scout Commissioner in southern West Virginia. During those years Guice organized the first Boy Scout camp in Kanawha County which was located on the banks of the Coal River. Ultimately, he organized six of these camps that operated successfully between the years 1913 and 1921. As time went on Charles Guice became the scoutmaster of Troop 40, which was affiliated with Fairview Junior High School in the St. Albans area.

During his many years as a scout leader, Guice kept copious notes on his many scouting adventures. A memorable one occurred at the Coal River camp during the Summer of 1914. A

in Mingo County. Then he quit schoolwork for two years as he was suffering from ill health. But it is in his work with the Boy Scout movement that Charles P. Guice became best known to thousands of people in West Virginia. In scouting activities he taught boys about the outdoors, hunting, fishing, camping, good citizenship and helping others.

He was director of camping and pioneering for 20 years at Camp Chief Logan, a summer scout camp near Chapmanville in Logan County. The camp today is a vital part of the Buckskin Council's properties, the council having acquired it with a merger in the early 1990s.

One of the distinguishing features of Guice's career is that he was the first person in the Buckskin Council to receive the Silver Beaver Award, the highest award that can be given to a volunteer at the local level. Guice received the Silver Beaver in 1932.

In an interesting twist of fate, he received his Eagle Scout award one year later, 1933, at the

This photo, which was taken in 1942, shows scouter Guice at age 60, still quite active in the Boy Scout movement.

scout by the name of Nancarrow was bitten by a copperhead snake one night while doing guard duty. Guice immediately summoned the first-aid team and instructed them to bring the boy to the council fire. He was horrified to learn that the first-aid equipment which contained a number of snake bite remedies had been left at the station in St. Albans.

There was no physician closer than Madison, West Virginia, and there were no good roads to travel to get help. It was strictly up to Guice to meet the situation as best he could. Without delay he made six deep incisions in the boy's leg, and then applied two tourniquets. Fortunately, he had brought his own first-aid kit before leaving St. Albans. He was able to clean the wounds with some hydrogen peroxide. He then ordered the camp cook to make one gallon of strong coffee which was administered to the boy during the rest of the night to keep him awake. Although the methods used by Guice would not be approved by most physicians today, forty-six hours later Dr. S. H. Phillips came to the camp by the first train available and pronounced the treatment suitable, and the patient was by then beyond all danger. Scout Nancarrow later became a successful businessman in Ravenswood, West Virginia and a great booster of scouting.

Upon receiving the Silver Beaver Award in 1932, Guice was quoted as saying, "Scouting has enabled me to build men from boy material and I mean MEN. The records prove the assertion. My old-timers are, for the most part, married men and doing well. They are respectable citizens. Few have died. They are a safe, sane group. I am glad to say that very few failures are reported. Get me an average boy and with the aid of scouting I will make him a man good enough for any community."

Charles P. Guice died on September 16, 1953 at age 71 after forty-three years in the scouting movement. Interestingly, Guice had never married and there were no known survivors at the time of his death. He had lived alone in a room in the Bank of St. Albans Building on C Street in St. Albans. He is buried in Teays Hill Cemetery, St. Albans.

Beginnings of Formal Council Organization 1919-1928

Any history of the Buckskin Council must focus on M.H.F. Kinsey, who was its first paid executive. Kinsey was hired to run the Charleston area council office in 1919. But his story begins earlier than that, when he was teaching in a small Presbyterian school in Williamson, West Virginia in 1902. There Kinsey organized a boys' nature studies club. Their activities included hiking and camping in the wilds of southern West Virginia. Later Kinsey would recall nights he sat around the dying campfire, the boys asleep. He would think about the future of the boys. He asked himself what sort of men would they make?

In those early years Kinsey developed a lifelong interest in making boys into men, men of well-rounded character, citizens who would

FIRST BUCKSKIN COUNCIL SCOUT EXECUTIVE M.H.F. KINSEY IS SEEN OVERLOOKING AN AREA OF THE KANAWHA VALLEY ON ONE OF HIS MANY TRALBLAZING HIKES.

make worthwhile contributions to the life of the nation.

In 1911 Kinsey accepted a position with the railroad YMCA at Richmond, Virginia. He organized an athletic program, and first saw the game of basketball. Soon, though, he took another job, in Portsmouth, Ohio, becoming the director of social and religious work in the Portsmouth YMCA. There Kinsey was initially disappointed with his efforts to organize the boys into the YMCA.

By chance one evening as he was walking home he noticed a group of boys playing baseball. As he talked to them he discovered what he felt was the underlying and basic philosophy of working successfully with boys—that to gain their attention and their confidence one must be vitally interested in the things that they are.

Soon he organized a group of boys from the YMCA into the first boy scout troop in Portsmouth, Ohio. The troop was successful and soon there was a citywide scout organization which Kinsey headed as Scout Executive for a period of seven years. The Portsmouth council was one of the first organized in the United States. At the time Kinsey became the Portsmouth Scout Executive in March, 1911, there were fewer than a dozen scout executives nationwide.

In June, 1918, Kinsey left Portsmouth to become the Scout Executive in the Kalamazoo, Michigan council. But the severe winter took a toll on Kinsey's health and that of some members of his family. Although he had initially felt a strong desire to remain in Kalamazoo for a minimum of five years, on the morning of June 6, 1919 he found himself being interviewed in Charleston, West Virginia, by George S. Laidley. Laidley was superintendent of Charleston's public schools and had recently been elected the first president of the Charleston Area Boy Scout Council. When Kinsey had departed Kalamazoo the ground was covered with snow. When he

GEO. S. LAIDLEY, President REV. W. C. HARTINGER, Vice President OKEY JOHNSON, Secretary W. O. ABNEY, Treasurer

BOY SCOUTS OF AMERICA

CHARLESTON COUNCIL

HEADQUARTERS: 31 MASONIC BUILDING

Charleston-Kanawha, W. Va.

M. H. F. KINSEY, Scout Executive

July 16, 1919.

Lieut. Ben. Brown,
City.

Dear Scout Worker:

There will be a public meeting of the Charleston Court of Honor Friday afternoonof this week, July 18, at five o'clock in the Supreme Court room. You are cordially invited to be present and watch the Court in "action". You will also be interestedin the examinations to be given the First Class scouts for Merit Badges.

Trusting you can arrange to be present, I remain

Yours sincerely,

M. H. F. Kinsey

SCOUT EXECUTIVE.

One of the initial letters by first Council Executive M.H.F. Kinsey, a few weeks after he assumed the job.

George S. Laidley (left) was the first Council President, 1919, and W.E.R. Byrne was Council President from 1923–30.

arrived in Charleston the trees were in full bloom, the birds were singing and spring was in the air. He was unable to overcome the temptation of the better weather. He described getting off the train at the C&O Depot in Charleston and walking across the bridge to downtown.

> I glanced up the river toward Kanawha City. My reaction was not unlike the famous Rodgers-Hammerstein lyric, "I saw what I liked, and I liked what I saw, and I said to myself that's for me."

George Laidley had checked Kinsey's references from Portsmouth and was ready to hire him after the interview. But Laidley felt that other members of the council committee, as well as members of the community, ought to meet Kinsey before any decision was made.

Laidley asked Kinsey to give a presentation to the local Rotary Club at noon that same day in the Kanawha Hotel. Kinsey had about two hours to prepare. Laidley also asked Kinsey to make another presentation at 4:00 p.m. that afternoon to the council executive board. Laidley asked Kinsey to outline for the board his policies and program ideas. Kinsey was ready, as he had prepared much of his information before leaving Kalamazoo.

Kinsey's topic was "Dollars or boys?" In his presentation he emphasized the search for wealth that seemed universal in that day. He pointed out how many times we overlook much that is of value, especially of value to boys. Scouting was one such important program. The presentation which took place in the Chamber of Commerce rooms atop the old Capitol City Bank on Capitol Street, was a hit with the board. One of the scout board members, attorney W.E.R. Byrne, quizzed Kinsey relentlessly, as only a lawyer could, as to his genealogy, experience, views on current events and more. As the years passed Kinsey and Byrne became close friends.

Scouts at Castle Rock; Record Hiker

Here, on Castle Rock, are Scouts Douglas Venable, Charles Bekenstein, Billy Wyatt and Jack Slaughter. At the right is Billy Wyatt, the 1,000-mile hiker, on a bird study tour.

Castle Rock Termed Beauty Spot of Kanawha by Kinsey

Place, 12.5 Miles From City, Visited Frequently by Boy Scouts on Their Expeditions

According to M. H. F. Kinsey, Boy Scout executive, the real beauty spot from a scenic standpoint in Kanawha county is "Castle Rock" in Huffman's hollow, near the headwaters of Davis creek and 12½ miles from Charleston.

"This rock," he said Saturday, "is a huge cliff close to 300 feet above the bed of Middlelick fork of Davis creek in what is known as Huffman's hollow. From this eminence one gets a panoramic view of mountains for a distance of 10 miles. Perhaps there is no more isolated section in West Virginia, and one can travel for miles without seeing the trace of a cabin. Unlike most sections in the upper stretches of Davis creek this is a vast tract of virgin timber; it has not yet become acquainted with the axe-man, thanks to the owners who are real conservationists."

"It is a real job," Mr. Kinsey said, "to reach this cliff. The path winds round through a mass of briers and underbrush, and takes a full hour for the best seasoned hikers to reach the top. It is well worth the effort, however, and after reaching it you fell just like you would like to stay there indefinitely. A wonderful place for over-night camping. Nature has made ample provision for shelter, and you are far, far away from the noise and grind of civilization.

Scores of Streams

"Nearby are scores of mountain springs pouring forth streams of cold sparkling water. We found this spot on last Saturday a riot of wildflowers, and with me were a number of high school students who availed themselves of this opportunity to make a collection for their botany class.

"On the spur just across from 'Castle Rock' is the beautiful 'Balance Rock.' Not so high as the former, but a real rock to study if one is geologically inclined. Beneath this rock in the lower folds will be found snug sleeping berths, which Mother Nature has created. A pile of leaves in these nooks will make a bed fit for the gods. No writer can do justice to these two splendid rocks. The only way to thoroughly enjoy them is to visit them, but you must be able to take it as the boys express it. You can't reach it in an automobile, and I am rather thankful for that, for once the great gasoline caravan gets headed towards these beauty spots they will lose their native charm, and become as common-place as filling stations and billboards. Inaccessibility is right now their protection, and let's hope that this will continue for a long time.

Covered in a Day

"The round trip to Castle Rock and Balance Rock is a good 25 miles, and is usually covered by our hikers between 9 a. m. and 8 p. m., allowing two hours for exploration. The hike is only strenuous in the vicinity of the rocks. The steep climb through the many obstacles already mentioned is the only discomfort one will experience. But this is really no discomfort to the gang who call themselves Trail Blazers, older Boy Scouts who are connected with the explorer group of scouting. Billy Wyatt is perhaps the best hiker anywhere. Since coming into the organization he has 1,000 miles of hiking to his credit. Wyatt has won every hiking honor offered by the Charleston council. He is an enthusiastic lover of nature, especially birds and trees."

Explorer scouting is gaining wide favor in the Boy Scouts of America, and is spreading rapidly in Charleston and environs, Mr. Kinsey said.

Kinsey's Trail Blazer Hiking Club, which included socuts and others, was the focus of frequent newspaper articles, such as this one from 1934.

M.H.F. KINSEY IN THE 1930S.

As the years passed Kinsey presided over developments in scouting in the Charleston Area that are too numerous, rich and varied to capture completely in this book. Some of the highlights of Kinsey's tenure included the establishment of the first two summer camps, Camp Pequoni which served from 1920 until 1925, and Camp Walhonde which served scouts of the Council from 1926 until 1945. As Kinsey neared the end of his years as scout executive, Camp McClintick opened and served the scouts of the area from 1946 through 1959. By 1960 the present camp, Buckskin Reservation, located in Pocahontas County, opened for business.

Prior to Kinsey's arrival in Charleston there had been several troops operating in the Charleston Area. One of these was Troop 2 which was sponsored by Sacred Heart Parish. Its scoutmaster was William Coffey. It had been Coffey's practice to take his troop members on hikes after Mass every Sunday morning, their packs on their backs, headed for the hills. As Kinsey recalled it in his memoir they were never stopped by the elements. Neither rain nor snow prevented them from taking their

After returning to Kalamazoo and conferring with his wife, Kinsey made the decision to move to Charleston and become the first scout executive of the Charleston Area Council. The first scout office set up shop on June 7, 1919 at 31 Masonic Building. Scouting had begun to operate in Charleston.

One month later, on July 18, 1919, Kinsey had the meeting of Charleston's first Court of Honor. Its chairman was William Burdette Matthews, who was Clerk of the State Supreme Court. Other members of the Court of Honor were Byrne, Arch Kreig, Leo Loeb, and A. M. Heydrick.

Kinsey Recalls Southworth Incident

M. H. F. KINSEY, Boy Scout executive, was pulling with all his heart in the World series for the St. Louis Cardinals and not because he has anything against the Yankees. Mr. Kinsey and Billy Southworth, St. Louis manager, are old friends. But let Mr. Kinsey tell about it:

"I first became acquainted with Billy Southworth in 1912 when he was playing with the Portsmouth Cobblers in the old Ohio State league. But it was later that I became intimately acquainted with him when he used to spend his winters in Portsmouth and served under me as assistant scoutmaster in one of our Portsmouth troops. At that time we used to promote several baseball leagues, and Billy would conduct a baseball school in a church gym. I recall how we would have a load of sawdust hauled to the gym and spread on the floor so that he could teach the boys the art of base sliding.

"Once he came to me and wanted permission to take a rifle on a hike he had planned for his troop. I told him that it was contrary to our custom to carry firearms on a hike, but he insisted, stating that he would be personally responsible. I finally relented. Much to his embarrassment one of the boys picked up the rifle while Billy's back was turned. It went off accidentally and shot another boy in the leg. You can imagine how he felt and the next day found him entering my office with a hangdog expression. He said, 'I'll always take an older man's advice after this. Tough luck, one of the boys was shot through the leg, but not seriously. I hope you'll forgive me. I promise you that it will never happen again.'

"I saw him here in Charleston a few years later when he and the team was playing—the Boston Braves—an exhibition game. We both laughed heartily about the incident. He was a great hero with the boys of his troop and was a very efficient leader."

* * *

KINSEY CALLED OUT THE SCOUTS TO FIGHT THE FIRE THAT BURNED THE ORIGINAL CHARLESTON AREA STATE CAPITOL BUILDING IN 1921. THE SCOUTS SAVED THE RECORDS OF THE DEPARTMENT OF EDUCATION.

PICTORIAL HISTORIES PUBLISHING COMPANY COLLECTION

HERE KINSEY IS SEEN ON A TRAILBLAZER DAY HIKE, SEATED FIFTH FROM THE RIGHT. THIS PHOTO WAS TAKEN IN THE EARLY 1930S.

PAGE FOUR JUNE 5, 1944 — THE CHARLESTON DAILY MAIL

Scout Executive Marks 25th Anniversary at Present Post

A quarter of a century of service to West Virginia boyhood is the record of M. H. F. Kinsey, who celebrates Monday his 25th anniversary as scout executive of the Charleston Area Boy Scout council. The affair was marked simply by a congratulatory message and a handshake from Council President J. W. Londeree.

Mr. Kinsey came to Charleston June 5, 1919 to start southern West Virginia's first organized Boy Scout movement. Scouting had been introduced in this area several years before, but it was not until the arrival of this benevolent, talented Virginian that an organization of adults was formed for the express purpose of spreading the scouting idea, finding and training leaders and working for the general welfare of boys.

As the senior executive of Boy Scout Region 4, comprising West Virginia, Ohio and Kentucky, he has an admirable record to his credit. Under his direction, the council has increased its membership from 150 boys and a negligible number of adult leaders in 1919 to a present all-time high figure of 4,365 boys and 1,341 men. In the council's ten counties there are now 3,787 Boy Scouts (ages 12 to 15), 481 Cubs (ages 9 to 12), and 97 Senior Scouts (15 years or older). The organization has made it possible for 12,500 boys to enjoy the healthful experiences of camping and has awarded about 200,000 merit badges to scouts who have participated in the personal attainment program of the Boy Scouts of America. Eagle Scout badges, symbols of the highest rank in scouting, have been awarded to 279 boys.

Mr. Kinsey was born and educated in Virginia. He attended a school for Y. M. C. A. secretaries and in 1912—two years after the Boy Scout movement was brought to this country from England—he became a scoutmaster at Portsmouth, O. He later was appointed scout executive there and organized the Portsmouth council, now headed by a former member of is scout troop. Immediately prior to coming to Charleston he was employed as a scout executive at Kelemazoo, Mich.

Mr. Kinsey is a writer, a musician, and, above all, a man who has a heart interest in boys.

"During my 32 years in this work," he said, "my confidence in scouting and as a youth program has grown steadily. I am proud of our finished product, especially in these war days. My pride soars to new heights when I pick up our local newspapers and read of heroic acts being performed almost daily by our former Boy Scouts. I am thinking particularly of one boy who, after every one of his companions had been killed in a plane battle, brought the limping machine back to base while suffering major injuries himself. I knew that lad when he was starting in scouting some ten years ago. I feel confident that a goodly share of the resourcefulness and courage he displayed on this occasion was

M. H. F. Kinsey Congratulated

J. W. Londeree (left) of South Charleston, president of the Charleston Area Boy Scout council, is shown congratulating M. H. F. Kinsey on his 25th anniversary as the council's scout executive. Mr. Kinsey has been a professional Scouter for 32 years—a record unequalled by any other scout executive of West Virginia, Ohio and Kentucky.

Sunday hikes. Coffey said of his hikes in the inclement weather, "I never had a boy to catch a cold on a hike, because they knew how to dress for such an occasion." Another active troop at the time was Troop 13 whose scoutmaster was Emmett Thaxton. In 1929 when the council expanded out of Charleston and became a twelve-county area, Thaxton was hired as Kinsey's assistant, mainly due to his outstanding volunteer record, going back to before Kinsey's arrival in Charleston.

Other pioneers during the initial five to ten years of the council included A. W. Paull, the Reverend B. F. Sparrow, Benjamin B. Brown, E. O. Leighley, John N. Abbott, J. C. McCoy, Harry Morris, Charles P. Guice, N. C. Howard, Howard Luckey, George Lewis, Paul M. Dreibelbis, and others.

Early Outdoor Activities

Kinsey was an outdoorsman who loved camping and hiking. One of his routine activities was a hiking club known as the Appalachian Trailblazers. This likely was the first hiking club in West Virginia. It survived for 20 years and was not exclusive to Boy Scouts, as Kinsey permitted other interested individuals to join in.

But most of the Trailblazers were Boy Scouts, and when they hiked, Kinsey was there. Most of the hikes were about 20 miles, and they usually occurred on Saturday. Kinsey plotted the route on his topographical maps and off they went.

To stimulate interest in the Trailblazers Kinsey gave awards for distance hiking. When a member completed his one hundredth mile, he was awarded a wolf emblem. At two hundred and fifty miles he received a patch with a pine tree. On completion of five hundred miles the boy would receive an Indian's head patch, and an "ATB" shield patch was awarded at 750 miles. Kinsey made the felt patches with the exception of one, a pirate's head given on completion of one thousand miles hiking. The first to receive the pirate's head, which Kinsey called the corsair, was Bill Wyatt, the scouter who inspired this book.

Often as Kinsey hiked he recited a poem to the boys. Its author was noted American poet Hamlin Garland.

> Do you fear the force of the wind, the slash of the rain?
> Go face them and fight them. Be savage again.
> Go hungry and cold like the wolf,
> Go wade like the crane.
>
> The palms of your hands will thicken,
> And the cheeks of your face will tan.
> You'll grow rugged, and weary and swarthy,
> But you'll walk like a man.

Later, himself a scoutmaster, Bill Wyatt frequently recited that same poem to his own scouts. It exemplified Kinsey's, and Wyatt's, thinking about the importance of a rugged outdoor life in the development of young boys into men.

The Trailblazers hiked many trails in the Kanawha Valley. One of their favorites began at the C&O Railway Station in Charleston and was twenty miles round trip to the headwaters of Huffman's Branch of Davis Creek where the boys found "castle rock" and nearby "balanced rock." There they enjoyed a panoramic view of the countryside. The state later purchased the land and the area became part of Kanawha State Forest.

Kinsey also frequently organized out-of-town hiking and camping trips. One of these occurred in August, 1935. He took three boy scouts, Stanley Wyatt (uncle of the author), Donnally Morris, Jr., and Charles Watts.

They camped near Carter Caves, Kentucky. After some initial exploration they found a route to an underground passageway. Morris was selected to mark the trail so that they would be able to enjoy a safe return. Watts looked after the lighting and Wyatt was elected the camera man.

After traveling a mile under ground, at times through knee deep icy water, they came upon a cavern filled with stalactites and stalagmite formations. Later, in a large room they found fluted columns, draperies in broad folds, cascades of snow white stone, and other formations seldom seen. With only two lanterns and fear that their kerosene supply was becoming low, they reluctantly returned to daylight.

"Mobilizations" were another important part of the early scouting program in the Charleston area. Each spring, leaders staged a full mobilization of the scouts. They tried to make it as realistic as possible, with no advance notice. Kinsey's assistant, Emmit Thaxton, had a flair for the dramatic and orchestrated the mobilizations himself. A system was devised whereby scouts could quickly communicate with one another by telephone after first receiving a coded message from a leader.

The code included details indicating what to bring and where to meet. For example, the code 1489-630 included location "1" which was the vacant lot where the C&P Telephone offices later stood. The number "4" stood for first-aid kit, "8" meant scout staff, and "9" was flashlight. 630 was the time for assembling. A message would be sent out as following: "Mobilize-1489-630."

One of these mobilizations occurred on April 6, 1928. Kinsey was sitting at his desk at scout headquarters in the Masonic Building that morning when the phone rang around 11:00 o'clock. The voice he heard was that of a forest ranger at Bee Mountain Tower. "Can you let me have some Boy Scouts at once?" he asked. "We have two bad fires on Cabin Creek, and we need some good firefighters."

By noon, troops and supplies were moving and by 3:00 p.m. 60 boys and a suitable number of leaders had traveled 25 miles, including crossing Kanawha River by ferry at Coalburg, to reach the fire site. Sixty additional scouts arrived from Cedar Grove and East Bank, towns close to the fire area. Scouts in the nearby communities of Kayford and Decota were notified to hold themselves ready in case more help was needed.

The scouts fought the flames at Piney Ridge that day. They were under the supervision of trained forest rangers and they worked in relays so as to have some rest. They had various jobs including beating out the fire in the underbrush, digging trenches and felling trees.

The scouts worked into the night in one-hour shifts. Finally, at 3:00 a.m. the fire was under control and by dawn all danger had passed. Rain began to fall at 7:00 a.m. as well. Forest lands and rural homes had been saved thanks to the scouts.

Scouts who participated in fighting the fire of Piney Ridge went on to have outstanding records as citizens as well. Some of them were Fred Scott who became a successful physician in Madisonville, Kentucky; Vinson Wilson who went to work for Carbide-Carbon Corporation in Charleston; Tom Robertson who operated a successful filling station on the west side of Charleston; Edwin Shepard who became a physician and eye specialist in Charleston; John Bruner who became the dean of a boy's prep school in Richmond, Virginia; Melvin Mathes and John Quinland who went into the retail business in Charleston.

Others were Edward King who became a physician at Pinecrest Sanitarium in Beckley;

For Kinsey's "Trailblazer" group a number of awards were earned. Kinsey made the awards by hand with the exception of the 1,000 mile award, which was a professionally made pirate patch, the "Corsair" as Kinsey termed it.

THIS 1912 PHOTO SHOWS EARLY SCOUTER CHARLES P. GUICE, REAR, SECOND FROM RIGHT, WITH A GROUP OF SCOUTS PREPARED FOR A CAMPING EXPERIENCE.

WEST VIRGINIA STATE ARCHIVES AND ST. ALBANS HISTORICAL SOCIETY

Lawrence Winter who went on to a career as a chemical engineer in Pittsburgh; and Tom Mathes who later became an important administrator with the Chesapeake and Potomac Telephone Company.

Still others were Ernest Garton who became a scout official in Charleston; Frank Clarke who became the assistant fire chief in Charleston; Gordon Wood who later became a professor at Davidson College in North Carolina; Lloyd Auer who developed a career as an orchestra leader and traveled from coast to coast; and Charles Albert who became an official with the WestVaco Company in South Charleston.

Perhaps the most important mobilization occurred on January 3, 1921 (photo, page 10) when West Virginia's State Capitol Building burned. The first capitol building in Charleston was located at the corner of Capitol and Washington

THIS 1924 PHOTO SHOWSL A GROUP OF ST. ALBANS AREA SCOUTS WHO WERE HIKING TO POINT PLEASANT. OBVIOUSLY, AN OVERNIGHTER.

WEST VIRGINIA STATE ARCHIVES AND ST. ALBANS HISTORICAL SOCIETY

THURSDAY EVENING, SEPTEBER 5, 1935

Unexplored Caves Penetrated by Boy Scout Executive and Three Youths of Charleston

Above are the three youths who accompanied Boy Scout Executive M. H. F. Kinsey on an exploration trip into the caverns of Carter county, Kentucky. Left to right, Stanley Wyatt, Donnally Morris and Charles N. Watts, Jr. Mr. Kinsey is shown in the photograph at the right before the mouth of Crooked cave, a supposedly haunted cavern the four visited. It is one of the hundreds of caverns in Carter county that are not generally known and which had great scenic possibilities, according to the scout executive.

Scout Executive M.H.F. Kinsey and three older scouts enjoyed an adventure in the caves of Kentucky.

Streets, where later the Diamond Department Store and Kanawha Valley Bank stood. Kinsey described it like this:

> I was returning to my office from lunch, and I was crossing Elk River on the Virginia Street Bridge. I could see a great volume of smoke rising from the roof of the State House. Soon there was the shriek of sirens. When I reached the scene of the fire I was happy to note that Boy Scouts were already on the job. Scoutmasters Abbott and Leighley had already assembled their troops for the purpose of removing valuable state records from the burning building. Local schools were notified immediately upon my arrival at Scout Headquarters, and more scouts were excused for duty at the fire. We had to work quickly as the fire spread rapidly, and the falling walls presented a real menace. Scoutmaster Thaxton's brother, who was a city fireman, lost his life soon after the fire started. In less than an hour every record of the State Department of Public Schools was saved by the scouts. The fire was so rapid that it was impossible to save other records with but a scout membership of slightly over 200. This service might well be called the Charleston Boy Scouts' first community good turn.

This patriotic parade, probably on Kanawha Street, occurred circa 1918. Notice some of the scouts are wearing helmets of captured Germans. At left, a scout carries a sabre and rifle as the boy in front of him marches "hands up."

West Virginia State Archives and Benjamin B. Brown Senior Center

Rallies, such as this 1935 Troop 71 event in Charleston were common arenas in which scouts could demonstrate the various skills including first aid. The scouts pictured here are, from left: Jim Bailey, Joe Thomas, Glenville Hayes, and Noble Wyatt. The scout on the ground is not identified.

CHAPTER TWO

Expansion, 1929–1991

The Council Expands, 1929

In April 1929, Ted Foley, who was Deputy Regional Executive of the Boy Scouts of America, came to Charleston to meet with the Executive Board. Foley told the board that their duties would no longer be confined to the corporate limits of Charleston. The council would become an area council. Foley told the board members that the area council would include twelve counties: Kanawha, Boone, Raleigh, Fayette, Greenbrier, Pocahontas, Webster, Nicholas, Braxton, Clay, Putnam, and Lincoln.

The Reverend Frank C. Brown was elected President of the Charleston Area Council. Emmett Thaxton, a man with many years' experience as a scoutmaster, was approved as the Assistant Scout Executive to Kinsey.

The increased job responsibilities made for an arduous task, a great deal of it falling on Thaxton's shoulders. He did much of the traveling from Hurricane to Marlinton, and from Sutton to Beckley.

The size of the job may be measured by the increased manpower that later was required. By 1946 the area had been reduced to nine counties and had a staff of ten to serve it.

By the late 1940s the council's name had been changed to the Buckskin Council. Over the years there were other mergers and consolidations of areas. For example, in June, 1990, the Chief Cornstalk Council with headquarters in Logan, West Virginia, was merged and became part of the Buckskin Council. In January, 1991 the Appalachian Council, whose office was in Bluefield, West Virginia, consolidated with the Buckskin Council as well.

There were several reasons for the mergers. First was economics. Employment in the southern coalfields had dropped dramatically by the 1990s, creating a financial burden on those two councils. With the national council downsizing, the Buckskin Council was affected as well. Presently the Buckskin Council consists of 23 counties, including three in Virginia and part of one in Kentucky.

The mergers were disappointing to many of the scouts, volunteers and executives in the Logan and Bluefield area councils. They had enjoyed long and proud traditions. Fortunately, most of the volunteer scouters in those two councils continued to work and help make Buckskin a strong council. Most of the professionals in the two councils were given opportunities to continue their positions as they became part of the Buckskin Council.

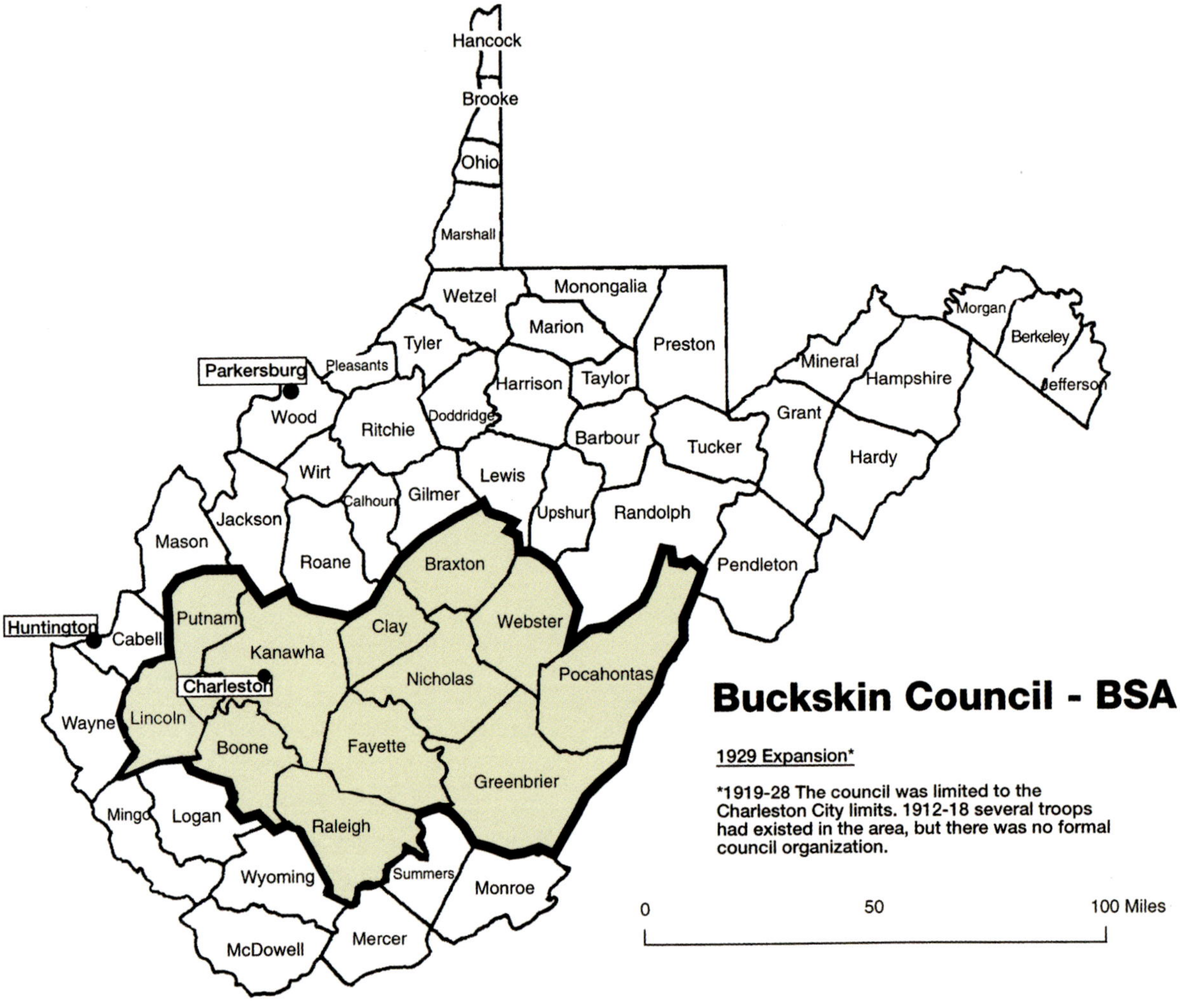

At the publication of this history the alignment of the Buckskin Council's districts was as follows:

Chief Cornstalk: Boone, Logan, and Mingo Counties in West Virginia, and the eastern third of Pike County, Kentucky.

Mountain Dominion: McDowell, Mercer, and Monroe Counties in West Virginia, and Tazwell, Bland, and Giles Counties in Virginia.

Mountain Rifle: Kanawha County east of Institute.

Pioneer: Western Kanawha County, Putnam County, Lincoln County.

Wilderness: Braxton, Clay, Webster, Nicholas, Greenbrier, and Pocahontas Counties.

The years leading to these mergers saw the council change and develop. The 1954 Annual Report showed that 10,796 cubs, scouts and explorers were registered in the council. They were served by 242 packs, troops and posts. That year 25 earned the Eagle rank. As the 1950s turned into the 1960s the council continued to serve greater numbers of boys. As but one "snapshot" example, the council's 1967 Annual Report showed that 49 new Packs, Troops and Explorer Posts had been organized that year, bringing the Council to a total of 389 units with 8,825 boys registered. That year alone 68 boys had achieved Eagle rank and 3,119 had advanced at least one rank. An all-time high of 1,913 boy-weeks were spent at Buckskin Scout Reservation that year, 53 explorers and older scouts camped at Philmont, New Mexico, and nine had participated in the XII World Jamboree.

The council operated eight districts in the 1960s. Changing times, mergers and the like have resulted in re-drawing of district boundaries and re-naming of districts. But in 1967-68 the districts were known by these names: Pioneer, Scowego, Long Rifle, Shawnee, Burning Springs, Fayette, Greenbrier Valley and Nine Rivers. Council officers at that time were: Bishop Wilburn C. Campbell, President; John B. Hover, Council Commissioner; Sam C. Hill, Vice President; James R. Thomas, II, Vice President; J. D. Treanor, Vice President; Art Greiner, Scout Executive; and Jack Richmond, Assistant Scout Executive.

As the 1960s turned into the 1970s times were changing. The Vietnam War burgeoned, then ended. To some extent the national pessimism that was discussed endlessly by sociologists and philosophers seemed to have an impact upon the council. Also, the booming days of 1950s West Virginia coal were behind us, finances again got tighter within the council, but the council pushed ahead to make scouting viable for boys and girls. The changes affected the council in various ways, but most evident were the declines in numbers of cubs, scouts and explorers registered, and in the number of units chartered. By 1977 the council showed 4,882 boys (and girls, as Explorers now accepted girls) registered, and 241 units in operation.

By the 1980s it had become evident that from a financial standpoint additional changes would be called for. Following mergers of 1990 and 1991, and the re-alignment of districts into those that we recognize today, there were 8,026 cubs, scouts and explorers registered in 353 units. Those numbers represented a 30% increase in registrations from the previous year, placing the council's growth first among the 85 councils in Buckskin's thirteen-state region.

But it was clear that not enough Cub Scouts had been making the transition to Boy Scouts, and older youth needed encouragement. Because of these concerns, the mid-to-late 1990s saw the council focus additional attention on those groups. One result was the establishment of the Learning for Life program which saw a 45 percent increase in Exploring registrations from 1997 to 1998.

At the publication of this book the council showed 9,958 registrations and 363 units, as the youth of Buckskin Council continued to be served by dedicated professionals and volunteers.

CHIEF CORNSTALK, VIRGINIA EXPANSIONS

IN 1990, THE CHIEF CORNSTALK Council, comprised of Boone, Logan, and Mingo Counties in West Virginia, and about one-third of Pike County, Kentucky, consolidated with the Buckskin Council. The consolidation was necessary because of changing times, and because of economic factors and the decline of the coal industry in Southern West Virginia and Eastern Kentucky.

The Chief Cornstalk Council has a rich history that predates the 1990 merger. The council was first organized in 1926 as the Logan County Council. It was chartered with six troops and 140 Boy Scouts. Dr. C. B. Morris was the first council president and served in that office for nearly 17 years.

In 1930, Boone County was added to the council, and in 1934, Mingo County and the sixth magisterial district of Pike County, Kentucky, were added. By 1955, the Washington and Duval Townships in Lincoln County had been added, and a year later the seventh magisterial district of Pike County, Kentucky, had been added. In October, 1954 the name of the council became the Chief Cornstalk Area Council.

The Logan Rotary Club had been the force behind the original organization in Logan

THE COAL CAMP COMMUNITY OF DEHUE, LOGAN COUNTY, FEATURED A SCOUT TROOP LED BY SCOUTMASTER ADAM JOHNSTON. THIS PHOTO, EVIDENTLY TAKEN JUST BEFORE CHRISTMAS AS EVIDENCED BY THE LIGHTS ON THE TREE IN THE REAR, SHOWS THE BOYS DOING A GOOD TURN BY COLLECTING FOOD FOR THE NEEDY. THE TROOP, WHICH WAS SPONSORED BY THE YOUNGSTOWN MINE CORPORATION, SHOWS THE FOLLOWING SCOUTS (LEFT TO RIGHT): BILL SCHRODER MAYS, FRANK MARIANO (IN HAT), JOHNNY PATRICK, PETER COZMYK, WOODROW DILLO, GIDEON DEAN, JOHN HATFIELD, PAUL BENCY, GEORGE LEWIS, TONY LEPETRONE, SILAS MARIANO (IN HAT), ______ PATRICK, SAMMY LEPETRONE, CLARENCE BAILEY, BILL MCCOY, VICTOR VIDOVICH, FRED SCHRODER, LOUIE ZETO, MILLARD "DIXIE" HOWELL, MANUEL DILLO, AND JIM BENCY. IN THE BACKGROUND, FROM THE LEFT, ARE THE DEHUE GRADE SCHOOL, THE POST OFFICE AND THEATER, AND THE COMPANY STORE.

County. The first scout executive, Carter Haley, was hired in 1926. He served until 1929 when he was succeeded by Dan Riley. Other scout executives over the years included Scottie McPherson, Edgar P. Christopher, O. B. Roberts, and Mark E. Lutman, who served the council well from the 1930s to 1961.

From the '60s through the '80s, the scout executives included Robert Justice, Kenneth Ackeret, William Fish, Sam Warner, Donald Cheek, and Richard Kelley.

During the tenure of O. B. Roberts, in the 1940s, the council acquired 805 acres on the Garrett's Fork of Big Creek for Camp Chief Logan. The acquisition was made possible by the Yawkey-Freeman Land Company, and the actual purchase of the land was made by the Island Creek Coal Company. The camp opened in the Spring of 1952. It continues to serve the Buckskin Council today as the Scout Training Center. During the two or three years prior to the publication of this book the camp sustained severe damage due to flooding. However, with the cooperation of many volunteers the restoration has been completed.

Over the years the Chief Cornstalk Council grew substantially. By January 1964, records

Troop 51 at a Show-And-Do, 1950s or early '60s.

ABOVE: THESE TROOP 51 SCOUTS ARE SEEN IN 1963 DURING A DEMONSTRATION BY BOBBY WALLS. THE SCOUTS TAKING IN THE DEMONSTRATION ARE, LEFT TO RIGHT: ALVIN GLEASON, ROGER BRYANT, RICHARD BRAY, AND T. V. HALL. THEIR SCOUTMASTER WAS DALE HARWOOD. INSET: DONNIE WILKS AND PETE LOWE OF TROOP 51 PRACTICE THEIR LASHINGS IN THIS 1963 PHOTO TAKEN AT CAMP CHIEF LOGAN.

showed a total of 184 cub packs, scout troops and explorer units, with a total of 4,666 scouts and leaders registered. For many years the council service center was located at 503 Stratton Street in Logan.

The first eagle scout in the council, whose name is unknown, is thought to have been a member of Troop 2, Holden, West Virginia (which later became Troop 36). Among early recipients of the Eagle badge from that troop were Dominic Dardi, Ralph Dodd, Bill Lee, and James E. Estepp. Another early Eagle Scout was Richard Brown whose troop was located in Chatteroy. Also of significance, Troop 2 Scoutmaster L. H. "Hutch" Hutchinson served as camp director and program director at Camp Chief Logan for 38 camping seasons, an amazing record. Many other dedicated leaders have served the Chief Cornstalk Council and District. Some of the names that come to mind are: Hivens Snodgrass, Quentin Howard, Doc Howard, Willard Peale, Bob Peale, R. B. Foster, Seaton Coleman, Andy Emody, Carter Williamson, Mr. Vickers, Newman Merritt, Bob Ross, John Coleman, Duffy Mays, Dale Harwood, Bill Epperly, Bob Padgett, Tennis Sampson, Paul Merritt, Whitney Warren, Brooks Lawson, Charles Albert, Joe Fish, and Harry White.

Much of the information about the Chief Cornstalk Council cited above came from a 1964 history of the council authored by Robert E. Justice who was then the council's Scout Executive.

Above: Chief Cornstalk Area Wood Badge Recipients seen at Camp Chief Logan. Below: A more recent Chief Cornstalk Wood Badge camp staff pictured here.

Much of the more recent history was obtained from long-time Logan Scoutmaster and attorney Douglas Witten. Witten was scoutmaster of Troop 217 in Logan for 31 years. He had an active troop and over the years about 75 boys of Troop 217 received the Eagle Scout award.

The Council Expands Again—1991

Six months following the 1990 expansion—in which the Buckskin Council embraced Boone, Logan, and Mingo Counties in West Virginia and the Eastern areas of Pike County, Kentucky (previously known as the Chief Cornstalk Council)—the council grew larger again, this time taking in three more West Virginia counties and three counties in Virginia.

The new additions to the Buckskin Council, now called the Mountain Dominion District, included McDowell, Mercer, and Monroe Counties in West Virginia, and Bland, Giles, and Tazewell Counties in Virginia.

Much of the interesting and varied history of the district comes from longtime Princeton, WV scouter, David Emanuel. His research shows that around 1925 there were seven boy scout troops in the Mercer and McDowell County areas, and the

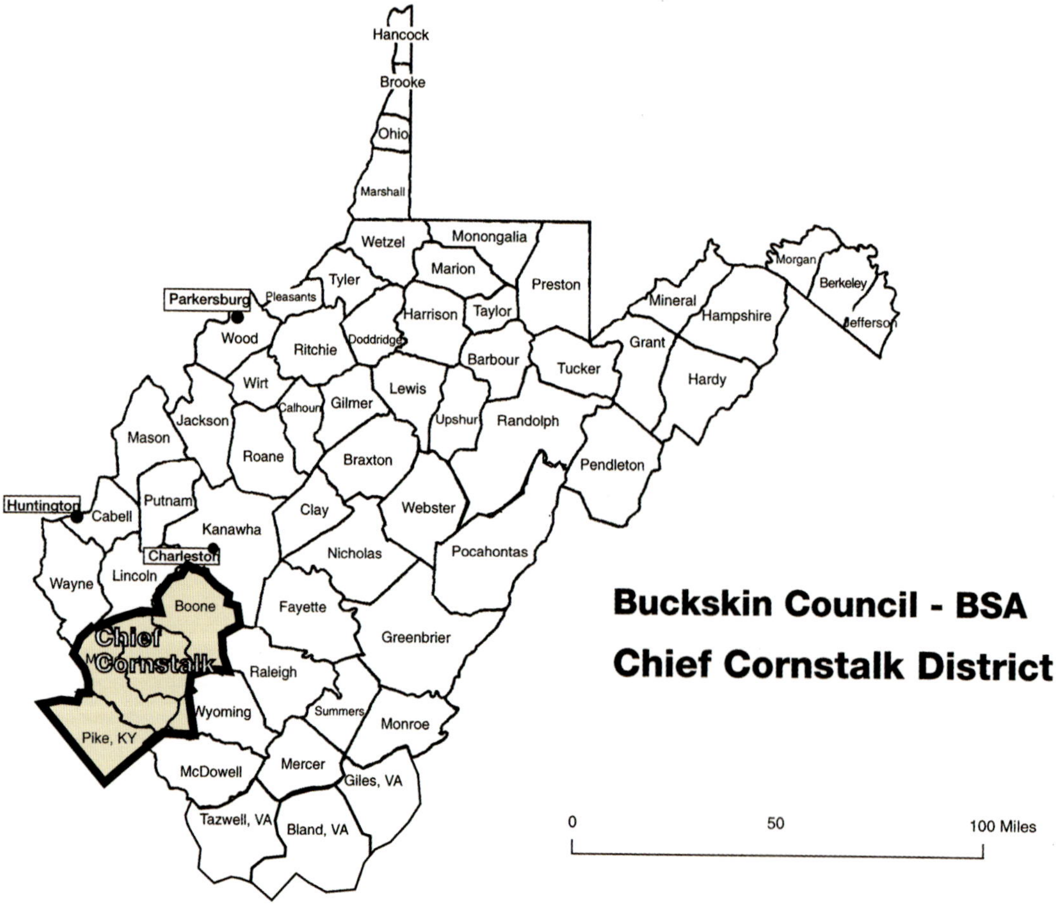

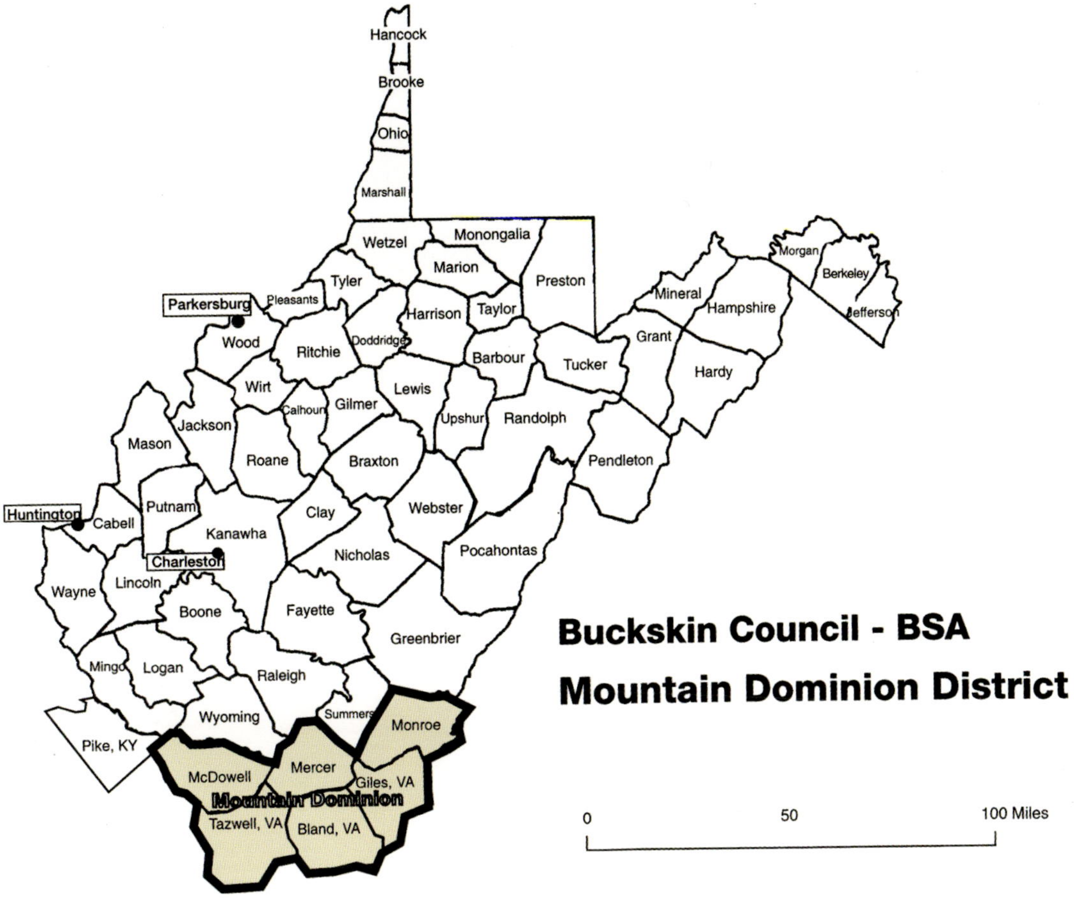

Boy Scout program was beginning to grow. As a result, the Welch, West Virginia, Rotary Club became interested in sponsoring a project to form some type of organization that would assist the already existing troops, and would help new ones become organized.

Rotarians from Welch, Keystone, and Bluefield, West Virginia, applied for and were granted a charter from the National Council of the Boy Scouts of America on April 1, 1935, and a formal organization was born. The council was given the name Southern West Virginia Area Council and included five of the six counties that make up the district today. The exception is that today's district includes Monroe County, while the original organization did not. Instead it included Summers County of West Virginia.

With the help of the Rotarians, one year later on April 17, 1936, the State of West Virginia granted a charter to the council with J. R. Anderson as president and C. H. Atkinson as Scout Executive.

In time a new Scout Executive named Roland took over. However, he was killed in an automobile accident on East River Mountain and J. C. Acuff was hired as the next Scout Executive. Some say that the council's summer camp, Camp Roland, which is located a few miles south of Bluefield in Bland County, Virginia, was named for the deceased Scout Executive, although it is not known for sure whether that is the case.

Camp Roland is a 100-acre site that was donated to the scout movement by Mr. and Mrs. Laurence E. Tierney, Jr., of Bluefield. Once the land had been donated, a major campaign was undertaken to raise $67,000 to develop the camp. At the time of that campaign in 1948 and '49, there were 104 cub packs, scout troops, and explorer units with 2,970 scouts registered.

In 1949, the council changed its boundaries. The National Council of the Boy Scouts of America removed Summers County and Wyoming County, West Virginia (which had been

Boys of Six Counties in Two States
Will Have Unsurpassed Camping Facilities

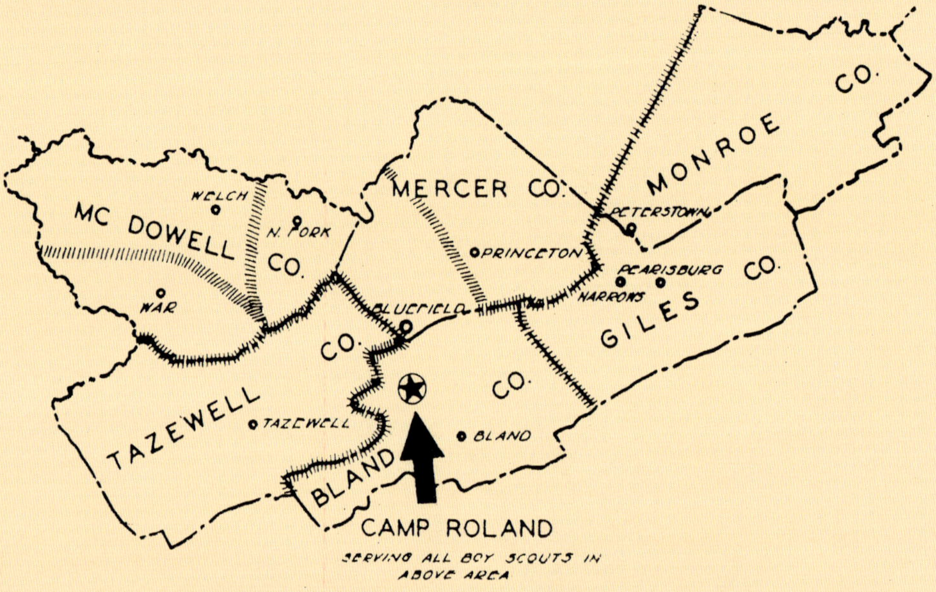

MEMBERSHIP AS OF DECEMBER 31, 1948

COUNTY	No. of Units	No. of Scouts
MERCER	34	991
McDOWELL	51	1361
MONROE	3	79
TAZEWELL	7	203
BLAND	3	85
GILES	6	251
TOTAL	104	2970

There are 7950 Boys of Scouting age in the area.
Our job is to give these boys a chance!

A 1949 BROCHURE SHOWED SCOUTING TO BE STRONG IN THE COUNTIES LATER TO BECOME THE MOUNTAIN DOMINION DISTRICT OF THE BUCKSKIN COUNCIL.

Archery is big at the Mountain Dominion District's Camp Roland, Virginia.

These Camp Roland Scouts are lashing a large tri-pod, suitable for cooking stew.

added to the council) and also took Raleigh County, West Virginia, which had been part of the Charleston Area Council, and formed the Appalachian Council which was then headquartered in Beckley, West Virginia.

By 1955, Jack L. Lewis succeeded the retiring Mr. Acuff as Scout Executive of the Council. Lewis had worked for Acuff as a Field Scout Executive in Middleboro, Kentucky, and was the Assistant Scout Executive in the Buckskin Council in Charleston at the time.

A year later the Appalachian Council of Beckley and the Southern West Virginia Area Council of Bluefield merged, with Mr. Lewis continuing as the Executive. The headquarters remained in Bluefield, West Virginia, and the new name for the combined councils became the Appalachian Council.

Lewis served the council long and well, retiring after 30 years of service on March 1, 1985. Don Voll, who had been with the Blackhawk Council of Rutford, Illinois, was selected as the new Scout Executive. However, two weeks later he resigned. Thus, in April, 1985, Paul Perkins became the Scout Executive. Perkins had worked under Jack Lewis as District Executive in the Seneca District of the Appalachian Council and was hired away from the Buckskin Council in Charleston where he had been Assistant Scout Executive.

Wayne Hartley leads singing at Camp Roland.

As times continued to change it was decided at the national level that six of the nine counties of the Appalachian Council would consolidate with the Buckskin Council headquartered in Charleston. That was accomplished on January 1, 1991, at which time the six counties became the Mountain Dominion District of the Buckskin Council.

THE KLONDIKE SLED RACE IS HELD AS PART OF THE WINTER CAMPOREE AT CAMP ROLAND.

BASTIAN, VIRGINIA, WAS THE SITE OF A MAJOR EAGLE SCOUT PROJECT. AN INDIAN VILLAGE IS UNDER CONSTRUCTION IN THIS PHOTO.

A LARGE INDIAN LODGE IS TAKING SHAPE AT BASTIAN, VIRGINIA.

CHAPTER THREE

The Depression and World War II

The Boy Scouts, like every other thread of the fabric of American life in the 1930s, was adversely affected by the Depression.

At a council board meeting in 1931 that fact was evident. The men around the conference table at that meeting were mostly businessmen whose enterprises were crumbling. Some had already lost their savings and lifetime investments.

The discussion focused on whether the council could keep going. A resolution was made that the

1930s CCC newspaper photo. Courtesy of Stan Cohen.

council cease its programs until better times returned. There were others at the table who agreed.

Then an old scouter who had helped lay the foundations of scouting in Charleston took the floor. His name has been lost to history but his words live on.

He made a passionate appeal as he pictured the moral disaster that would result from the abandonment of social agendas of all kinds. Abandonment of these programs would be more disastrous, he contended, than anything imaginable.

His timely appeal saved the day, and a few weeks later the largest budget to that time had been raised.

As part of the solution to the problems of the Depression, Kinsey dropped his assistant, Emmett Thaxton. Thaxton had given up a good paying job to enter scouting full time as a new profession. Kinsey also gave up his full-time secretary and took a fifteen percent pay cut in order to keep things going. The council's appropriation to operate summer camp was lopped off, and it was not restored until 1944. As Kinsey put it, ". . . we were fighting for our very existence . . . many men today (1948) will sit down and coolly write a check for one thousand dollars . . . but during the Depression they deliberated at great length before they could make up their mind to make it ten."

It was through the determination of many long-time scouters that scouting in the Charleston area survived the Great Depression of the 1930s. Some area councils in other states did not survive. It is to the credit of those who worked long and hard through the dark Depression years that the council made it.

The World War II Years

During World War II the scouts were intensely active in the Charleston Area Council. They collected aluminum, scrap iron, and paper. By the first months of 1943 the scouts operated their own collection depot on Virginia Street near the Elk River Bridge. The proceeds from the sales were divided among various social agencies such as the Red Cross and the Salvation Army.

During World War II virtually all of the council staff members, except one, were in the age category for military service and were no longer available to the council, having entered the military. Additionally, many scoutmasters entered the military and this created a problem in recruiting volunteers.

To deal with the shortage of both professional and volunteer staff, Executive Kinsey called on numerous former scoutmasters who, though older, quickly answered the call to take over the leadership roles of various troops. Their outstanding service enabled numerous troops to continue operation during the World War II years.

On December 10, 1941, three days after the Japanese bombing of Pearl Harbor, Council Scout Executive M.H.F. Kinsey wrote a letter to all scoutmasters in the council. In it he pointed out that he had been a Scout Executive during World War I and at that time there had been confusion as to the roles that the Boy Scouts would play in the war effort. He wrote that this time things would come together. Now the roles of scouts would involve various kinds of emergency service activities. He called for a meeting to be held five days later at Calvary Baptist Church, the home of Troop 4.

At that meeting (similar meetings followed in other council locations) he outlined the roles scouts would play in the war effort. They would

BOY SCOUTS OF AMERICA

Charleston Area Council

To All Scoutmasters of the Charleston Area Council:

War has been declared!

Every true Scouter knows his duty. This is contained in our Scout Oath. We will not become a member of the armed forces of our Nation, but there are many other things just as important that Scouts can do. I was a Scout Executive during World War I, and I know that at first there was much confusion on the part of our leaders as to how our organization would fit into the picture. Some very foolish things were done. There will be no confusion this time. I think every man of us knows that our job is one of EMERGENCY SERVICE. For that reason the great majority of our activities will be along that line. Fortunate are those Scoutmasters who a year ago organized and perfected emergency units. How unfortunate that any should neglect this vital preparation. IT IS NOT TOO LATE.

Beginning on the evening of December 15th, an Emergency Service Training School will begin to operate in Charleston at the Calvary Baptist Church, Troop 4 Headquarters. Other schools are being organized in the Fayette, Raleigh, and Allegheny Districts, announcements of place and time to be made later. I know that we will not have to urge men to attend these schools. There will be no need for any extensive promotion measures. Every patriotic leader will be there. He will realize that to make our boys efficient and effective scouts in this crisis they must have the kind of training that is recommended by our National Emergency Council. The way to get this training and this information is to attend these Schools.

Every troop under this Council should be in the Emergency Rallies now on. We are not promoting these just for fun, just for pastime, but there is a deep, solemn motive back of them. Read your newspaper and you will know why this is so important.

Undoubtedly Boy Scouts are going to be called upon during this war for many types of service. We have already participated in the Aluminum and waste paper drive. We have been assisting the Red Cross. Our tasks for the future are going to be a great deal heavier. Much of our time will be demanded. Let's have the united support of our organization in the performance of these patriotic duties. No one can hold back now. No one can make excuses. Alibis don't go in war-time.

Our Scout office will lend its every facility in cooperating with you. We will all work together for AMERICA!

Cordially yours,

M. H. F. KINSEY,

Scout Executive.

December 10, 1941.

Executive M.H.F. Kinsey began to mobilize the scouts just three days after the attack on Pearl Harbor.

BOY SCOUTS OF AMERICA
Charleston, W. Va.

March 22, 1943

Dear Scouter:

In connection with the war effort the County Agent of Kanawha County has asked us to cooperate in a Victory Garden program for this spring and summer. Our part in this program is to compile a list of all the Boy Scouts who want to work during this season. When a person wants to hire a boy to work in his garden he will call one of our sponsors and he in turn will call one of the boys to do the job. This will afford employment for the boys and also help the war effort.

You have been selected as one of the sponsors for this program. I hope you will watch the papers for further information. Secure your list of boys and be ready when garden time rolls around. You and the boys can set a fair minimum wage if you think it advisable. If there is any questions in regard to this program, please contact this office.

Yours truly,

R. A. Bennett
Field Commissioner.

SCOUTS RAISED VICTORY GARDENS AND HELPED OTHERS RAISE THEIR GARDENS.

collect scrap metal and scrap paper. They would grow "victory gardens" and toil in the gardens of other, older citizens who needed help. They would assist the Red Cross in various ways. And leaders would step up their recruitment efforts. An Emergency Service Training School was established. There was much to be done. And, as Kinsey wrote, "Alibis don't go in war-time."

The results were clear. As but one example, the scouts of the Charleston, South Charleston and St. Albans Districts alone collected 186,437 pounds of scrap paper during the two-months of the General Eisenhower Paper Salvage Campaign, March and April, 1945.

During the World War II years council activities, including rallies, were given such names as "Victory Meet" and "Victory Campaign." At rallies, first aid, semaphore message-sending and

September 9, 1943

Mr. Lloyd Hilbert
1033 Kanawha Terrace
St. Albans, W. Va.

Dear Commissioner:

I am calling a meeting of all Commissioners for the coming Tuesday night, September 14th at Boy Scout Headquarters, new address - 330 Professional Building, 8 p.m.

This will be an important meeting as we will discuss our fall and winter program, and our coming War Conference to be held in October.

Our new Field Executive, Grant Collins, will be present to meet all of our Commissioner Staff and consult with them about our future plans.

Looking forward to seeing you and with kind personal regards, I am

Cordially yours,

M H F Kinsey

M. H. F. KINSEY
Scout Executive

MHFK:mf

THE WAR PERVADED SCOUTING, AS THIS 1943 LETTER FROM EXECUTIVE M.H.F. KINSEY SHOWS.

Malden Boy Scout Troop Speeds Aluminum Drive This Week Toward Goal of Half-Ton For Uncle Sam

Spurred by collection of about 650 pounds of aluminum toward their 1,000 pound goal for national defense, these members of the Blazing Arrow Boy Scout troop, of Malden district, this week again will swing into action for Uncle Sam.

Pictured left to right, standing: Stanley Pascavin, co-sponsor of the drive, James Harlor, Daniel Carter, Charles Hall, Frank Hall, jr., Jack Albert, Oscar Cochran, William Cochran, Tommy Atkins, Ralph Hensley, Samuel Frazier, Tommy Young, Billy Pascavin, Charles Curry and Patrol Leader Robert Dickson. Seated, Tommy McDowell, Fred Hall, jr., Robert Wickiser and Charles Shannon.

The Scouts will make a house to house canvas today at Snow and Dry Branch, Reed and Malden tomorrow at Levie and Belle, Wednesday at Putney and on Campbells creek towns.

(Gazette photo)

the like took on defense themes. Scouts were urged to support the war effort by buying defense bonds and stamps, working with their parents on civilian defense matters, and more. Points were awarded for those activities and others such as recruitment of new troop members, advancement in rank, and participation in civilian defense demonstrations.

As we look back it may well be said that the World War II years were Kinsey's "finest hour" as Council Executive. The Council had held together and flourished as it played its role in the war effort.

These Troop 146 scouts are collecting scrap metal. The scout carrying the can is Robert Barnett who later served many years as a St. Albans police officer and chief at Yeager Airport. The photo is from 1943.

The scouts shown in this scrap metal collection drive are J.W. Thompson (left) and Billy G. Thompson.

HALF A MILLION SCOUT GARDENS

Dear Judge Jones:

Your call for continued Boy Scout service in food production and conservation into 1945 could have but one answer. We will do our best. Under Scouting's ideals of service and its charter from Congress we can do no less.

Sincerely yours,

Boy Scouts of America

Elbert K. Fretwell

Chief Scout Executive

War Food Administration
Washington, D. C.
January 24, 1945

Hundreds of thousands of Scouts have served their country during the war years in Victory Gardens and on farms.

During 1945 there is an unprecedented need for food production and more than ever we must count on your support in this vital war service.

Sincerely yours,

Marvin Jones

War Food Administrator

THE NEED IS VITAL

This year fresh vegetables must be produced more abundantly in America than ever before. Other countries have suffered from drought; trucks are wearing out and the commercial supply will be harder to deliver; the occupied countries must be fed. Not since the war began has the home food supply of fresh vegetables and fruit seemed so critical.

SCOUTS RESPOND

Acting on the request of the War Food Administration, the Boy Scouts of America plans its fourth war year of food production and conservation. Last year Scouts worked one hundred and eight million hours growing food for freedom. We must produce more food than ever in 1945.

Thousands of Scouts will work on farms where help is short, and in crop rescue projects. Scout camps will be set up in critical crop areas; permanent Scout camps will grow food. And everywhere throughout America Cub Scouts, Boy Scouts, Senior Scouts and Scouters will grow gardens, — home gardens, Pack and Troop gardens, gardens large and small. A half million Scout gardens is the objective for 1945.

"GREEN THUMB" GARDEN PROGRAM

Many years ago people used to say that any one who could make things grow had a "Green Thumb." And so, because Cubs, Scouts and Scouters everywhere will grow things this year we are using the Green Thumb for the symbol of Scouting's big 1945 gardening program.

YOUR RECORD AND REPORT BLANK

This is your record form which you should keep faithfully through the summer and send to your Council headquarters at the end of the season as an indication that you too have done your best. On receipt of the certified blank your Council will recognize you with the "Green Thumb" Garden Service Certificate, and add your record to the final report made to the nation.

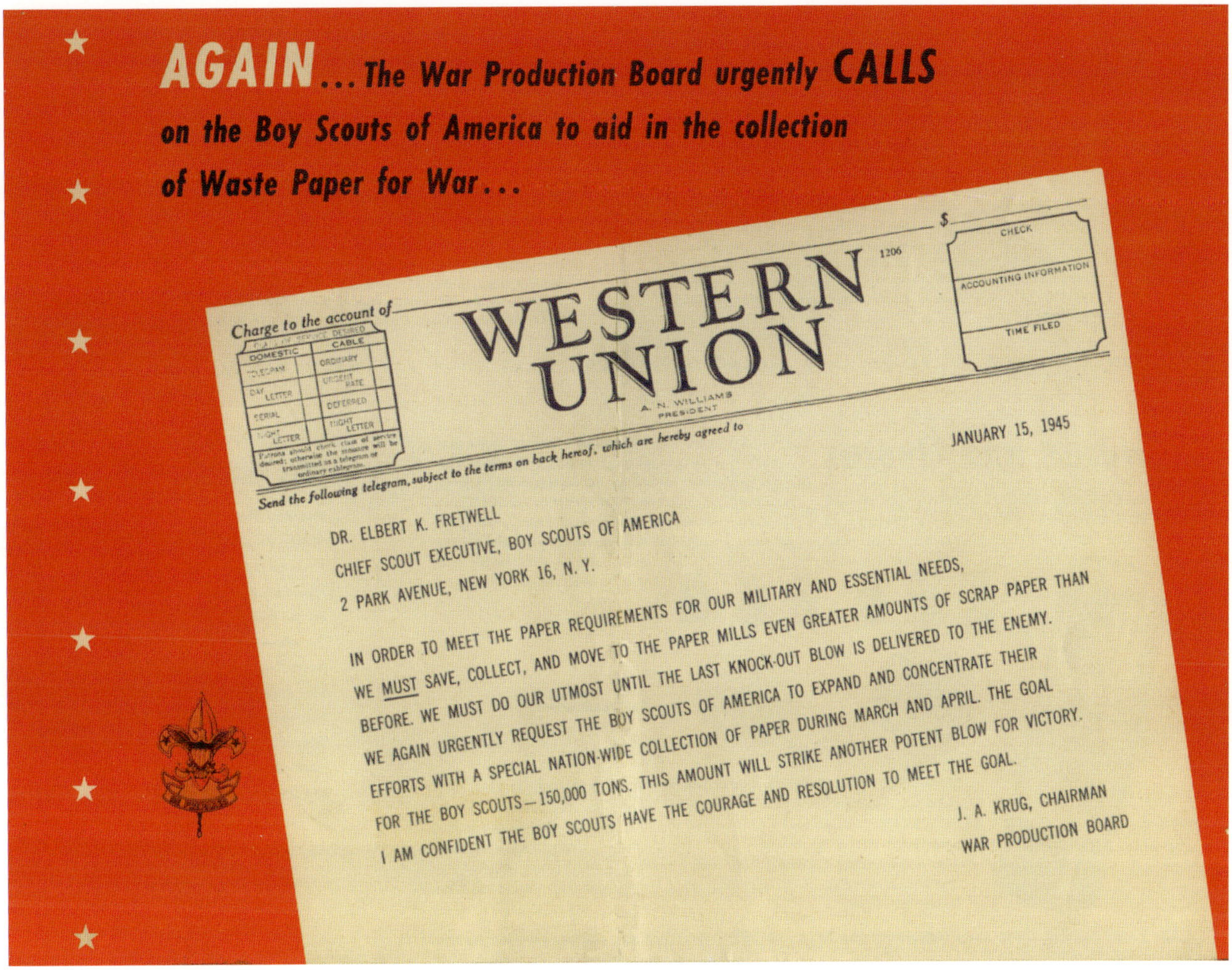

AGAIN ... The War Production Board urgently CALLS on the Boy Scouts of America to aid in the collection of Waste Paper for War ...

WESTERN UNION

A. N. WILLIAMS, PRESIDENT

Charge to the account of

Send the following telegram, subject to the terms on back hereof, which are hereby agreed to

JANUARY 15, 1945

DR. ELBERT K. FRETWELL
CHIEF SCOUT EXECUTIVE, BOY SCOUTS OF AMERICA
2 PARK AVENUE, NEW YORK 16, N. Y.

IN ORDER TO MEET THE PAPER REQUIREMENTS FOR OUR MILITARY AND ESSENTIAL NEEDS, WE MUST SAVE, COLLECT, AND MOVE TO THE PAPER MILLS EVEN GREATER AMOUNTS OF SCRAP PAPER THAN BEFORE. WE MUST DO OUR UTMOST UNTIL THE LAST KNOCK-OUT BLOW IS DELIVERED TO THE ENEMY. WE AGAIN URGENTLY REQUEST THE BOY SCOUTS OF AMERICA TO EXPAND AND CONCENTRATE THEIR EFFORTS WITH A SPECIAL NATION-WIDE COLLECTION OF PAPER DURING MARCH AND APRIL. THE GOAL FOR THE BOY SCOUTS—150,000 TONS. THIS AMOUNT WILL STRIKE ANOTHER POTENT BLOW FOR VICTORY. I AM CONFIDENT THE BOY SCOUTS HAVE THE COURAGE AND RESOLUTION TO MEET THE GOAL.

J. A. KRUG, CHAIRMAN
WAR PRODUCTION BOARD

The War Department called on the scouts for help during World War II.

Charles McCabe, Sr., was Council President, 1942–46.

The scouts were out in force at a ceremony at the State Capitol Building in 1945 honoring the late President Roosevelt.

Scouts bow in reverence at the Franklin D. Roosevelt Memorial Service, 1945.

CHAPTER FOUR

The Camps

CAMP PEQUONI, 1920–1925

UPON BECOMING THE first Council Executive, M.H.F. Kinsey decided that one of the first orders of business would be the construction of a summer camp. Kinsey had been hired as executive in the Summer of 1919 and was determined that the Boy Scouts would have a summer camp for the 1920 camping season.

One of the members of the first court of honor, W.E.R. Byrne, was appointed as the first council camping chairman. Early in the Spring of 1920, Byrne, Kinsey, and G. S. Weistling visited the community of Porters on the B&O Railway, twenty-eight miles up Elk River from Charleston.

The Coal and Coke Land Company, a subsidiary of the B&O Railroad, owned a six-acre tract of land near the Porters station. This was one of the few level tracts of land anywhere between Charleston and Clay, West Virginia.

On arriving at the site, however, the men observed that crops had been planted by squatters who had been living on the property for a number of years. Otherwise, the river seemed to provide a suitable swimming area and there were no other noticeable problems that would prevent a camp from being constructed.

The three men returned to Charleston and met with George E. Price, who was the local attorney for the B&O Railroad and a member of the scout council. Mr. Price quickly obtained a lease on the property for the scouts, and construction of the camp could go forward.

CAMP PEQUONI WAS THE FIRST COUNCIL SPONSORED SUMMER CAMP. IT OPENED IN 1920 AND WAS LOCATED 28 MILES EAST OF CHARLESTON, UP THE ELK RIVER.

The squatters were determined to stay on. Although the scouts had legal control of the property and could have taken possession at any time, Kinsey realized that the squatters had invested money and labor in the planting of several acres of corn and other produce. It was decided that the scouts would buy the crops and plow them under. They settled with the squatters for $150.00.

Camp Pequoni, located at Porter, West Virginia, was accessible only by train.

This photo shows the original mess hall at Camp Pequoni, August 26, 1920. Notice the Troop 4 flag.

There were other problems besides the squatters. First, construction had been going on for about a week when a load of lumber was lost. Then, once the lumber was found and construction resumed, the well driller reported that he had struck a vein of salt water at the one hundred foot level. A new well was started in another location nearby. This was a surface well which ultimately produced sufficient drinking water. The final obstacle was a lack of shelter. The scouts had been promised tents by the National Guard, but at the last minute the National Guard had to withdraw its offer. So the scouts contracted with the Hughes Awning Company to make eight large tents. The job was done in three days and the tents were delivered to the camp site.

The camp opened on July 7, 1920. It was raining hard that day and the camp committee decided to wait for clear weather to have its dedication. On Saturday, July 10, the dedication was held.

The new camp could only be reached by rail, so on the morning of July 10 a delegation of scout officials boarded the train in Charleston at 6:00 a.m. and headed for the camp. As the train rumbled toward Porters Station, it occurred to the men on the train that the camp had no name. Mr. Byrne, the camping committee chairman, huddled with several of the men and decided that the dedication could not be held until a name was decided upon.

Fortunately Kinsey, the Scout Executive, had

Pequoni featured a variety of standard outdoor activities such as volleyball.

First scout executive M.H.F. Kinsey spent a great deal of time at the camp site. To Kinsey's left is John H. Hendricks.

TOP PHOTO: SCOUTS OF TROOPS 1 AND 5 OF CHARLESTON ARE SEEN IN THIS 1920 PHOTO AT CAMP PEQUONI. ABOVE: A DRUM AND BUGLE FORMATION AT CAMP PEQUONI, AUGUST 26, 1920. LIKELY, THIS EVENT WAS ORCHESTRATED FOR THE PHOTOGRAPHER.

been giving the matter some consideration already and had read about the history of the Elk River area. He told the men assembled that each Indian tribe had a different name for the river and that the Delaware Tribe had called it Pequoni. Thus the camp had its name. John L. Dickinson, president of the council, turned over the keys of the camp to Harry Waggoner, the first camp director, and the new camp was officially recognized. Waggoner had just turned twenty-one years of age, but he put together a program that was met with great enthusiasm. Every camp session was filled to capacity, and a large number of scout leaders attended along with the boys.

Camp Pequoni served the Charleston Area/Buckskin Council well for six summers, 1920 through 1925. But the camp was twenty-eight miles from Charleston, there was no phone communication, and the only means of transportation was two trains a day. There was no improved road leading into the camp, and the nearest doctor was ten miles away. The only way the doctor could have reached the camp was by picking his

ABOVE: VIEW OF THE GENERAL CAMP AREA. LEFT: ANOTHER VIEW SHOWING THE MESS HALL TO THE LEFT AND ROWS OF TENTS TO THE RIGHT AND BEYOND THE MESS HALL, AUGUST 26, 1920.

way over a steep mountain trail. Fortunately, there were no serious injuries or accidents to any of the boys or leaders during those six years.

There was, however, an indication of what could happen in such a remote location. One morning at about ten o'clock a screaming woman ran into the camp exclaiming that she was dying. She had been bitten on the arm by a copperhead snake. Her arm was beginning to swell and turning a dark color. Joe Cook, an Eagle Scout who happened to be in camp, ran to his tent and brought a razor blade. He made an incision which started the blood flowing freely, then bandaged her arm.

A crew of section hands were working on the railroad nearby. Although first reluctant to abandon his work, the foreman finally agreed to allow the scouts to use his hand car. The woman was placed on the car as comfortably as could be arranged and Cook, along with another scout named Peel Hyde, pumped the car to Clendenin where the woman was successfully treated by Dr. Max Goldman.

While Camp Pequoni had been a success from many standpoints, the lack of access caused the council committee to look for a more accessible camp. Their search led to the opening of Camp Walhonde in 1926.

Camp Walhonde, 1926–1945

1929 Camp Walhonde staff pictured here: Lawrence Winter, James "Bus" Bibby, Dr. Bivaugra, Banks Shepherd, Brenley Michie, Jack Caldwell, Ed Shepherd, John Bruner, Harold DeAtley, Lloyd Auer, Jim Williamson, Charles Albert, Gordon Ward, Melvin Mathes, Ed Warner.

Because the council's first camp, Camp Pequoni, was isolated with no physician readily available, the council decided to develop another camp closer to town and more accessible. One of the local scoutmasters, Friend Cochrane, recommended a site on the Coal River. The site became Camp Walhonde and it is still accessible today with an easy Sunday afternoon drive. The camp later became known as Cliffside and was used for the children of Union Carbide employees. It was located close to town and may be seen today by driving south on Corridor G from Charleston and turning right at Alum Creek beside the Marathon oil station. The camp is located about 1.5 miles west of Corridor G, on the lefthand side of the road.

On September 12, 1925 the council president, J. D. Woodroe, along with Mr. Byrne, who was the council camping chairman, visited the site. The land belonged to Mr. and Mrs. Tom Keeney.

Woodroe had barely stepped from his automobile when he said, "Gentlemen, I see no use in going any farther. This, in my opinion, is the place." The other members of the camping committee agreed. They decided to immediately get an option on the fifty acres of land that would become Camp Walhonde (Wall-hon-de).

Woodroe requested a sheet of paper from Mr. Keeney in order to draft the option, but Keeney could not find a sheet of paper anywhere in his home. Woodroe reached in his pocket, took out an envelope, and wrote the option.

The option was to expire on December 10, 1925 at noon. Early in December the property was surveyed and the deed was prepared. On December 10th the scout executive, Mr. Kinsey, along with the scoutmaster who had originally recommended the site, Friend Cochrane, drove to the Keeney property to close the deal. But en route the car got stuck in a muddy quagmire and the men had to work nearly an hour trying to extricate it. As the clock was ticking toward noon, the men decided they would have to abandon the car and walk the rest of the way. It had recently come to their attention that some others were interested in securing the land for a resort park. Thus, waiting until another day did not seem to be feasible.

They reached the Keeney home at 11:45 a.m. and told the Keeneys that they were there to close

THE TOMAHAWK
CAMP NEWS
of the CHARLESTON AREA COUNCIL
BOY SCOUTS OF AMERICA

Vol. II CHARLESTON, W. VA. No. 1

SCOUT CAMPS TO OPEN JULY 5TH

Three Area Council Camps to be Operated This Year

CHARLESTON—The Charleston Council will conduct three camps this summer, all conveniently located for scouts in every section of the Area. Camp Walhonde will be conducted at Alum Creek, Camp Wah-Tal-A at Cliff Top, and Camp Wilderness at Beaver, W. Va. There will be all types of camping, leaving it up to each camper to select the camp he desires. Troop Camping will feature both Camp Wah-Tal-A and Camp Wilderness. Provisional troops will be provided at Camp Walhonde as in past years.

Parents should plan right now to have their sons spend their vacations in one or more of these camps. We guarantee safe conditions. All drinking water is analyzed weekly, and food supplies are inspected by duly accredited health officials. Swimming is supervised by Red Cross Life Saving Guards. Our leaders are men of the very highest type, and daily association with them develops in the boy a fine, well rounded character. To the Scoutmasters, we add: Come with your boys to camp.

The Camp Committee considers this so important that no charge is made for the attendance of Scoutmasters in camp, The real purpose of our camps is to strengthen troop morale, and we think the best way to do this is to have the Scoutmaster in camp with his boys. For further particulars regarding these camps write or call: Boy Scouts of America, Charleston Area Council, 215 Professional Bldg., Charleston. Branch offices: Oak Hill, W. Va., and Beckley, W. Va.

Scout Executive Tells of Camp Features for the 1943 Season

CHARLESTON—M. H. F. Kinsey, Scout Executive, reported that while in the Council Camps a Scout learns to do things worthwhile and has a good time while he is doing it.

Scouts will have an opportunity to learn how to swim or to pass tests for the qualified swimmers.

We will have crafts and activities that every Scout may choose from. Some of these include wood craft, model airplane building, archery, photography, dramatics, obstacle training, nature lore, O. C. D. training, campfires, first aid, Scout commando games, leathercraft, pioneering, hiking, life saving, Emergency Service training, Field Meets, soft ball, and tennis.

Since the camps are in different parts of our Council and different types, each Camp will provide and feature different activities.

Scout advancement will have its place in all of our Camps. Boards of Review will be held at each Camp. Only Merit Badges actually passed at Camp will be credited during the camp periods.

"What Will My Boy Get Out Of Camp?"

He will benefit physically from the exercise, regular hours, plenty of sleep, fresh air, ample well-prepared food and a happy vacation with boys of his own age.

He will benefit from the instruction in wood craft, camp craft, and Scouting. He will develop endurance, self-control, self-reliance and to respect others' rights.

Scouts Told What to Bring to Camp

OAK HILL—R. K. Hopkins, Camp Director, urges all Scouts to bring adequate clothing and equipment.

Clothing necessary for any of the camps include extra pairs of shorts, extra pairs of stockings, shoes, underwear, pajamas, two or more heavy blankets, sheets, small pillow, toilet articles, towels, handkerchiefs, latest Scout Handbook, flashlight, sweater and swimming trunks.

Equipment which a Scout may desire to bring are Scout knife, notebook, pencil, Scout axe, canteen, compass, signal flags, first aid kit, camera, or musical instrument.

The Director also urges that Scouts who plan to attend Camp Wilderness or Camp Wah-Tal-A and are in the tent units, bring their own cots or ground cloth, and candles or lantern. Troops coming to either of these Camps must bring their own tent and eating equipment.

Scouts should mark all their equipment with their name.

"Will My Boy Be Able to Attend Religious Services?"

Council Camps arrange for a boy's fulfillment of his religious duties. The twelfth point of the scout Law says "A Scout is Reverent" and goes on to explain that he is "Reverent toward God. He is faithful in his religious duties and *respects the convictions of others* in matters of custom and religion."

The Camps attempt to make it possible for each Scout to attend religious services conducted by leaders of his own and his parents' religious faith.

BY THE 1940S, THE BUCKSKIN COUNCIL'S GEOGRAPHY LED TO CONSTRUCTION OF THREE SUMMER CAMPS. THEY WERE LOCATED AT ALUM CREEK, CLIFF TOP AND BEAVER, WEST VIRGINIA.

the deal. The deed was signed . Mr. Keeney pointed out that the option stated that one thousand dollars would be paid upon receipt of the deed, with the balance of four thousand dollars to be paid in annual installments.

Kinsey and the others, in their haste to get the deed signed, had overlooked the important item of the down payment. It was too late to get a council check prepared. Worse, Kinsey knew that the council did not have a balance sufficient to cover a check of a thousand dollars.

Camp Walhonde was later purchased from the Boy Scouts and renamed Camp Cliffside. It was then used as a camp for the children of Union Carbide employees.

Kinsey gave his personal check in the amount of a thousand dollars, aware that he didn't have sufficient funds for the check to clear the bank. The deal was closed, the men returned to their mired car, hired a team of horses to pull it out of the mud, and returned to Charleston.

Before there was a pool, swimming was done in the river at Walhonde as is shown in this 1930s era photo.

Early the next morning Kinsey searched frantically for the chairman of the finance committee, R. C. Montelius. Kinsey told Montelius what they had done the previous day, and that he did not have sufficient funds in the bank to cover his personal check. Montelius called in his secretary and directed her to issue a personal check on Montelius' account for seven hundred and fifty dollars payable to the Boy Scouts of America. Kinsey breathed a sigh of relief and went straight to council treasurer W. O. Abney, got the check credited to the Boy Scouts of America, then secured a check for himself to maintain his own solvency. Camp Walhonde was born.

A few days later, Walter E. Clark was elected president of the council. He was intent on getting camp construction underway and appointed an energetic camp committee, along with a building committee.

But construction of the camp went slowly. In late March Clark called Kinsey and said, "The board is meeting today and I'm going to call for a showdown. Have prepared by that time no less than fifty pledge cards and bring them with you."

When the meeting got underway, Clark addressed the members saying, "I have asked the Scout Executive to drop every item of business from today's agenda, except one, and that is action on camp construction." With that encouragement and a handful of pledge cards, by the end of the meeting the council had in hand sufficient pledge funds to start construction work. In less than ten days more money came in.

Contractor John Moore proceeded with the work. Architect Herbert Kyle already had plans prepared and by April 15, 1926 the first signs of a camp began to appear. On June 24, 1926, Camp Walhonde opened its gates to a capacity crowd of campers.

GAZETTE, 7-28-29

One Hundred Boys At Camp Walhonde For Fourth Period

Much Interest and Some Excitement Mark the Best Season for Boy Scouts

One hundred boys were registered into Camp Walhonde last week for the fourth period of this season's camp. This period is proving to be the very best of the season as there has been plenty of good hot weather, and the program full of "pep." The boys arrived at camp Tuesday afternoon after some real excitement on Rable's mountain. A car in front of them toppled over the hillside and

EDWIN WARNER
Director of Indiancraft at Camp Walhonde

two persons were injured. First aid was administered by Scouts Charles Albert, Charles Eskey and Loren O'Dell, and the injured parties were then carried to a hospital in Charleston.

Joe Woody's airplane again carried off first place honors in the aviation meet held on last Saturday afternoon. Many other fine planes were on exhibition and some splendid records hung up. The meet scheduled for next week will bring out a round dozen new planes, and some real fun is expected. John Bruner and a group of boys working for the pioneer merit badge are building a 30-foot observation tower on the knoll just back of the St. Albans cabin. This when completed will command a fine view of the Coal river valley below.

Harold DeAtley, one of the Indian Village counselors, led an interesting hike on Friday through the hills toward Ruth. The entire distance covered was 14 miles.

Badges Presented

At the closing campfire ceremonial of the third period held on last Monday night, first class badges were presented to Scouts Ernest Byrd of Troop No. 22; James Meadows of Troop No. 32; Tommy Bryan of Troop No. 13, and Oden Goshorn of Troop No. 5. At this campfire ceremony three boys were initiated into the third degree of the little chief of the Indian Village. These were the first boys in camp this year to win this honor. The lucky boys were John Moore, Lowell Warner and Paul Newlon. The three degrees of the Indian Village are as follows: First degree brave, second degree warrior, and third degree little chief. To reach the latter degree is considered on of the greatest honors that can come to a Walhonde camper. This initiation is a very elaborate ceremonial based entirely on Indian tradition, and has been dramatized by Edwin Warner, nature study teacher at camp and chief of the Indian Village.

Possibly no feature in recent years at Camp Walhonde has been so popular as that of the Indian village. Each of the five tents i.. the village has an Indian name, as well as each camper. Warner leads them in their war dances, and directs the ceremonials at the council fire.

The following boys are residents in the Indian village this week:

Edwin Warner, chief.

Counselors: Lloyd Auer, Harold DeAtley, James R. Williamson.

Campers: Lowell Warner, Albert Foster, Robert Stewart, Ronald Spence, Everett Rowsey, Ivan Lowery, William Hopper, Curtis Brewer, Ronald Burnette, Paul Newlon, Arthur Newlon, Malcolm McConnell, Robert Bird, Jas. Rhodes, Oliver Hawkins, Charles Eskey, Bill Hager, Eddie Bowman, Vernon Dixon, John Crites, Carleton Osborne, James Moore, Dana Evans, Alexander Rice, Billy Rice, Tommy Bryan, Gilmer Jones, Wilbur Frankfort, Kermit Lockhart, Edward Mills, Richard Rectenwald, Charles Rectenwald, Edward Merrifield, Francis Krouse, O. B. Bobbitt, jr., and Edgar Mallory.

"Scalping" Game

One of the most interesting games played by this group is the game called "Scalping," and calls for some real strategy. Sometimes it takes an entire afternoon to complete it. There have been two sessions of it this camp season, and the boys have proclaimed it the best game on the week's program.

Carter Haley, regional scout executive, was a visitor at camp on Friday and Saturday, and made an official inspection. On Saturday members of the Charleston camp comittee were present, and inspected the camp in company with Mr. Haley.

The following boys are in the cabin community this week:

St. Albans cabin: Lawrence Winter, counselor; Elvert Easter, Harry Frank, Danny Kirwin, Tom Kirwin, Ben Swint, Robert Smith, Anthony Foy, George Foy, Joe Groves and John Goshorn.

Lions cabin: Melvin Mathes, counselor; Chance Morris, Ed King, Bill Miller, John F. Hann, Charles Barlow, William Isaac, William Barringer, Joe Barringer, Lon Barringer, jr., Otho Wright, Ronald Ownby and Dana Keesaer.

Kiwanis cabin: Edward Shepherd, counselor; Carlyle Wade, David Swarts, Richard Drumheller, George Roberts, Charles Probst, Franz Thayer, Bus Bibby, Arthur Holz and Robert Kincaid.

Hopper cabin: Gordon Wood, counselor; Francis Burks, Jack Burntett, Eddie Hoover, Dick Hoke, Gene Hoke, Earl Knighton, Charles Blaine, James Shelton, Ernest Hays and Thomas Lynn.

Lebow cabin: John L. Bruner, counselor; Charles Albert, John Albert, Walter Wiley, Joe Woody, Owen Garred, Clarence Pharr, Morton Levin, Loren O'Dell, Joe Carney and David Isaac.

Lindbergh cabin: Jack Caldwell, counselor; Raymond Lightner, Bobby Miller, John Hickman, Claude Keller, Bill Keller, Francis Thayer, Budd Meredith; Russell Dye, Don Corrwell, Frank Mairs and Gordon Grisinger.

Camp Walhonde consisted of four cabins and a large dining hall. Several thousand dollars had been spent on grounds improvements. The dining hall was designated as "Rotary Hall" in appreciation of a generous gift from the Charleston Rotary Club.

The four cabins were also given names: Kiwanis, Lions, Hopper, and Lebow. The two former had been built by the Charleston Kiwanis and Lions Clubs and the two latter cabins were memorials to two prominent Eagle Scouts who had died just a few months prior to the opening of the new camp.

The dedication of the camp was observed on July 4, 1926 with Council President Clark presiding at the ceremonies. Over the next twenty years, through 1945, Camp Walhonde provided a summer camping experience to more than ten thousand boys.

The camp had taken its name from the Delaware tribe words for "Hill River." Legend has it that an old Delaware chief stood on the mountain overlooking the forks of the Coal River where the camp is located and was moved to exclaim, "Walhonde."

The first camp director was Red Hopkins who had transferred from Camp Pequoni to the new camp. Hopkins had been hired in 1923 as co-director of Camp Pequoni, with its original director Harry Wagner. Illness had overtaken Wagner who was not able to complete the 1923 season. As a result, Hopkins had become the camp director and continued in that capacity in 1924 and 1925 at Camp Pequoni. In 1926 he took charge of Camp Walhonde. In 1927 Ronald Wilson became the camp director. Banks Shepherd led the camp from 1928 through 1932, followed by Edwin Shepherd from 1933 to 1935, Paul Newlon in 1936, and Charles Loeb from 1937 through 1938. All of these men had worked under Hopkins and continued his tradition of aggressive, well-organized camping experiences for the boys.

The camp grew rapidly as more and more boys attended. The four cabins were outgrown. As a result, many lived in a tented section known as "Indian Village."

THE CHARLESTON DAILY MAIL, SUNDAY MORNING, JULY 21, 1929

WHERE YOUTH GETS CLOSE TO NATURE—SCENES AT BOY SCOUT CAMP

Center: a human "W", made by swimmers in the "old swimmin' hole " at Walhonde. Left: on the archery range at the Boy Scout camp. Right: a sample of the airplanes made in the Walhonde shops. Below: living quarters at the camp on Coal river.

BOYS FIND IDEAL IN WALHONDE, BOY SCOUT CAMP ON COAL RIVER

Swimming, Boating, Baseball Games and Other Activities Keep Youths Busy; Present Season Best in History; Large Staff of Instructors Busy

During the Banks Shepherd administration there occurred an incident which was recounted by Scout Executive Kinsey as "Turning my hair gray overnight."

Kinsey had been out to lunch in Charleston and when he returned, a telegram lay on his desk. Opening it he found the following message from Camp Director Shepherd, "Rush ambulance and doctor, two boys drowned."

This was a week or so before the camp season was to open, a time when only the camp staff was at Walhonde as they made preparations for the official opening. Kinsey knew that all the camp leaders and staff were excellent swimmers, and that during the training there was little opportunity for swimming. He could not understand how two boys might have drowned.

There were no phone lines to the camp nor

Swimming, boating, baseball games, plenty to eat.

Asked in the middle of July as to his idea of heaven, such might be a small boy's answer.

Yet all these things and more are to be had at Walhonde, the Boy Scout camp, on the banks of Coal river.

Not only do the scouts have the opportunity to spend a week under canvas or in a cabin at the camp, but the parents have the assurance that their sons will be well looked after by competent camp leaders who are specially trained for their tasks.

Contests of skill and strength are on the program in abundance. There also is instruction in the various branches of scouting and the certainty to escape, for the time being, the dangers of city heat and traffic.

Charleston council opened its tenth summer camp July 2. The first was held at the old camp site on Elk river, known as "Camp Pequoni", and for six seasons successful camps were held there. The growth of scouting made a new and larger site imperative, so in 1926 a large tract was purchased on Coal river and Camp Walhonde was built and equipped. This new camp was opened and dedicated in July, 1926, and since that date capacity crowds have been in attendance.

Present Season Is Best

The present season is by far the best in its history, according to officials. The camp has been full since the opening date and the program has surpassed that of any previous season. Camp leaders with years of experience to their credit are in charge. The present director, Banks Shepherd is now serving his second year in that capacity. Previous to this he had served as assistant director at Walhonde, and as camp counselor at old Camp Pequoni. Shepherd believes that the summer camp is the golden opportunity for character building, for in camp the boy learns the spirit of the scout oath and law, and through contact with men of high type he acquires the character values of scouting. In other words the objective of camp is more than skill and knowledge—it is character.

Director Shepherd is assisted by a staff of camp leaders. His first assistant is Beverly L. Michie, who is in charge of swimming and life saving activities. His job is to teach the boys' how to swim. Scores of them learn every season at Walhonde.

Camp Naturalist

Edwin Warner is the camp naturalist, and chief of the Indian village. He is about the busiest fellow in the whole camp. Before sunrise each morning he starts out with his bird study class. The boys are taught the varied species of bird life in the vicinity of Walhonde. In the afternoon nature study hikes are on his program, where trees and plant life are studied and explained. In the evening he and his tribe of "redmen" gather around the campfire for the evening ceremonial. The latter is possibly one of the most interesting as well as one of the most colorful events of the day. These "Indians" have their own village. They live in tents, tepees, and some in the open. In a few days they have acquired a bronze complexion.

Next on the staff is John L. Bruner, Eagle scout, and director of instruction. He heads up all scout advancement, and works out various schemes to stimulate study along scouting lines. The work embraces all phases of scoutcraft, carpentry work, leathercraft, and archery. He has under his direct supervision eight instructors, who direct the educational work.

"Bus" Keeps Commissary

James A. Bibby, Jr., better known to the scouts as "Bus" is camp clerk and in direct charge of the commissary department. It is Bus' job to see that 114 hungry boys are fed three times a day, that all meals are served on time, and that every boy is filled.

Edwin Shepherd is the builder of morale, for his job is that of activities director. He keeps the campers "pepped up" by finding something interesting for each to do. This might include craftwork, hiking, leathercraft, baseball, tennis, archery, or what not. He sees that every fellow enjoys himself and that homesickness is banished from the camp. He is the song leader, too, and it is he who directs the music around the campfire in the evenings and in the devotionals Sunday morning.

Harold DeAtley and James Williamson direct the work of model airplane building. These boys have as many as 20 scouts working each morning on model planes. Last Monday afternoon the first meet was held. The material for building these planes is sold to the boys at practically cost so that a plane might be built for the low sum of 75 cents. Melvin Mathes, a new counselor at Walhonde this year, looks after leathercraft instruction and the making of archery sets.

Serving Third Season

Jack Caldwell, assistant swimming instructor, is serving his third season as counselor at Walhonde. He is one of Director Shepherd's right hand men and an instructor in aquatics.

Other counselors who are serving in the capacity of instructors are Lawrence Winter, Eagle scout; Gordon Wood, Lloyd Auer, and Dymock Smith.

Dr. Arthur Bevacqua is the camp physician. He looks after the health of the campers, and directs the sanitary work of the camp. He spends his entire time at the camp. Weekly inspections of health conditions at the camp are also made by Charleston physicians. Each boy entering camp must be examined by a physician before leaving the city.

Camp Walhonde campers are divided up into two groups, half of them living in tents, and the other half in cabins. Those in tents comprise the Indian village population, and those in cabins, the "pioneers." There is strong rivalry between the two groups, and many contests of an interesting nature are held.

The Charleston Boy Scout camp committee includes Charles E. Krebs, chairman; Walter E. Clark, Herbert S. Kyle, Dr. B. H. Swint, Dr. John Thames, C. C. Alberts and E. S. Tisdale.

Campers This Week

The following boys are in camp this week:

Indian village: counselors, Edwin Warner, chief; Lloyd Auer, Harold DeAtley, James Robert Williamson and Dymock Smith.

Campers, Lowell Warner, John Moore, Irving Bass, Albert Foster, Morton Levin, Paul Newlon, Robert L. Bird, William Dabney, Malcolm McConnell, Joel Belknap, John Crites, William Goff, Dana Evans, Hugh Wood, Woodrow Grubb, John Spence, Alexander Rice, William Rice, Cecil McClung, Edward Shelton and Tommy Bryan.

Pioneer cabins: St. Albans cabin, Lawrence Winter, counselor; Ben Pierce, Harry Frank, John Goshorn, Earl Wood Hall, James Meadows, Otho Wright, Joe Barlow and Homer Pierce.

Lions cabin, Melvin Mathes, counselor; Charles Campbell, Harry Diesher, Wilbur Summerfield, Edward King, Dana Keesaer, John Hann, William Miller, Orville Arnett, Clay Robinson, James Robinson, and Howard Arnett.

Kiwanis cabin, Edwin Shepherd, counselor; Carlyle Wade, Robert Kincaid, Oden Goshorn, Richard Drumheller, Jack Shanklin, Ogden Willis, Arthur Shawkey, Nick Cooke, Julius deGruyter, Roscoe Noble, Cledith Morgan, George Roberts, Clayton Clere and Robert Yates.

Hopper cabin, Gordon Wood, counselor; Norman Fitzugh, David Swarts, Chance Morris, Charles Newman, Howard Hiserman, Francis Thayer, Robert Loeb, Charles Holz and Noyes Kinder.

Lebow cabin, John Bruner, counselor; Joe Woody, Robert Newton James Mottesheard, Richard Ault Eddie Bowman, Mitchell Schwartz Gordon Grisinger, Don Cornwell Owen Garred and Clarence Pharr.

Lindbergh cabin, Jack Caldwell, counselor; Ernest Byrd, Leonard Rodgers, Forrest Hill, Raymond Lightner, Clarkson Watts, Russell Dye, Charles Peters and Robert Wille.

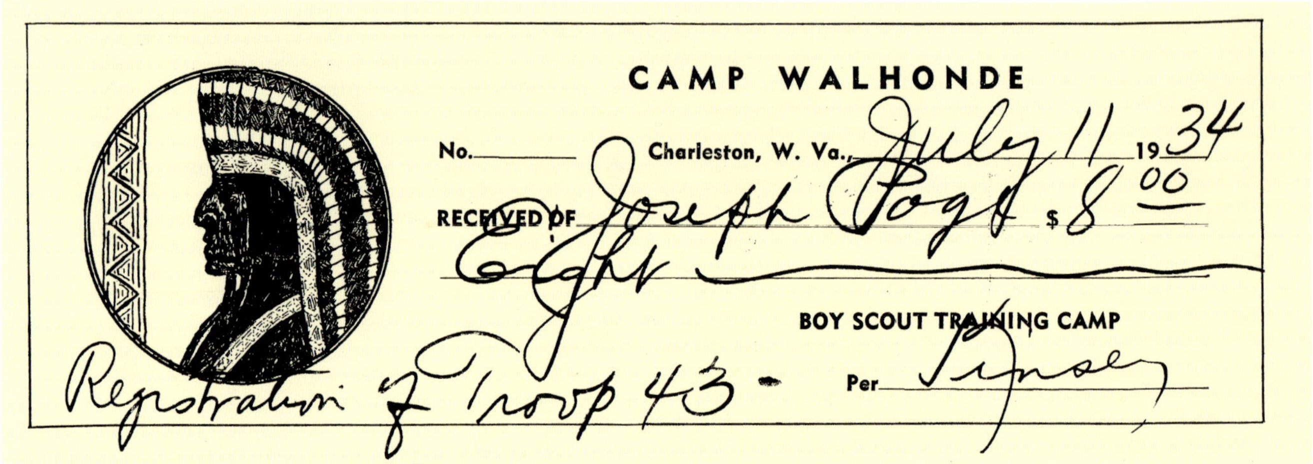
CAMP WALHONDE

No._____ Charleston, W. Va., July 11 1934

RECEIVED OF Joseph Page $ 8 00

Eight

BOY SCOUT TRAINING CAMP

Registration of Troop 43 - Per Kinsey

In 1934 it cost only $8 to go to Camp Walhonde, as this registration for scout Joe Page of Troop 43 shows.

This 1930s era photo at Camp Walhonde shows several staff members and campers, most of whose names are not known. However, on the far left is Edwin Warner, third from left is Melvin Mathes, to his left is Rondel Lyons, and fourth from right is Lowell Warner.

anywhere else on that section of Coal River. Kinsey went to his car, drove to the office of Dr. Hugh Nicholson and set out for the camp at 1:30 p.m. Nicholson stopped at a local drugstore to pick up some adrenalin and they were on their way. They reached the camp at about 2:30 and could see a group of Coal River natives and members of the camp staff huddled together near the camp entrance. On a wagon near the entrance Kinsey could see a boy partly covered with a white canvas. Kinsey knew the boy was dead. Nicholson examined the body quickly, and he returned to the car where Kinsey sat. "They are not our boys," Nicholson said.

Camp Director Shepherd soon told the story. At about 9:00 o'clock that morning a Sunday School teacher and his class of boys from St. Albans had arrived at the camp and asked Shepherd if they could swim at the camp's swimming hole in the river. Shepherd had explained to them that no swimming was permitted unless lifeguards were on duty. So the man and his boys went up the river about

This 1935 photo shows numerous scouts at General Swim at Camp Walhonde. Note the close oversight of the lifeguards in boats.

Camp Walhonde, swimming on a hot summer day in 1935.

In 1935 Scouts Jim McCabe, Grant Fletcher, and John LaRue made for an interesting fife and drum corps.

In 1935 the camp was operated by Director Ed Shepherd (right). The camp's physician, Dr. Moore, is at left. Assistant director Paul Newlon is between them.

The Camp Walhonde staff of 1935 posed for this picture.

leader could not swim and both boys sank to the bottom.

The Sunday School teacher rushed to the camp to ask for help. Shepherd and his camp staff, all expert swimmers, ran to the spot. One boy, Beverly Michie, who had Red Cross Lifesaving Instructor credentials, went into the water along with Shepherd looking for the boys. Five minutes later Michie came up with the body of one boy and, after getting him to shore, began artificial respiration. He and a relay of other staff members worked on the boy for over an hour, but to no avail.

The second boy's body was not recovered until after Kinsey and Nicholson had arrived. He too was pronounced dead by Nicholson.

200 yards and began to swim. Coal River was near flood stage and the current was swift and treacherous. The boys had plunged into the water and almost immediately two boys had gone under. They were in trouble, but their

Before long an automobile arrived and a huge man appeared on the scene. He bounded from the car and made inquiry about the Sunday

By 1936 this camp staff photo clearly showed one of the major advantages of Camp Walhonde over the previous council camp, Camp Pequoni. Camp Walhonde had much more open space in which to conduct various scout activities. Additionally, Camp Walhonde was much closer to town and was accessible by car. This meant that medical care would be relatively close by.

This 1936 photo of the Camp Walhonde main lodge will be familiar to many individuals who remember the dark wood siding on the buildings when they attended "Camp Cliffside."

These scouts look completely comfortable camping at Walhonde, about 1940.

The Walhonde dining hall, about 1937.

School teacher. He was the father of one of the boys who had died. He attempted to attack the Sunday school teacher but Shepherd and others prevented it.

As Kinsey described it in his memoir, the boys had died because of the neglect of a leader who had been unprepared to lead boys, especially on a trip of this kind where there were so many potential perils.

Because the incident had taken place so near the Boy Scout camp, Kinsey became fearful of how the newspapers might treat the deaths. He hurried back to Charleston and conferred with the city editors of both newspapers, giving them the facts of the case.

During the Walhonde era it was often the case that the council operated other camps. For example, Camp Wah-Tal-A was located on grounds formerly occupied by the Civilian Conservation Corps, on the edge of Babcock State Park near Lookout, West Virginia.

Wah-Tal-A became a council camp in about 1943. It had over twenty buildings and featured hot water showers. The camp was operated on a chartered troop basis only and troops had to provide their own adult leadership.

Similarly, Camp Wilderness was located seven miles south of Beckley near Beaver, West Virginia, and operated on a troop basis. Troops had to provide their own cooking in this particularly rugged experience which featured only a small central staff to assist with crafts and other activities.

In camps such as Wah-Tal-A and Wilderness there were no provisional troops in which boys from smaller troops that lacked leaders could be placed. It was Walhonde that provided for those scouts, as well as for the majority of council chartered troops.

Camp Clifton McClintic, 1946–1959

In the fall of 1945 the Charleston Council was given a camp in Greenbrier County. The donor was Dr. Clifton F. McClintic, who had been involved in scouting for many years. The property was more than one hundred acres and included several nice buildings. It was the consensus of the council members that Camp Walhonde should be sold and the proceeds used to make improvements at the new camp. The new camp was named Camp Clifton McClintic.

In the Spring of 1946 Camp Walhonde was sold to the Carbide-Carbon Corporation for $20,000. Carbide used the camp for many years thereafter as a camp for its employees' children. Although many of the old-time scouters regretted to see Walhonde end its years as the council camp, most agreed that it was in the best interest of the program to move the camp. Camp McClintic was located about six miles west of Lewisburg, West Virginia, off of Route 60, and then seven miles north near Williamsburg, West Virginia, near the area of Old Fort Donnolly.

Thousands of scouts and leaders passed by this sign on the way to Camp McClintic.

Culverson Creek, where the camp was located, ran through the camping area. This creek flowed out the side of a mountain about five miles above the camp site and ran through the woods until reaching the camp. At the upper end of the camp a dam was constructed across the creek, thus forming the swimming area. The pool was quite small, about 150 feet long by 40 feet wide, and it was always cold as the water never had a chance to warm up after leaving the underground. Culverson Creek was quite short. It disappeared into the side of a hill about two miles below the camp. The water was never much above 60 degrees F. Despite the limited facilities, the young scouts were able to pass their swimming and life saving merit badges.

The camp had a combined office and health lodge, a modest sized kitchen and dining hall, plus four tent platforms with canvas tops, and one full sized log cabin. In addition there were a number of tents in the small flat areas directly adjacent to the creek. The rest of the property was hilly, and it was exceptionally slippery when it rained. In spite of the somewhat primitive con-

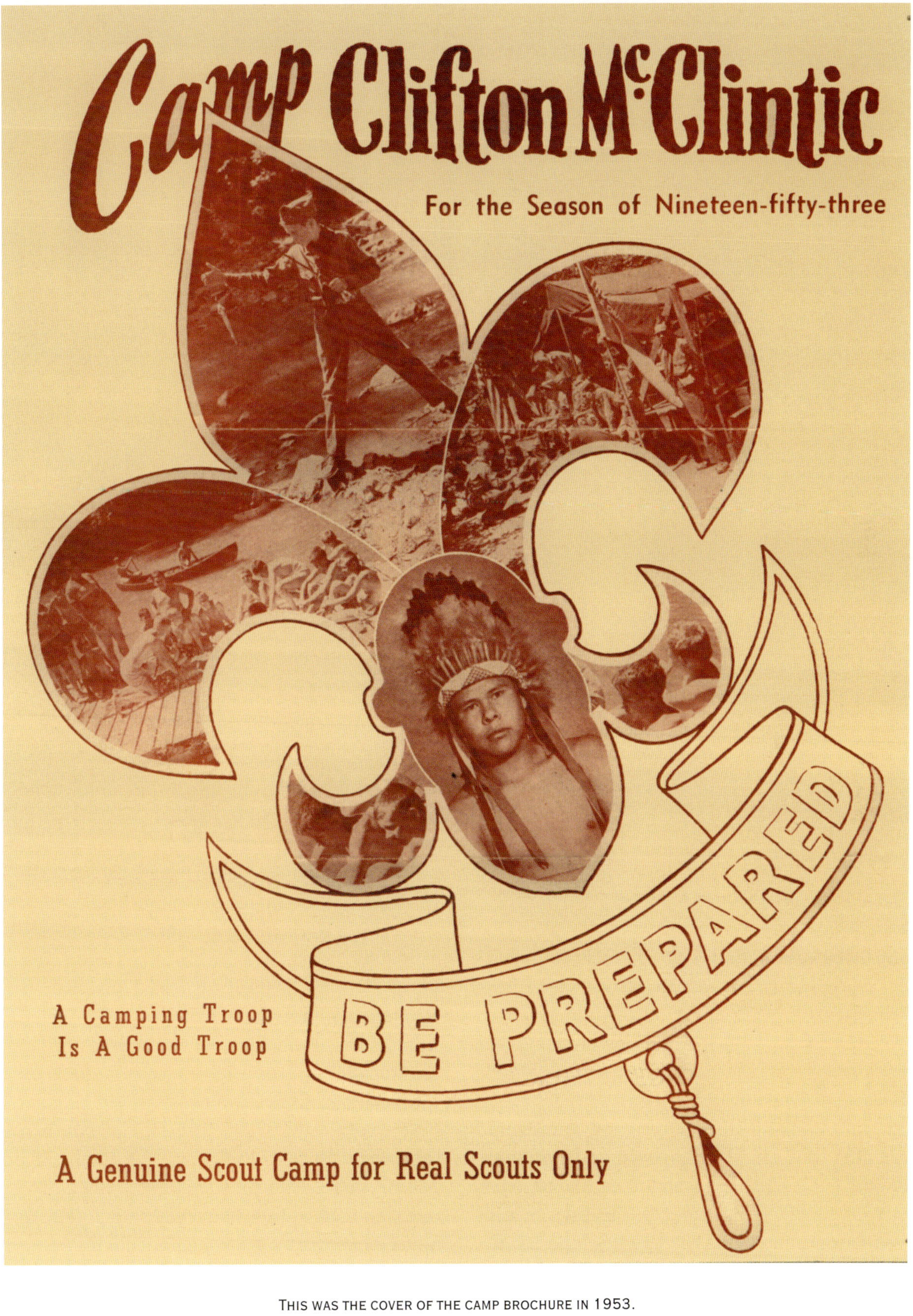

This was the cover of the camp brochure in 1953.

Checking in at the Camp McClintic Health Lodge, July 1950.

ditions, the scouts had a good learning experience. Some of the camp directors were Jack Lewis, Burns Powell, and Creed Wood.

Greenbrier County is limestone country, and consequently there are numerous caves. Gunpowder Cave was located about two miles south of the camp just off the narrow road from Route 60 leading to Camp. In the 1940s and '50s there was still evidence of the activities of confederates who mixed gunpowder in the cave in hollowed trough-like logs. The story behind its discovery is that a hunter was chasing a rabbit and suddenly the rabbit disappeared. The hunter was attracted to the cave entrance by some cold air. He pulled away the brush and discovered the entrance. Many scouts explored it.

In 1957 John Howell, who was the acting scoutmaster of Troop 11 of Christ Church United Methodist in Charleston, took seven scouts on a hike exploring various caves. The camp truck took them near Alderson and let them off on a country road. They hiked about 5 miles and found one small interesting cave. After lunch they found a large hill with a 10 to 12 foot high opening in front. They learned that this cave was named Horse Cave. The residents had used the cave to

Left: The swimming was cold and the river was narrow but, as at previous camps, the lifeguards were always watchful.
Above: At Camp McClintic scouts had the advantage of level wooden platforms and steel-framed beds. Here we see scoutmaster Grant Turner of Troop 77 with several of his scouts. They hailed from Spencer, West Virginia.
Below: These Camp McClintic scouts posed for a hastily arranged group photo, circa 1950.

Scouts line up to enter the health lodge at Camp McClintic, about 1958. Note two sea scouts at the far right.

Above: Building a "Monkey Bridge" at Camp McClintic in the 1950s. Right: The archery range.

TOP: ROPE WORK AT CAMP MCCLINTIC. ABOVE: A VIEW OF THE ADMINISTRATION BUILDING IN THE DISTANCE.

THESE CHARLESTON AREA TROOP 71 SCOUTS HAD JUST COMPLETED A TEN-MILE HIKE AT CAMP MCCLINTIC. SCOUTMASTER HOWARD MILLER IS FRONT, CENTER.

hide their horses and cows from marauding armies during the Civil War. The scouts took their shoes off and waded in the pitch dark for about three-quarters of a mile until the cave's shrinking size prohibited them from safely going farther. On that trip they also visited an old water-powered grist mill with wooden gears and large sandstone grinding wheels named Blaker's Mill.

Anecdotes such as this fill the memories of

ABOVE: ABOUT HALF OF THOSE PICTURED IN THIS 1954 CAMP MCCLINTIC STAFF PHOTO HAVE BEEN IDENTIFIED. ON THE FRONT ROW LEFT TO RIGHT ARE CHARLIES GREENMAN, TOMMY THOMAS, DAVE LONGWORTH, AND ON THE EXTREME RIGHT JESS RICHARDS. MIDDLE ROW EXTREME RIGHT IS HENRY RUTKER. IN THE BACK ROW LEFT TO RIGHT ARE BOB HOWELL, BEECHER HINKLE, HARRY CAPERTON, STANLEY YOUNG, BILL HALSTEAD, ALLEN JONES, AND BILL CONKLIN.

former scouts who camped at "McClintic." However, as the council continued to grow, it became clear that larger and more adequate facilities were needed to handle the larger enrollment. 1959 was the last year of operation for Camp Clifton McClintic. Buckskin Scout Reservation opened in 1960 as the new council scout camp.

THIS PHOTO FROM THE LATE 1940S SHOWS MEMBERS OF TROOP 146 OF ST. ALBANS, WEST VIRGINIA, ON THE STEPS OF THEIR TENT AT CAMP MCCLINTIC. THEY ARE, TOP TO BOTTOM, IN THE LEFT ROW: EDDIE VAUGHN, CHARLES HUTCHINSON, JACK LANIER, TOM ROBERTSON, AND DAVID TERRY. ON THE RIGHT, TOP TO BOTTOM, ARE BILL HENSLEY, JAY MCCORMICK, NEIL FRIETS, HOWARD RIMMER AND SCOUTMASTER BILL WYATT.

BUCKSKIN RESERVATION, 1960–PRESENT

BUCKSKIN SCOUT RESERVATION, located in Pocahontas County, West Virginia, consists of twelve hundred acres west of Route 28 and six hundred acres east of Route 28. Referred to as Dilley's Mill by the old-timers, the council acquired the title to the land in July, 1957. One of the people who helped secure the land was Sam Hill. Hill was a telephone company executive in Charleston, but he loved the beauty of the Pocahontas County area.

The land was bought through the generosity of Mr. Palmer Stacy. Additionally, three neighbors of the property donated 44 acres of their own land to allow deeper flooding of the lake site.

A dam 500 feet long, 200 feet wide at its base and 20 feet wide across its top was built. It is 35 feet high. The dam created a lake of approximately 16 acres that is suitable for swimming, boating and fishing.

The camp was dedicated on July 23, 1960. John G. Fox was chairman of the capital campaign to raise the funds to construct the camp.

Many companies were responsible for building the new camp. Their donations of money, time and materials made the camp possible.

The camp construction committee was headed by Sam Hill as general chairman. Committee members included E. A. Bartells, J. W. Bell, Jr., John G. Fox, Roy D. Koch, Charles P. McCabe, Eugene L. Pleninger, E. W. Poinier, Jr., Myron R. Renick, Ed W. Rexrode, W. W. Rogers, Donald C. Shonk, Dr. J. H. Thornbury, E. V. Wickline, and William W. Withrow. At the time of the camp's dedication, special plaques and memorials were provided. Specific camp areas were dedicated to people who had contributed to the securing of property and construction of the camp. Those people and organizations were:

MANY SCOUTS WILL RECALL ROLLING INTO THE BUCKSKIN SCOUT RESERVATION, PASSING THROUGH THESE GATES.

HEALTH LODGE	Doctors and dentists of the Buckskin Council Area
DINING HALL	Mrs. Ruth B. Thomas
CENTRAL SHOWER FACILITY	Godfrey L. Cabot
UTILITY DISTRIBUTION SYSTEM	Frank B. Lamb
M.H.F. KINSEY ROAD	M.H.F. Kinsey
CAMP SITE	Harold Wehrle (The area's first Scoutmaster)
CAMP SITE	The Kanawha Valley Mining Institute
CHAPEL	W. O. Abney (First Council Treasurer)
FLAG POLE PARK	Colonel Walter C. Phillips
ENTRANCE GATE	M.L. "Johnnie" Johnson (Scout Executive)
PROGRAM SHELTER	Harry Brown
ADMINISTRATION BUILDING	D. W. and Frances Stubblefield
PROGRAM SHELTER	John D. Hover
TRADING POST	Howard Wehrle (First Boy Scout)
LAKE	Sam C. Hill
CAMP SITE	William A. Boone
RIFLE RANGE	Citizens of Charlton Heights
AQUATIC FRONT	Citizens of Upper Kanawha Valley
TRAIL	John G. Fox
CAMP AREA	Dr. Clifton C. McClintic
DAM	Charles P. Guice (Council's First Silver Beaver)
DONALD C. SHONK ROAD	Donald C. Shonk

From its opening in 1960 to the present, Buckskin Reservation has served the council for 45 summers—longer than the previous three camps combined. Tens of thousands of scouts have hiked its trails, splashed in its lake, worked toward advancement in rank, and more. At this writing, scouts and former scouts from 11 to 61 years of age can look back with fond remembrance of one or more summers they spent at "Buckskin."

The lake and chapel at Buckskin Scout Reservation.

An early "Buckskin" brochure.

The Buckskin Camper

Published By Buckskin Council, W. Va. March 22, 1961 Scouting Is Outing

Six-Day Scout Camp Program Opens June 18, Closes Aug. 5

OA Planning Fellowship June 2, 3, 4

The Order of the Arrow is planning a fellowship weekend at the Buckskin Council Scout Reservation in Dunmore, June 2, 3, 4 this year.

All OA members in good standing (that means if you've paid your OA dues) are invited to attend. There will be a business meeting, some work on the OA ordeal grounds, repair and making of Indian costumes, recreation and a regular fellowship.

There is a fee for this one, to cover the cost of mess hall meals during the weekend. It's $2.50 per head, so if you're planning to bring a carload, be sure someone in the crowd is rich.

There are about 240 OA members in good standing in the council at present, so the weekend of June 2-4 ought to be a ball.

PLAN NOW, CAMP LATER

Use Camp Session For Advancement

Scout advancement can and should be a big part of your camp program. Most advancement can be handled in the course of regular Patrol and Troop activities and should be a natural result of a good Unit program — planned before you come to camp.

Special helps are available through your Troop Commissioner at camp for training purposes (not examination) on advancement skills.

Be sure every Scout brings his own advancement card and handbook to camp.

SCOUTING IS OUTING

Physical Exam Is Camp 'Must'

All campers must be given a health examination by a medical doctor within two weeks prior to attendance at camp. Boy Scout medical forms will be given to scouts upon registration.

A medical recheck is given at the camp upon arrival of the unit. This is to prevent the spread of communicable diseases.

PAUL HACKNEY of Troop 4, Charleston, packs out after spending an unforgettable week at the Buckskin Scout Reservation last summer. Early reservations hint this year twice as many Scouts will go to camp. Second week period is completely taken.

Trail to Scout Reservation Leads Through Marlinton

We didn't hear of too many Scout trains getting lost and wandering around the wilds of Pocahontas County last summer trying to find the way to the Buckskin Reservation, but just in case you're on the trail for the first time this year, here are simple directions for getting there.

Take the Seneca Trail (U. S. 219) to Marlinton. At Marlinton take State Rt. 39 east to the first fork (it's about 7 miles out of Marlinton). Take the left fork. (It's Brown's Creek Road but you may never see a sign) for 7 miles. Just before you come to the Reservation entrance, you'll come to first a horseshoe bend and then a narrow culvert sitting on a diagonal, as you might expect.

Don't speed up after slowing down for the culvert, the gate is the next turn off to the right.

If you're being stubborn and coming south on 28 or west on 84, pick your own landmarks, but don't say we didn't warn you.

Who would ever want to come that way?

WILL YOU BE THERE?

Scout Camping at the Buckskin Reservation this year is being set up on a six-day cycle to eliminate the coming in-checking out confusion that marked weekends last summer. The saddest experience the camp staff members had last year was the incoming rush of new campers that prevented them from saying the kind of farewells they wanted to those departing.

This season, check in time is Sunday afternoon from 2 to 5 p.m. Check out time is the next Saturday after lunch.

The first meal at the mess hall for incoming campers will be Sunday evening dinner. The mess hall will open at 5 p.m. immediately following the retreat ceremony in front of the Memorial Flag Pole.

There will be a Protestant Chapel service at dusk on Sunday evening followed by an Opening Campfire on the lake front.

At present two leader orientation sessions are scheduled on Sunday evening. The first will be after dinner, the second after the opening campfire. These will be the times when leaders post the times for their Troop swims, troop shoots on the rifle and archery ranges; Troop boating, Troop use of the ax and rope lot and volunteers for the camp flag ceremonies.

Taps will be blown at 10 p.m. Sunday and every night at the Reservation.

On Monday morning, those who did not get their swim checks Sunday afternoon will get them at the waterfront.

Clip and fill out coupon on page four of this newspaper to make your reservation for Buckskin Camping this summer.

The only camp-site activities scheduled for Monday, Tuesday and Wednesday are the morning Flag raising, mess hall meals and the retreat ceremonies, which will be held every day except Wednesday and Saturday.

Troops are urged to use the old, familiar, "exchange campfire" on Monday and Tuesday evenings. It's a great chance to get the boys together and let them test their skills with Scouts from other Districts.

On Wednesday, the mess hall will close after lunch and remain closed 'til breakfast Thursday. All units will be given food for cooking out Wednesday evening and Thursday morning.

Mess Hall breakfast Thursday is optional to permit overnight hikes.

A word of warning to Units which aren't accustomed to dehydrated cookery. The mess hall supplies are dehydrated, which allows them to be packed on overnight hikes without refrigeration. They're not too difficult to prepare and, cooked right, downright tasty, but some practice with dehydrated cookery before you come to camp will stand

(Continued on Page 3)

Keep This Camping Check List

Here is a list of the things you should pack for Camp.

Registration Card
Health blank completed by family doctor.
Sleeping bag or blankets
Changes of underwear
Toiletries with 2 towels
Work clothes
Extra shoes
4 pairs of socks, handkerchiefs
Pajamas
Sweater or jacket
Poncho and raincoat
Scout handbook
Complete summer uniform
Swimming suit
Scout knife (no sheath knives allowed)
Mess kit
Compass
First aid kit
Sheets (if you use blankets)
Small Bible or prayer book
Cook kit

In addition to the above, here are some things you'll find downright handy.

Inexpensive camera
Notebook and pencil
Rain boots
Scout ax
Pillow
Flashlight

PLAN NOW, CAMP LATER

Bucky Says . . .

"Two weeks in a tent doesn't equal Scout Camp!"

It is hard for thousands of scouts to imagine it, but before any buildings were built this was what would become Buckskin Scout Reservation's dining hall and trading post area.

This July 1969 photo was taken during retreat (flag lowering). Some of those pictured are, front row (nearest camera) Troop 146 Scoutmaster Charles Evans and Scout Stan Wyatt (in campaign hat). Second row (nearest camera) Roger Rasmussen (in civvies), Paul Priddy, scouts C.W. Eaker, (unknown), Bill Endicott, Steve Kraft.

A church service, July 1969.

Let's Go Camping at...

The Buckskin Scout Reservation

A Boy Scout Camp

OPERATED BY THE

BUCKSKIN COUNCIL

OFFICE SERVICE CENTER—1414 KANAWHA BLVD., E.

CHARLESTON, WEST VIRGINIA 25301

This camp staff photo was taken in 1970 or 1971.

The waterfront provides ample swimming and boating at Buckskin Scout Reservation, as this 1985 photo shows.

OUTDOOR LIFE

Scout Camp Offers Badges And 'Break'

By LYNN WITHROW
Of The Daily Mail Staff

DILLEY'S MILL — Roger Dahmer keeps going to Boy Scout camp to get merit badges. "They're easier to get here," he said.

Jeff Boggess likes camp because it gets him away from the city.

To Eddie Massie it's "just kind of a break from home."

Whatever their reasons, the boys were enjoying their week at Buckskin Council Boy Scout Campheee in Pocahontas County.

The camp opened for the summer in June and will have different groups of scouts through early August.

"We may have had 900 boys here by the end of the session," Robert Wilson, camp director, said. "The cost is $33 per boy and we provide tents, food and all facilities. The only things the boys bring are their bodies and gear."

Wilson said he thinks more troops but fewer boys will use the facilities this year since the number of boys per troop has been declining.

The 2,800-acre camp is in the Monongahela National Forest about 12 miles from Marlinton.

The camp offers a variety of activities. Scouts can earn Merit badges, hike (the camp has two 50-mile trails through the forest), swim, go boating on Lake Sam Hill, learn archery or riflery.

Dahmer, 17, is a fifth-year camper. The son of Mr. and Mrs. Harlen Dahmer of St. Albans and a member of Troop 126, sponsored by the United Methodist Church in River Lake, he hopes to be a staff member next year.

Another Troop 126 member, Bogess said he likes swimming best of all.

The 11-year old son of Mr. and Mrs. Ted Bogess of St. Albans, he is working on four Merit badges — music, buglary, fish and wildlife management, and basketry.

Massie, 12, a first-year camper, said he enjoyed the break from home.

A resident of Frankford, Greenbrier County, Massie is a member of Troop 181, sponsored by the Williamsburg Fire Department.

"My favorite activity is fishing," the first-year camper said. "I'm pretty sure I will be coming back next year."

Paul Westefield, 14, son of Mr. and Mrs. George Westefield of Charleston, said, "I've gone to camp at Bluestone, and I think this one is more educationally busy, but it's fun to do."

Westefield, a second-year camper, and Kelly Angel, a first-year camper, hoped to get four Merit badges during camp.

"I'd like to come back," Angel, 11, said. He is the son of Mr. and Mrs. Michael Angel of Charleston.

Church ana Angel is a member of Troop 68, sponsored by the Cross Lanes Methodist Church.

Third-year camper Rob Lilly of St. Albans said he has advanced in rank eact time he has come to camp.

"I wouldn't come if I didn't like it," said the 15-year-old son of Mr. and Mrs. Robert Lilly of St. Albans. He is a member of Troop 126.

"The days seem long around here, but they're not at all boring," commented Freddie Dodd of Eleanor.

Dodd, son of Mr. and Mrs. George A. Grimm, is a first-year camper and member of Troop 164. "I'm sure I'd like to come back," he said.

St. Albans resident Tom Morton, 12, said he thought the camp was good. The son of Mr. and Mrs. Donald Morton, he is a member of Troop 126.

Boys between the ages of 11 and 18 are attending the summer camp.

Wilson said girls also could attend as long as they brought a female advisor with them.

The council has plans to expand the camp this summer.

"From July 13 to 26, two units of the National Guard will do some construction work," Wilson said. "The Guard will build us a new road in the Pioneer area (land across the lake from the facilities), a new commissary and three staff cabins."

ROW, ROW, ROW YOU
Boy Scouts Learn Pro

Daily Mail City
PAGE 1B
CHARLESTON, WEST

:ARN A MERIT BADGE
·edure on Lake Sam Hill

—Daily Mail Photos by William Tiernan.

Page *LOCAL NEWS*

:SDAY EVENING, JULY 8, 1975

MORE THAN JUST CAMPING — Boy Scouts do more than camp when they spend a week at Buckskin Council Boy Scout Camp in Pocahontas County. Varied activities are offered to scouts, who earn merit badges while attending the camp. Above, staff member Bob Burnette of South Charleston practices his archery. At left, camper Shawn Howley, 11, of St. Albans, spends his spare time whittling.

TROOP 250'S JAMIE JARVIS SCORES IN THE GREASED WATERMELON CONTEST, JULY 1973.

TAPS, JULY 4, 1996.

July 2003, cooking dinner at Buckskin are, left to right, Neil Reynolds, Jonathan Davis, Don Sargent, Andy Caudill, and Sam Jackson. Dennis Hanshew in background.

It isn't always summer at Buckskin. Sam Jackson, Bobby Hypes and Bobby Shamblin enjoy breakfast on this backpacking trip in March 2003.

Chapter Five

Heroic Deeds & Council Activities

This photo, taken at Fola, West Virginia, around 1955, was for the purpose of presenting a lifesaving medal. The scout to whom the medal was to be presented is unknown. Behind the table are Fred Parish, John Hover, Ward Eister, and Scout Executive Johnny Johnson.

Acts of Heroism

One of the important facets of scouting is the training scouts receive in first aid, rescue activities, and the like. Throughout the history of the Buckskin Council there have been many acts of heroism in which scouts used the training they had received to save lives and property.

One of these occurred in the late 1920s when a South Charleston scout named Dale Johnson saved a life. A great crowd of people looked on as a residence was burning one winter morning. The news soon spread that an aged woman was trapped on the second floor. Johnson knew her well and knew which room she occupied. Quickly he rushed into the smoke-filled house, ran up the stairs, and was soon seen emerging from the house, staggering under the weight of the woman whom he was carrying by means of the "fireman's lift." Both Johnson and the woman were suffering from suffocation and minor burns, but they lived through the experience.

For many weeks and months afterwards, neighbors recognized the scout. Seeing him coming they'd say, "That's Dale Johnson. He saved a life." The Scout Council made application to the National Council for an Honor Medal which was presented to the youthful hero several months later.

Years later Scout Executive M.H.F. Kinsey was at a scout rally in one of the church gymnasiums. He overheard one of the scoutmasters checking over his attendance and caught the name of Dale Johnson. Kinsey found the boy and told him of a Dale Johnson who had saved a life a number of years earlier. Kinsey was surprised to hear the boy say, "He was my father."

Another act of heroism occurred July 29, 1927, when several scouts who were camping and hiking near Dundon on Buffalo Creek near Clay, West Virginia, looked down from a high point near Eagle Bend. They saw that a large tree had fallen across the B&O Railroad tracks.

The boys knew it was near the time when the afternoon passenger train would be coming through. They also saw that the sharp curve in the tracks would make it nearly impossible for the engineer to see the tree in time to stop the train. Four of the boys ran a mile and flagged the speeding train with their neckerchiefs. The train was able to stop in time. The boys were members of Troop 50, of Clay Courthouse. Their names were Wilbur Frankfort, Denville Moore, Richard Shelton, and Clifton Summers.

Another well known scout was Charles Albert of Troop 20 at Rufner Memorial Presbyterian Church in Charleston. He was an Eagle Scout, had won the Harmon Foundation Scholarship, and had saved the lives of several people. He had been awarded the Veterans of Foreign Wars medal for heroism, having saved at least six lives from drowning.

A tragic incident involving Albert occurred on a January afternoon in 1928. It was Sunday and Council Executive Kinsey was at home when his phone rang. He was told that some Boy Scouts were drowning in the river at a location near Veazey and Kanawha Streets. Kinsey immediately went to the spot near the Kanawha City Bridge where a large crowd of spectators had gathered on the riverbank.

The three boys were Charles and John Albert and another scout, Freeman Kyle. All three boys were expert swimmers, but in the icy river swimming was not generally possible for more than a few minutes.

The boys had not intended to swim. Rather they had built a small boat and were trying it out on the river that afternoon. They were attempting to row

12 VICTIMS PULLED TO SAFETY IN SINGLE DAY

Rescuing Swimmers 'Old Story' To Coal River Youth

Rescuing drowning men, women and children at the Upper Falls of Coal river is getting to be an old story with young Creed Wood, who is only 24 years old and who went to the assistance of the first threatened victims of the stream 12 years ago.

If you saw the young man in a crowd he would probably be other than the one you would choose who has a record of at least 20 rescues, perhaps more because he has kept no record.

Creed, who graduates from Morris Harvey college in August, weighs but 140 pounds and is five feet and eight inches tall. He plans to make a career of school teaching and will be a member of the Nitro elementary school faculty this coming year.

Quiet and unassuming and not one to seek publicity, the young man was most recently in the news last week when he expertly assisted in applying artifical respiration to two girls who narrowly escaped death at Upper Falls and were revived after being on the river bottom for four minutes.

HE LIVES with his parents, Mr. and Mrs. C. E. Wood directly above the falls and it is second nature for him to run to the river when he hears a call for help from the popular swimming spot.

Last week he partially revived a 15-year-old girl and a 19-year-old girl at the falls and then accompanied the younger to the hospital in an ambulance, administering respiration all the way. He still has two big blisters on his knees that he got during the wild ride as he bent over the unconsciois girl.

CREED WOOD

Crede got into the habit of rescuing people when he was 12 years old. He saw an elderly man and two girls get into the water beyond their depth in front of his home. Being a little small to be of much help, he did the next best thing. He jumped in the river and pushed a small log to them to cling to.

The most exciting day that Crede has experienced occurred last summer when the river spot was thronged with swimmers. Crede sat on the bank until somebody got into distress and then went to their assistance. He pulled 12 from the stream during the day, a remarkable accomplishment even at a metropolitan beach, and this is the first word of it that has been printed.

ANOTHER TIME last year the river was high and swift when three boys began yelling for help, one about to drown the other two. Crede got two of them free to go to shallow water and then went to the third. The boy grabbed him tightly and down they went.

"I got lose from him under water and thought I had him secure," he related. "I got my hand in his hair to hold him and it was so short I could not get a grip. I lost him and he drowned."

THE BOY'S father later told Crede that his son had gotten a crew haircut the day before.

One experience he does not like to recall occurred when he was in a small boat while the river was being dynamited in an effort to raise a drowning victim. Through a misunderstanding, the operator on the boat had it almost directly over a charge of dynamite when it exploded.

His life saving activities are what he considers a responsibility to people in trouble. He is not a paid life guard, instead just a young man who lives near the swimming spot.

"I can't sit on the bank when somebody needs help," he said.

On a recent morning Mr. and Mrs. Wood were awakened at 3 a. m. by a woman screaming for help. They jumped up and started for the river without awakening their son, a sound sleeper.

ONCE THEY reached the river, the woman who was standing in shallow water and hiding in the dark from a party of other swimmers, began laughing and said it was all a joke.

"If I had been awake," said Crede, "I would have held her head under water until she would have needed help.

across from the south shore to the north when in midstream a large river steamer passed and the waves upset the small boat. The boys began to swim back to the south side.

As they desperately swam, Charles Albert, looking back, noticed that Kyle was in trouble. Charles, himself stiff and cold, turned and started back to help Kyle. At that point he saw the unfortunate Kyle sink and he knew it was hopeless.

Albert, now drawing on his own reserve of

energy, could do little but attempt to save himself, and he was finding it hard to move his arms and legs.

In the meantime, someone had obtained a boat and was rowing toward the boys. He managed to rescue both Albert boys, but it was fifteen minutes more before Kyle's body was brought up. The boy was dead.

The Albert brothers, unhurt and recovering quickly from the exposure and freezing they had experienced, attended the funeral of Freeman Kyle two days later.

In another incident that took place during the Summer of 1929, Kinsey was taking some boys, including Charles Albert, to Camp Walhonde. There was little in the way of improved road and Kinsey had to cross Rabel's Hill. When they reached the crest of the mountain they saw a car in front of them topple over the side of the hill, down some 40 or 50 feet. In the car were a man and a woman.

Scout Albert ran to the front of the bus, jumped out, and was soon over the hill with his first aid kit. The man and woman were injured and still in the badly demolished car. The man's arm was badly lacerated and he was losing blood quickly. Albert made a tourniquet and applied it to stop the hemorrhaging. The man was taken to a Charleston hospital where the emergency room doctor said that Albert's quick actions had saved the man's life.

Charles' father, C. C. Albert, was himself an outstanding scouter who served on the council board for a number of years. During much of that time he chaired the finance committee. He passed away while his boys were still involved in scouting. Charles Albert, Jr., became an executive with WestVaco Corporation in South Charleston and his brother John became an Episcopal rector in Cincinnati.

LIFESAVERS— Williard S. Jones thanks Berry Rogers, center, and Wade Myers for saving his life. He suffered a heart attack at a Cub Scout meeting, and the two boys gave artificial respiration until medical aid arrived. They received national medals of merit for the action.

NATIONAL LIFESAVING AWARDS

Medals For Scouts

Putting into use techniques they learned in Scouting resulted in a saved life and national awards for two South Charleston boys.

Wade Myers and Berry Rogers, both 10, are credited with saving the life of Williard S. Jones, 33, of South Charleston, who suffered a heart attack last February. The seizure came as Jones was leading a Webelos den meeting.

The youngsters were awarded the national Medal of Merit during a dinner last night at Christ Church United Methodist, Quarrier and Morris streets.

Robin Meadows, Scout executive, in speaking of the heroics of the two Webelos, said Jones fell to the floor after suffering the seizure and suffered a broken jaw, crushed teeth and a severe cut.

"Wade and Berry reacted cooly and skillfully as they administered artificial respiration and controlled bleeding from the cut. They also sent for help," Meadows said.

Berry is the son of Mr. and Mrs. John Rogers of King Street and Wade is the son of Mr. and Mrs. Thomas D. Myers of Southerland Drive, South Charleston.

A July 20, 1951 story in the *Charleston Daily Mail* detailed heroics of former scout and scout leader Creed Wood who lived near Upper Falls of Coal River near St. Albans. Wood, by that time 24 years of age, had rescued about two dozen swimmers who had found themselves in water beyond

Life Saver Scout Award Winner

By MARK PAXTON
Of The Daily Mail Staff

The highest honor ever given a West Virginia Boy Scout was to be awarded today to a Wyoming County boy who pulled a drowning teen-ager from the Greenbrier River even though he was outweighed by 115 pounds, scout officials say.

Byron Alfrey, an 11-year-old seventh grader at Kopperston Grade School near Oceana, was awarded the Honor Medal for Lifesaving by the National Council of the Boy Scouts. Gov. Rockefeller was to present the medal to Alfrey at a ceremony in the Governor's Reception Room at the capitol.

Alfrey is believed to be the first West Virginian to be awarded the medal, and is the first in the nation to receive the honor this year.

A shy, 85-pound resident of Kopperston, Alfrey was fishing from a small boat along the Greenbrier River near Alderson last July when he heard screaming from the bank. Eddie Highlander, a 200-pound 13-year-old, had been wading in the water and stepped into a hole, plunging him suddenly below the surface.

As Highlander's mother and a neighbor, both nonswimmers, watched in horror, Alfrey quickly ripped off his shoes and dove into the water. Twenty feet away, Highlander, also a nonswimmer, went under for the second time.

"We didn't see it happen," said Alfrey's mother, Judy. She and her husband, James Martin, had been at their campsite nearby when they heard the frantic screaming. "By the time we got to where we could see what was happening, he already had pulled Eddie to shallow water.

"It scared us all to death when we saw his boat empty. We knew he was a good swimmer, but I guess you think the worst when something like that happens."

What the Boy Scout of one year did was grab the heavier Highlander around the neck and pull him to shallow water. Although Alfrey had been taking swimming lessons for about three years, he said he had never had a similar experience.

Now 12 years old and five pounds heavier, Alfrey doesn't say much about the award other than he's "exited, real happy" about the Charleston trip and meeting the Governor.

His mother, though, is a bit more excited. She admits that she and her husband are "proud of him for thinking so quickly."

Six fellow Boy Scouts from the Kopperston area were expected to accompany the young hero to Charleston today for the awards ceremony.

Wyoming County scout Byron Alfrey saved a life in the Greenbrier River.

Hamon Recieves Heroism Award

Boy scout, John Hamon, whose dad is Ray Hamon of R and D was recently presented the Certificate of Heroism from the National Scouting Council.

The incident that qualified John for the award happened this past Summer at Riverlake Estates in St. Albans. A neighbor boy, Tom Martin, had been swimming across the Lake and evidently tired and was in trouble when John heard his cries for help. A strong swimmer, John immediately rushed to his aid and assisted Tom safely to shore.

John, who is 11 and a student at Lakewood Elementary School, is a member of Troop 126 sponsored by Lakewood Methodist Church. The Hamons are quite a scouting family ... Ray is the Pioneer District Commissioner and is a former scoutmaster and another son, David, earned his Eagle Award last year.

This report appeared in the Union Carbide newsletter in 1975.

their depths. As Wood recalled it, his home was located so near the unsupervised swimming area that several times he heard screams of, "He's drowning." Wood rushed to the beach and pulled the swimmers to safety. Doubtless numerous individuals went on to live productive lives that otherwise would have been stopped short, had it not been for scouter Creed Wood's heroics. A few years later Wood served scouting as a full-time paid Field Executive over the Shawnee and Scowego Districts.

Another heroic act occurred at a scout meeting. Scouts Berry Rogers and Wade Myers, both of South Charleston, were expecting to lead a routine Webelos meeting in

February, 1974, when leader William S. Jones fell to the floor. He had suffered a heart attack. To make matters worse, Jones had a severe cut and was bleeding profusely as a result of his fall. The scouts administered CPR and controlled the bleeding. Ultimately help arrived and Jones, whom they had saved, survived and was present later when both boys were awarded the BSA Medal of Merit on September 12, 1974.

There have been many other scouts, too numerous to mention, who have done heroic deeds. Two others include John Hamon of Troop 126 in St. Albans who swam to save the life of Tom Martin in 1975; and Byron Alfrey, II, of Oceana who saved the life of 13-year-old Eddie Highlander who had stepped into deep water while wading in the Greenbrier River in 1979.

At the publication of this book one of the most recent heroic feats was accomplished by Scout Andy Morrison, 13, of Troop 68 in Cross Lanes, West Virginia. While riding bikes with several buddies, he saw one of them, William Smoot, miss a curve and fly off the road and into a telephone pole guy wire. The wire all but amputated Smoot's right foot. Smoot had come to rest in a mud-filled narrow creek.

"In Boy Scouts, they give you first-aid training and tell you what to do," Morrison told the *Charleston Sunday Gazette-Mail*. "I was scared half to death . . ." Scared or not, Morrison applied pressure by wrapping a towel tightly around the dangling foot and held on while a neighbor called 911. Medical professionals credited Morrison with saving Smoot's life. Smoot's mother, a registered nurse, said, "There is no question in our minds that Andy's clear thinking and fast actions saved William's life." Morrison has been recommended for the Boy Scout's Heroism Award.

Scout training and the Scout Motto, "Be Prepared," have contributed much to the people of the Buckskin Council region. Nowhere is that more evident than in its rich history of heroic deeds.

Council Activities

Aside from weekly troop meetings, camporees, and National Jamborees, Buckskin Council activities have always been many and varied. They include Cub Scout day camps; Webeleos weekends; scout rallies; scout fairs, expositions, day hikes, canoe trips and more.

The fall of 1920 marked the beginning of the council's fall district rallies. At that time there were only three scout districts in the city. Districts one and two were on the east side and district three covered the entire west side of Charleston.

The rallies included knot tying, fire building, first aid, signaling, rope spinning, rope throwing and more. In the early 1920s troops competed against each other. But over time it was discovered that this was not the best plan as it caused injurious competition between members of troops. Thus, a new policy was adopted, that of competing against a set standard rather than against other troops.

The district rallies led up to an annual Jamboree held during scouting's anniversary week in February. In the early years the troop winning the highest number of points in its district rally would be proclaimed district champion and would compete for its district at the larger Jamboree. The team scoring the greatest number of points in the Jamboree was declared city champion.

These 1920s St. Albans area scouts are shown in an unknown activity, possibly an awards ceremony.

Right: The same scouts assembled this display.
Below: Scout activities are typically denoted with a patch.

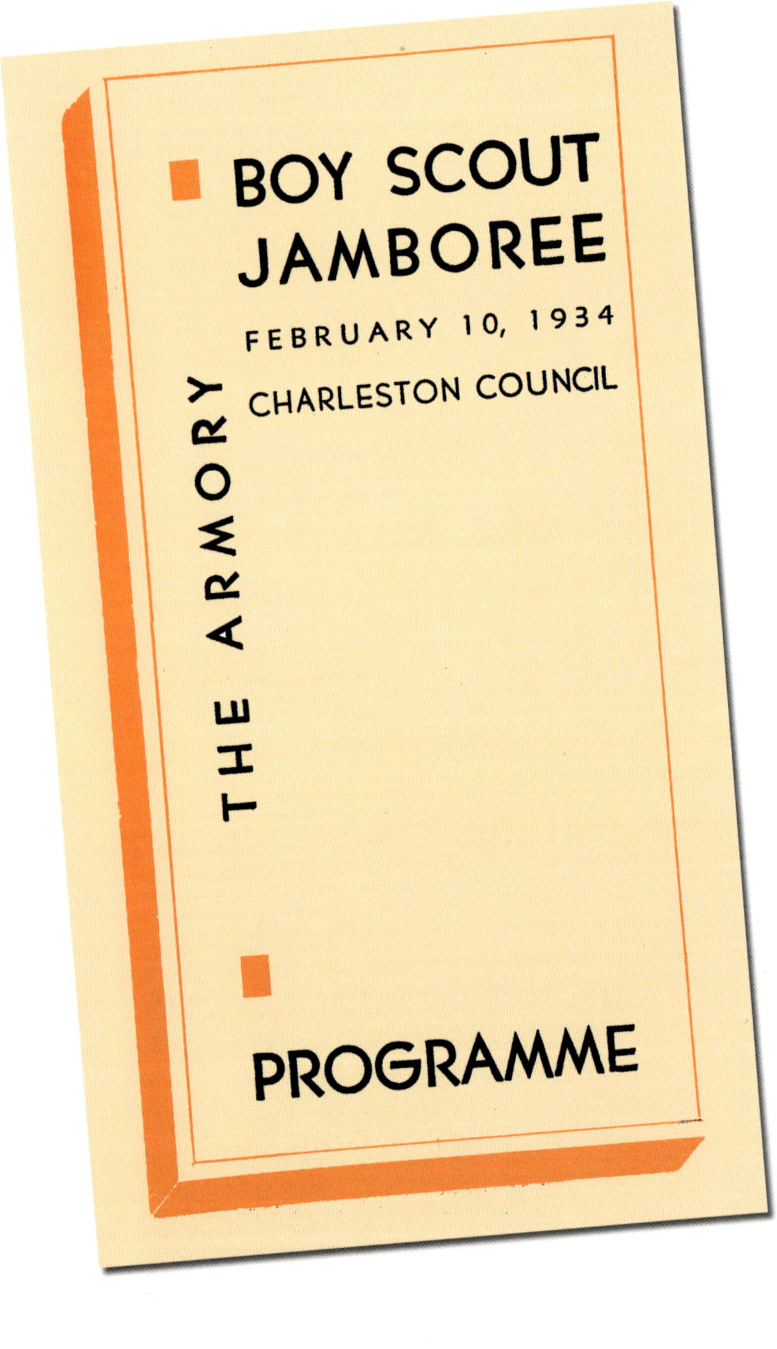

Shown here are the covers of programs for two typical 1930s era scout activities. Contents of the program, above right, appear on the facing page.

PROGRAM

ARCHERY .... Troop 22
Scoutmaster—George Belsches
Sponsor—American Legion

ART .... Troop 71
Scoutmaster—J. Ross Dowler
Sponsor—Warren Sign Co.

ASTRONOMY .... Troop 71
Ass't Scoutmaster—Sebert Brown
Sponsor—The Diamond Dept. Store

ATHLETICS .... Troop 26
Scoutmaster—C. C. Schwerha
Sponsor—The Sport Mart

AVIATION .... Troop 10
Scoutmaster—K. L. Pratt
Sponsor—Frankenberger Co.

CAMPING .... Troop 21
Scoutmaster—W. J. Graham
Sponsor—Manny's Store

CHEMISTRY .... Troop 5
Scoutmaster—A. L. Johnston
Sponsor—B. Preiser & Co., Inc.

COOKING .... Troops 21 and 46
Scoutmasters—W. J. Graham and Charles Wharton
Sponser—Appalachian Elec. Power Co.

CUBS AND EQUIPMENT .... Cub Pack 4
Cubmaster—C. C. Schwerha
Sponsor—Frankenberger Co.

ELECTRICITY .... Troop 5
Scoutmaster—A. L. Johnston
Sponsor—United Neon Co.

FIREMANSHIP .... Troop 26
Scoutmaster—C. C. Schwerha
Sponsor—United Fuel Company

FIRST AID .... Troop 11
Scoutmaster—V. V. Tilton
Sponsor—First M. E. Brotherhood

FORESTRY .... Troop 32
Scoutmaster—J. A. Poe
Sponsor—McClung & Morgan

INDIAN LORE .... Troop 7
Scoutmaster—Henry Smith
Sponsor—Pile Hardware Co.

LEATHERCRAFT .... Troop 65
Scoutmaster—Wentworth Williams
Sponsor—Coca Cola Co.

MARKMANSHIP .... Troop 31
Scoutmaster—Dr. P. A. Haley
Sponsor—Goshorn Hardware Co.

MINING .... Troop 60
Scoutmaster—Roy Kesee
Sponsor—Crab Orchard Improvement Co.

MINING .... Troop 66
Scoutmaster—O. O. Williams
Sponsor—Beckley Kiwanis Club

PIONEERING .... Troop 46
Scoutmaster—Charles Wharton
Sponsor—Dunbar Lions Club

PIONEERING .... Troop 16
Scoutmaster—Evan L. Harris
Sponsor—First M. E. Church, South

RADIO .... Troop 30
Scoutmaster—Howard Wiest
Sponsor—Virginian Electric Co.

SCULPTURE .... Troop 12
Scoutmaster—T. T. Vernon
Sponsor—Baird Hardware Co.

SIGNALING .... Troop 13
Scoutmaster—C. E. Mudd
Sponsor—Bream Brotherhood

STAMP COLLECTING .... Troops 27 and 76
Scoutmasters—Troop 27—M. L. Bush
Troop 76—Ray Ellis
Sponsor—Community of Nitro

TAXIDERMY .... Troop 2
Scoutmaster—Paul M. Barlow
Sponsor—Joseph Popp

WOODCARVING .... Troops 12 and 100
Scoutmasters—Paul McKinney and T. T. Vernon
Sponsor—Appalachian Trail Blazers

WOODWORK .... Troop 71
Ass't Scoutmaster—Sebert Brown
Sponsor—A. W. Cox Co.

This 1935 merit badge show at the Charleston Armory featured numerous troop demonstrations of expertise.

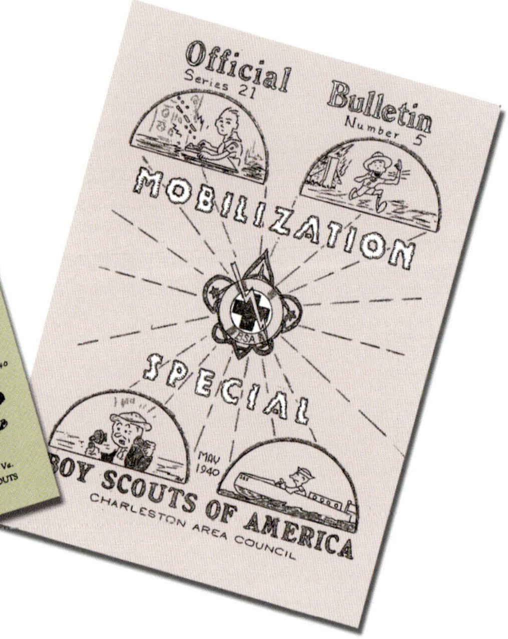

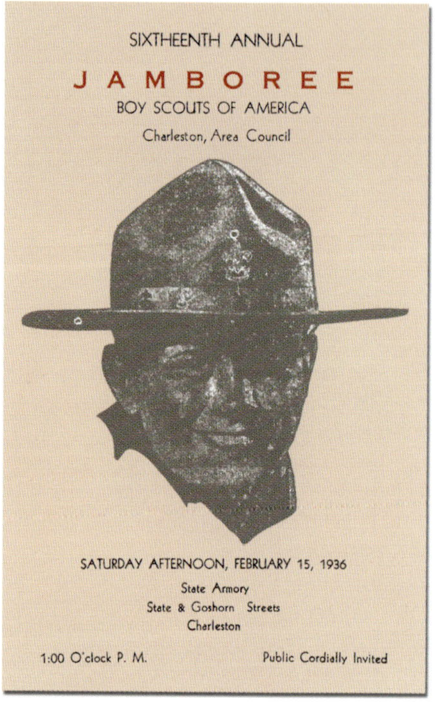

Above and right: Covers of programs for several major scouting events.

Scouts to Serve as Guides for P.T.A. Meeting

Gazette Photo

Approximately 50 properly uniformed Boy Scouts have been selected from the Charleston area council to act as pages and guides Thursday, Friday and Saturday for the thirteenth annual meeting of the West Virginia State Parent and Teacher congress. These Scouts held the honor rank in scouting as Star, Life and Eagle scouts. Twenty-one are of the senior high school age, efficiently trained in the line of duty.

In the group above are 22 of the 50 boys who are to assist the visiting delegates. Reading from left to right, front row—James Riordan, Robert Taylor, Robert Counts, Ted Treadgold, Siton Preston, George Merryman, Robert Blagg, Charles Strong, George Cunningham, Henry Swoope and William Watson. Back row—Robert Shingleton, Warren Point, Richard Hill, Douglas Venable, Robert Johnson, Robert Martens, Reavey Giles, Jack Holz, William Johnson, Arthur Newlon, Stanley Wyatt and H. R. Eggleton, district commissioner of Boy Scouts, in charge of pages for the parent and teacher convention.

These scouts served as pages and guides when the West Virginia State PTA held its meeting in Charleston in the mid-1930s.

AWARDS MADE TO BOY SCOUTS

Youths of Area Perform at Jamboree Before Crowd of 3,000

A crowd estimated at more than 3,000 attended the 18th annual jamboree of the Charleston area council of the Boy Scouts of America at the WCHS auditorium Saturday. Ten events were featured on the program and Charles C. Dickinson, president of the council, presented Eagle Scout badges to Andy Comrey of troop 5, Charleston, and to Guy Reynolds of troop 4, Charleston.

The eagle rank is the highest a scout can attain and placed the two Charleston scouts among the 56 active Eagle Scouts in the entire council, which has a registration of more than 2,000.

The jamboree events included field first aid, semaphore signaling, wig wag signaling (international code), rope spinning, lariat throwing, fire lighting by flint and steel, a compass relay race, a fire rescue and a sack race.

Judged on Point Basis

The 25 participating troops were scored on a point system with troops receiving the same scores receiving the same awards. Out of about 500 possible points, those who received 450 or more received blue streamers, white streamers were awarded for 425, and red for those receiving 400. President Dickinson made the presentations.

Blue streamers were awarded to the following: Troop 9, Charleston, M. M. Hartz, scoutmaster; troop 12, Belle, J. R. Mitchell, scoutmaster; troop 22, Charleston, George H. Belsches, scoutmaster; troop 65, Beckley, Wentworth Williams, scoutmaster; troop 68, Raleigh, Robert Thompson, scoutmaster; troop. 70, Lewisburg, C. W. Burr, scoutmaster; and troop 71, Charleston, Sebert Brown, scoutmaster.

White streamers were given to troop 10, Charleston, K. A. Pratt, scoutmaster; troop 11, Charleston, Virgil V. Tilton, scoutmaster; troop 15, Charleston, Geoffrey P. Jones, scoutmaster; troop 48, Spring Hill, Rev. L. Robert Stump, Scoutmaster; and troop 113, Powellton, Glenn Nelson, scoutmaster.

Red Streamer Winners

Red streamers were presented to troop 4, Charleston, Bernard Simms, scoutmaster; troop 8, Charleston, Louis Mobley, scoutmaster; troop 34, Fayetteville, Milton Propps, scoutmaster; troop 38, Charleston, Earl Crawford, scoutmaster, and troop 98, Beckley, Chester Lynch, scoutmaster.

Jamboree officials included Kenneth A. Pratt, H. R. Eggleton, Geoffrey P. Jones, Sebert Brown, V. O. Raines, T. K. Campbell, C. H. Wiest, Charles Bekenstein, J. Banks Shepherd, Grant Fletcher, Douglas Venable, William Gentry, Guy Belcher, Jr., Harry Martin, Paul M. Barlow, Simon Bailey, Alfred Gardman, George H. Belsches, Evan L. Harris, Carl Householder, Walter Johnson, Charles A. Albert, William P. Coffey, Charles Meadows, Dr. A. L. Bryant, Melvin Mathes, W. J. Graham, Dr. Peter A. Haley, Fred Glover, Harry Bekenstein and Leo Nicaise.

SERIES 25 — *Official Bulletin* — NUMBER 1

SECOND ANNUAL

SCOUT-O-RAMA

Boy Scouts of America

CHARLESTON AREA COUNCIL

Saturday Afternoon, February 12, 1944

CHARLESTON ARMORY

1:00 O'CLOCK

ERNEST L. GARTON, Director

Compliments of

FRANKENBERGER'S

BOY SCOUT TRADING POST

Official Boy Scout Outfitters Since 1916

104 Capitol Street — Charleston, W. Va.

Below: Many scouts will recognize some of these patches in their own collections. Patches play a large role in scouting and are frequently issued to signify participation in a scout activity.

Left: It was common for the scouts to hold annual track meets as this 1946 program cover shows. Right: Much later, as this May 1961 photo shows, Boy Scout track meets continued to be held. The enthusiastic scouts had just finished winning both the 440 and 880 yard relay races. They are James Albert, Robert McClelland, Paul Edwards and Steve Hopkins.

Scout-O-Ramas such as that depicted in this brochure were highly popular in the 1950s and '60s and remain so today. At such events scouts demonstrate various scout skills. Usually these skills follow along the lines of merit badge topics such as nature study, cooking, camping, astronomy and others. At this 1958 event two dozen troops, cub packs and explorer posts put on demonstrations at the North Charleston Recreation Center.

In 1949 a group of scouts from several troops paddled their canoes from Charleston to Cincinnati. Here the scouts are seen ready to depart from the capitol building in Charleston.

West Virginia Boy Scouts Traveled 263 Miles; 12 Youngsters in Six Canoes Happy

BY RALPH BRADY

A drama reminiscent of the days when Indian canoes were standard travel equipment on the Ohio River was enacted Monday when 12 West Virginia Boy Scouts paddled six canoes into Public Landing.

It was the end of an 11-day 263.5-mile river trail for the tanned and rugged members of the "Scouts of the Mountains," an honor group of Buckskin Council, Boy Scouts of America, Charleston, W. Va.

Awaiting the adventurers were parents and relatives and a tractor-trailer ready to transport the youths, their canoes and their duffle back home by motor.

"It was a great trip, except for five straight days of rain, and it'll be an annual event for selected Eagle Scouts of the Buckskin Council," declared Thomas A. Beaver, council field executive and trip leader.

"We pulled into Coney Island two days ahead of schedule and fooled around, took a rest and saw the Cincinnati Reds' double-header Sunday," Beaver said. "Everyone's in tip-top shape—not a paddle blister in the crowd."

The party paddled by day and camped at night on both the Ohio and Kentucky shores except for one night when they drifted in the moonlight cooking breakfast next morning in the canoes, 'just to see how it would go."

"Best day's mileage was 45 miles between Manchester and New Richmond," Recalled Jim Dillon, So. Charleston, trip historian. "That was the day a skipjack leaped out of the water right over my canoe."

"The chow? It was swell, all the way," the group chorused as the last canoe was hoisted out of the water onto the trailer. Cooks on the trip were Jack Lanier, of St. Albans, and Elmer Selby, of Charleston.

Scouts who completed the trip in addition to Beaver, Dillon, Selby and Lanier were: Travis Knight, Robert Crawford, William Pauley and Paul Heavener, of Charleston, Jack Habert, of Bomer; William Dodrill, of Clay; Patrick Donally, of South Charleston, and Richard Johnson, of Rupert.

Scouts were in attendance at the dedication of the "Bear Trek" Scout Lodge at Kanawha State Forest in 1952. Dewey Kuhns is in the dark suit at the right. Ernie Bartels is holding the microphone.

FEBRUARY 12, 1950

West Boy Scouts, Cubs Make Annual Report to State

West Virginia Boy Scouts presented their annual report to the governor Saturday in colorful ceremonies in the house of delegates chamber of the state house. Boys from the two "honor" councils of the state, those having the largest membership increases in the state during the last year, made the reports.

Representing the Cub Scouts was Charles E. H. Bartelos, of Cub Pack 2, at left. Others left to right are Scout Robert Bowman, of Troop 25, Fairmont; Scout Jack Lanier of Troop 146, St. Albans; Governor Okey Patteson, and Charles C. McCape, Sr., vice chairman or Scout Region IV, who supervises Scouting in all the states adjoining West Virginia as well as the Mountain State.

★ ★ ★ ★

Governor Tells Boys They Are Part Of 'Greatest Youth Organization'

Governor Patteson said Saturday that the Boy Scout organization is the "World's greatest and most far-reaching youth organization," and said that the Scouting activities in the state are "most outstanding."

He spoke briefly at ceremonies in the state house at which representative Boy Souts presented the third annual report to the governor by the nine councils of the state.

At the ceremony, held in the house of delegates chamber of the capitol, the governor also presented to the Scouts a state flag which will be flown by the West Virginia contingent at the national jamboree in Valley Forge this coming summer.

In his remarks Gov. Patteson said that the Boy Scout code is one of the very few positive codes of living in the world today.

The Scout reports were presented by representatives of troops and cub packs having made the greatest gain in membership during the year. The governor was told that the Scout membership in the state now is more than 33,000, an increase of some 4,000 during the year. Scout activities included, he was informed, the collection of some 25 tons of clothing, nearly 1,000,000 pounds of waste paper, tree planting, wild life protection, forest fire protection and support of international Scouting activities.

Charles P. McCabe of Charleston, vice chairman of Scout region 4, which includes Ohio, West Virginia and Kentucky, presided.

The invocation was delivered by Rev. Frank Donaldson, pastor of the First Christian church of Charleston.

National headquarters was represented by Howard Knepper of Cincinnati, executive of Region 4.

Prior to the ceremony, members of Troop 91 of Mount Hope were introduced to the governor in his office. Governor Patteson was a charter member of the first boy scout troop organized in his home town of Mount Hope.

An annual report to the governor is a highlight for scouts lucky enough to be included. Above Gov. Okey Patterson poses with the boys who had just delivered the 1950 report.

During the presidential campaign of 1952 Dwight Eisenhower visited Charleston and received a coonskin cap to signify his honorary membership in the Buckskin Council. Left to right in this October 28, 1952, photo are Assistant Scout Executive Burns W. Powell, Eagle Scouts Joe Earl Neff of Troop 88 and Robert Jones of Troop 15, "Ike," Cub Scout Walter Witschey of Pack 7 and Explorer Clarence Dillon of Post 48.

Scouts have typically been involved in, and benefitted from, the support of members of the community. This gathering in 1956 signalled the kickoff for a fund raising campaign. The location is Lee Street Triangle in downtown Charleston.

CAMPING IS THE ACTIVITY MOST TYPICALLY ASSOCIATED WITH SCOUTING. MANY SCOUTS HAVE EARNED THESE CAMPOREE PATCHES.

BUCKSKIN SCOUTS HAVE ENJOYED A WIDE VARIETY OF ACTIVITIES, AND OFTEN SOLD TICKETS TO THEM.

Cub Scouts and Boy Scouts have fun climbing across rope bridge at this expo. West Virginia State Archives, Frank Wilkin photo

This cover, along with the booklet's inside pages that follow, show how Scout Expositions had become huge events by the 1960s.

1961 SCOUT EXPOSITION COMMITTEE

RICHARD KRONMILLER
General Chairman

JIM GIBBS
Arrangements Chairman

C. I. ADKINS
Participation Chairman

J. D. TREANOR
Judging & Awards

CHARLES P. McCABE, JR.
General Vice-Chairman

RALPH A. MOORE
Safety Chairman

DAVID W. BROWNE
Commercial Relations

DEWEY E. S. KUHNS
Special Guests Chairman

JACK SCHEALL
Advisor

RAY BAIL
Competitive Events

B. W. Howard
Ticket Chairman

BEN EDWARDS
R. E. "DICK" SCHAFER
Co-Publicity Chairmen

WELCOME to the 1961 Scout Exposition

Welcome to the 1961 Buckskin Council Boy Scout Exposition. The things you will see here are the result not of a few days or even a few months of preparation. They are rather the result of years of training by volunteer and professional scout leaders; and more particularly of years of learning and doing by Cubs, Scouts, and Explorers.

The actual physical arrangements of booths, displays and events have been nearly four months in preparation. However, you can readily see that to have attained this finished product in only four months would be an impossible accomplishment. It has been possible only because these young participants have in their daily scout training developed the skills which you see displayed here.

These boys and their leaders have worked long and hard to produce an exposition which they hope will be pleasing to you as you see it unfold. But more importantly, you will see in evidence those skills which are designed to prepare these boys to be proper American citizens of tomorrow—young men well trained to meet the ever-increasing responsibilities of an ever-changing world.

This then is the true goal of Scouting—to Build, Serve, Achieve. And this 1961 Exposition is a public report to you in our stewardship of the responsibility which has been entrusted to us, that of the early training of the boys of the Buckskin Council.

J. Alex Gettman

J. Alex Gettman, General Chairman
1961 Scout Exposition

UNITED FUND

The members of the Buckskin Council, Boy Scouts of America, wish to recognize and thank the UNITED FUNDS in our various communities in Kanawha County, and the local independent campaigners, for the support they provide to the council program.

UNITED FUND

SUPPORT UNITED GIVING

BUCKSKIN COUNCIL
BOY SCOUTS OF AMERICA

SCOUT EXPOSITION

APRIL 21 and 22, 1961 CHARLESTON CIVIC CENTER

BOOTH DIRECTORY

SHAWNEE DISTRICT

Unit No.	Booth No.	Chartered Institution	Leader	Subject
Troop 1	70	St. Mark's Methodist Church	Frank Vigneault	Rope Craft
Troop 2	24	Sacred Heart Catholic Church	John P. Swint	W. Va. Camping Sites
Pack 28	47	Sacred Heart Catholic Church	Frank Hill	Kitchen Craft
Troop 3	77	First Baptist Church	Henry H. Hale	Safe Shootin'
Troop 5	14	First Presbyterian Church	D. C. Carlson	Signal Towers (2)
Post 5	81	First Presbyterian Church	Robert K. Barnes	Mt. Hiking & Camping
Pack 18	37	First Presbyterian Church	Harry W. Adams, Jr.	Plastic Handicraft
Pack 5	124½-25	Fort Hill P. T. A.	Charles E. Rogers	Air Adventure
Troop 9	138	Brotherhood Va. St. Temple	M. A. Mendel	Civil Defense
Troop 10	131	St. John's Episcopal Church	Owen Mahan	Compass
Troop 11	65	Christ Church Methodist	G. B. Pullen	Railroad Merit Badge
Pack 11	34	Christ Church Methodist	John W. James, Jr.	Friends of Other Lands
Post 111	87	Christ Church Methodist	Frank N. Clark	Fly Tying
Troop 12	10	Asbury Methodist Church	Harold L. Cook	Primitive Transportation
Troop 16	22	St. Agnes P. T. A.	B. H. Swint	Railroading
Pack 29	74	Charleston Baptist Temple	W. E. Holt	Paper Mosaics
Troop 31	8	Baptist Temple	H. K. Townsley	Printing
Post 31	68	Baptist Temple	John B. Holden	Dutch Oven Cooking
Post 4	12½-11	Kanawha Presbyterian Church	J. D. McGrew	Personal Fitness
Troop 93	108	Simpson Methodist Church	Benjamin Toliver	Axemanship
Pack 93	62	Simpson Methodist Church	Henry C. Haynes	What Cubs Can Do
Pack 84	103	Oak Hill P. T. A.	Denzil O. Wood	Paper Mache
Troop 98	19	Village Chapel Presbyterian Ch.	E. R. Blake	Electricity
Pack 98	66	Village Chapel Presbyterian Ch.	Charles E. Powell	Indian Country
Troop 144	76	St. George Orthodox Church	Michael Howard	Chemistry
Pack 144	119	St. George Orthodox Church	Geo. Jas. Russell	Coal Jewelry
Troop 201	91	Ruffner Memorial Presbyterian	Joel C. Bennett, Jr.	Space (Static Missile)

ST. ALBANS-NITRO-PUTNAM DISTRICT

Unit No.	Booth No.	Chartered Institution	Leader	Subject
Troop 25	145	First Presby. Ch. of St. Albans	R. D. Webster	Safety
Pack 26	20	St. Marks Episcopal Church	F. Harvey Herbert	Cub Scout Chemistry
Troop 27	140	Nitro First Presbyterian	Wm. N. Westlund	Making Merit Badge Replicas and Patrol Flags
Troop 50	106	Highlawn Baptist Church	Jim Roberts	Sculpture
Troop 75	115	Highlawn Presbyterian Church	R. G. Kronmiller	Patrol Equipment
Troop 77	146-47	E. K. Perrow Mem. Presbyterian	J. L. Johnson	Tumbling & Acrobats
Troop 83	12½-13	Mr. Vernon Baptist Church	Wm. R. Newman	"Camp Living"
Troop 128	27	Evangelical United Brethren Ch.	Jeremiah Poe	Radio
Troop 146	107	St. Andrew's Methodist Church	Wm. H. Wyatt	Rope Work
Post 146	32	St. Andrew's Methodist Church	Ray Robertson	Hi Fi Sets & AM Radio
Troop 151	96	St. Paul's Methodist Church	Joe F. Holstein	Models and Handicrafts
Pack 51	113	Methodist Men St. Paul's Meth.	T. N. Clark	Things Cubs Can Do
Troop 162	102	Poca Methodist Church	Darrell L. Brown	Pioneering
Troop 200	73	St. Francis Roman Catholic Ch.	John J. Dlugos, Jr.	Cooking
Pack 200	144	St. Francis Roman Catholic Ch.	Karl J. Mixson	Salt Modeling
Troop 232	143	Chemical City Chapel of First Presbyterian Ch. of St. Albans	W. J. Watson	Models
Pack 232	149	Chemical City Chapel of First Presbyterian Ch. of St. Albans	Dwight C. Webb	Plaster Craft
Troop 250	30	Riverlawn Presbyterian Church	R. F. Trowbridge	Indian Dancing Costume
Pack 250	29	Riverlawn Presbyterian Church	Carl Cobb	Indian Lore
Post 250	40½-41	Riverlawn Presbyterian Church	Paul Dunkle	Mechanics
Pack 31	128	St. Andrew's Methodist Church	Paul M. Churton	Plaster Casting & Painting

NINE RIVERS DISTRICT

Unit No.	Booth No.	Chartered Institution	Leader	Subject
Troop 135	33	Gassaway Baptist Church	Van Allen Smailes	Ancient & Modern Lighting Methods
Troop 155	137	Gassaway Methodist Church	Donald Greenleaf	Plaster Casts of Animal Track
Troop 192	130	Hope Baptist Church	Fred L. James	CP Gadgets & Equipment

BURNING SPRINGS DISTRICT

Unit No.	Booth No.	Chartered Institution	Leader	Subject
Troop 8	94	Imperial Colliery Company	Harold Walker	First Aid Team
Troop 19	39-40½	Judson Baptist Church	G. S. Lewis	Camping
Pack 19	78	Judson Baptist Church	Hubert B. Fout	Indian Craft
Troop 37	82	Godfrey L. Cabot, Inc.	Ralph W. Moore, Sr.	First Aid
Troop 55	132-33½	Mt. Juliet Methodist Church	James Johnston	Railroad
Post 55	129	Mt. Juliet Methodist Church	Clarence Mauzy	First Aid
Troop 85	133½-134	Pt. Lick Gospel Tabernacle Assn.	Allen L. Burdette	Camping
Troop 121	123-124½	Reynolds Memorial Method. Ch.	Clark Lamp	Outdoor Living

FAYETTE DISTRICT

Unit No.	Booth No.	Chartered Institution	Leader	Subject
Troop 63	53	Montgomery Rotary Club	Art Pierce	Printing Merit Badge
Post 63	54-55	Montgomery Rotary Club	Peter Mintreas	Pottery Merit Badge
Pack 63	52	McClung Bible Class Presby. Ch.	David S. Long	Minstrels
Post 91	44	Mt. Hope Lions Club	Ray Hughes	Electricity
Troop 100	48	The Old Kanawha Baptist Ch.	D. H. Brown	Home Repairs
Troop 115	105	Semet Solvay Division Allied Chemical Corp.	Jack McCoy	Pioneering
Troop 125	109	Church of God	Charles H. Prather	Scouting
Troop 141	45	Charlton Heights Methodist Ch.	K. F. Robbins	Signaling
Post 225	135	Charlton Heights Methodist Ch.	R. M. Arnold	Personal Fitness
Troop 225	21	Falls View Presbyterian Church	J. L. Workman	Fishing
Troop 240	126	Gauley Bridge Methodist Church	Earl Kincaid	Archery
Pack 240	15-16	Gauley Bridge Vol. Fire Dept.	H. N. Walker, Jr.	Pinewood Derby
Squadron 3	58	American Legion No. 149	Frank K. Thomas	Air Progress
	56	Alpha Phi Omega Mu Tau W. Va. Institute of Technology	Raymond Rose	College Careers

LONG RIFLE DISTRICT

Unit No.	Booth No.	Chartered Institution	Leader	Subject
Troop 4	63	Calvary Baptist Church	John S. Keeney, III	Camp Craft
Post 104	31	Calvary Baptist Church	Guy O. Davis	Disaster Preparedness
Pack 15	38	J. E. Robbins Elementary School	J. H. Vollmer	Clown Game
Troop 20	98	First Church of God	Bruce Garrett	Rope Making
Troop 22	36	Coopers Creek Church of God	John A. McQuain	W. Va. Native Shrub & Trees
Troop 30	93	Central Methodist Church	Charles E. Smith	First Aid
Troop 38	101	Humphreys Memorial Methodist Men's Bible Class	H. C. Gadd	Leatherwork
Post 38	121	Humphreys Memorial Methodist	Preston B. King, Jr.	Firemanship
Troop 42	97	Sixth Street Methodist Church	Rev. Cue M. Canterbury	Conservation
Troop 47	67	Trinity Methodist Church	Charles McClain	Weather
Pack 47	75	Trinity Methodist Church	Max W. Richardson	History of Aviation
Pack 62	127	Glenwood Grade School	Glen M. Colby	Craft Display
Troop 71	26	Wesley Methodist Church	Herbert M. Young	Screen Printing
Pack 71	51	Wesley Methodist Church	Alfred Atkins	Paper Mache
Post 71	49	Wesley Methodist Church	H. B. Miller	Explorer Hobbies
Troop 107	71	Randolph Street Baptist Church	Fred Gilmer	Fishing & Fly Tying
Troop 120	85	Rebecca Littlepage Presbyterian	George G. Quinn	Compass
Troop 124	42	Starcher Baptist Church	George Shawver	Crafts
Pack 124	141	Starcher Baptist Church	John Brady	Popsicle Stick Craft
Troop 130	17	Fola Missionary Baptist Church	J. C. Legg	Scout Hobbies
Squadron 130	86	West Charleston Kiwanis Club	Harry A. Martin	Radio
Troop 163	69	St. Anthony School	Robert Elliott	Distillation
Troop 172	111-12½	Blue Creek Advent Christian Ch.	Jack Blackwell	Indian Lore & Taxidermy
Pack 172	139	Blue Creek Advent Christian Ch.	Daris Nida	Basket Making
Troop 193	88	Church of Jesus Christ of LDS	Jennings Taylor	Troop Specialty
Pack 193	64	Church of Jesus Christ of LDS	Glen E. Pennington	Bird Houses

SCOWEGO DISTRICT

Unit No.	Booth No.	Chartered Institution	Leader	Subject
Ship 2	35	Group of Citizens	Dr. W. B. Goff	Sea Scouting
Pack 6	142	The Holy Name Society—Ch. of Christ the King Catholic	Bill Feldhaus	Carnival Prizes
Troop 32	84	Lions Club of South Charleston	J. W. Copley	Survival
Post 32	18	Lions Club of South Charleston	Thomas Cox	Aviation
Pack 25	95	First Presby. Church of So. Chas.	S. A. Kendall	Alaska
Troop 45	151	Blessed Sacrament Rom. Cath. C.	T. F. West	Pack Frame Making
Post 45	46	Blessed Sacrament Rom. Cath. C.	Larry Schmidt	Auto Mechanics
Troop 46	83	First Baptist Church	E. W. Smith	Pioneer Craft
Pack 146	25	First Baptist Church	Wm. A. Wilkinson, Jr.	Wood Working
Troop 129	116	Men's Barraca Class of First Baptist Church	Ray Bail	Basketry Merit Badge
Post 129	114	First Baptist Church	H. L. Flippin	Radio
Troop 175	9	First Presbyterian Ch. of Dunbar	H. R. Slaughter	Home Repairs
Pack 175	148	First Presbyterian Ch. of Dunbar	Emmett H. Skeen	Bird Houses
Troop 189	122	John S. Rumbaugh Bible Class of St. Paul's Methodist Church	M. A. Aitken	Maps
Pack 189	72	St. Paul's Methodist Church	Edward Caflisch	Winding Things
Post 289	118	John S. Rumbaugh Bible Class of St. Paul's Methodist Church	Herman E. Mattox	Social Activities
Troop 195	59	First Methodist Church	O. C. Loyd	Geology
Post 195	150	First Methodist Ch. of So. Chas.	J. H. Ankeney	Air Plane Cockpit
Troop 197	7	McKinnon Memorial Presby. Ch.	R. W. Fogarty	Electricity
Pack 197	92	McKinnon Memorial Presby. Ch.	Ken E. Steele, Sr.	Tin Craft
Pack 237	117	E. U. B. Church of Dunbar	Carl W. Johnson	Railroad & Trains
Troop 244	23	Darlington Methodist Church	Bob Dumont	Firemanship
Pack 244	104	Darlington Methodist Church	Edgar L. Burns	Reed Weaving

COMPETITIVE EVENTS

Unit No.	Chartered Institution	Leader
Pack 28	Sacred Heart Church	F. B. Hill
Pack 172	Blue Creek Advent Christian Church	Daris Nida
Pack 93	Simpson Memorial Methodist	Henry Haynes
Pack 121	Reynolds Memorial Methodist	W. J. Reese
Pack 152	St. Timothy's Lutheran	W. F. Hill, Jr.
Pack 189	St. Paul's Methodist	E. G. Caflisch
Troop 2	Sacred Heart Catholic	John Swint
Troop 3	First Baptist of Charleston	Henry Hale
Troop 4	Calvary Baptist	J. S. Keeney, III
Troop 5	First Presbyterian of Charleston	D. C. Carlson
Troop 6	First Presbyterian of St. Albans	D. L. Ellis
Troop 20	First Church of God	Bruce Garrett
Troop 22	Coopers Creek Church of God	John McQuain
Troop 30	Central Methodist	C. E. Smith
Troop 47	Trinity Methodist	Charles McClain
Troop 50	Highlawn Baptist	Jim Roberts
Troop 55	Mt. Juliet Methodist	J. G. Johnson, Jr.
Troop 75	Highlawn Presbyterian	Dick Kronmiller
Troop 107	Randolph St. Baptist	John A. Deahl
Troop 123	Clay Rotary Club	W. A. Sutphin
Troop 125	Carlisle Church of God	Charles Prather
Troop 130	Fola Missionary Baptist	J. C. Legg
Troop 162	Poca Methodist	D. L. Brown
Troop 172	Blue Creek Advent Christian	W. J. Blackwell
Troop 189	St. Paul's Methodist	M. A. Aitken
Troop 244	Darlington Methodist	Bob Dumont
Troop 229	Group of Citizens	E. G. Kincaid
Troop 232	Chemical City Chapel	W. J. Watson
Troop 240	Gauley Bridge American Legion Post 129	E. C. Kincaid

SPECIAL BOOTHS

Booth No.	
1-2-3	1961 SCOUT EXPOSITION OFFICE
4-5-6	COUNCIL SERVICES
57	COUNCIL EXPLORER CABINET
99-100	DIAMOND DEPT. STORE "SCOUT OUTFITTER"
136-120	FRANKENBERGER'S "SCOUT OUTFITTER"
89-90	ENGINE SALES & SERVICE CO., INC., AND R & K SALES & SERVICE
Lobby	SPECIAL GUESTS
3	INFORMATION BOOTH
	U. S. AIR FORCE RECRUITING
	U. S. NAVY RECRUITING
	U. S. ARMY RECRUITING
	SOAP BOX DERBY REGISTRATION

OFFICERS OF THE BUCKSKIN COUNCIL

PRESIDENT
Alex Gettman

COMMISSIONER
Dr. Ivan Stafford

TREASURER
Paul Hinkle

VICE-PRESIDENTS
Fred Otto
J. D. Treanor
Sam C. Hill

COUNCIL EXECUTIVE STAFF

Richard Lebetsamer,
Scout Executive

Jack Scheall
Assistant Scout Executive

Creed Wood
Shawnee and Scowego Districts

Rex Johnson
Greenbrier Valley and Nine Rivers Districts

Bill Stewart
Fayette and Burning Springs Districts

Charles Hoffman
Long Rifle District

Dale Holsopple
St. Albans-Nitro-Putnam

OFFICE STAFF

Mrs. Mary Eddins
Mrs. Velda Monk
Mary Jean Zain
Mrs. Aileen Robertson

ACKNOWLEDGMENTS

We also want to take this opportunity to thank the many men and women who served on our committees, the council office staff, the many leaders and assistants and committeemen, and the Cubs, Boy Scouts and Explorers, and each and every person or organization, without whose time and efforts this show could not have been produced.

Our thanks also are extended to the NEWSPAPERS, RADIO AND TELEVISION STATIONS in our area for their fine assistance in keeping the public informed of our SCOUT EXPOSITION.

TICKET SALES GIFTS DONATED BY:
KANAWHA SUPPLY ____ Camp Lantern
McCLUNG & MORGAN, South Charleston ____ Pine Wood Derby Cars
KELLEY DYER DEPT. STORE, St. Albans ____ Trail Cook Kit

FRONT COVER — Copy of original Norman Rockwell Painting for the Boy Scouts of America reproduced by Mrs. Paul Jochim of Charleston, W. Va.

BOY SCOUTS OF AMERICA
BUILD — SERVE — ACHIEVE

Trips to Philmont Scout Ranch in New Mexico are a highlight for many scouts and their leaders.

Boy Scout Goodwill Day To Be Held Saturday, Jan. 26 with 'Bag Drive'

Saturday, January 26th, is Boy Scout Goodwill Day in St. Albans.

At 9 o'clock that morning approximately 19 Troops of the Boy Scouts of America in St. Albans will begin an extensive "bag drive" for Charleston Goodwill Industries. Containers for usable and repairable discards will be distributed to all homes in the city.

An estimated 500 boys—cubs, scouts and explorers—will take part in the volunteer drive. At least 50 adults—Den Mothers, Scoutmasters and assistants—will guide the efforts of the youths during Saturday's initial step in the project. The Scouts will deliver the bags to households in St. Albans, with the request that residents fill them with discards—including shoes, clothing, rags, small appliances, books, toys and allied items.

Ralph A. Moore, Scout Commissioner of the St. Albans-Nitro-Putnam District, who will direct the campaign, said he expected full cooperation from the city householders.

"This is the first time a Goodwill Industries drive will have been undertaken by the Boy Scouts within the Buckskin Council," Moore stated, "and its success is of vital importance to our youths and to the handicapped employees and trainees of Goodwill.

"Similar drives have been sponsored by the Boy Scouts of America in 46 cities throughout the United States," he added, "and with success. If they can do it—then so can we!"

Aiding Moore in the supervision of the Goodwill drive are E. W. Poinier, district chairman, and W. H. (Uncle Bill) Graham, a well-known figure in local scouting.

The final phase of the drive will take place Saturday morning, Feb. 16. At that time, crews of Scouts will carry out a pick-up program. These units, each assigned a definite section of the city in which to work, will collect the filled Goodwill containers and place them in storage space being furnished by the Bank of St. Albans.

Transportation of the discarded materials to the Goodwill receiving station at 628 Kanawha Blvd., E., in Charleston, is expected to take from three to four days.

The following is a list of the Cub Packs, Scout Troops and Explorer Posts expected to participate in the city-wide Boy Scout Goodwill Day program, their sponsors and leaders:

Troop 6 and Pack 66, First Presbyterian Church, Donald Campbell and H. G. Kirtley; Troop 25, Packs 40 and 46, First Baptist Church, Tom Estep, Edgar Baxton and Faust Dambrosia; Troop 50, Pack 150 and Post 150, Highlawn Baptist Church, James S. Roberts, Ernest Foster and James Samples; Troop 75, Pack 10, Highlawn Presbyterian Church, Alex Rice and Dallas M. Harper; Troop 128, Evangelical United Brethren Church.

Troop 134, St. Paul's Baptist Church, James T. Johnson; Troop 146, Pack 31, St. Andrew Methodist Church, W. H. Wyatt, Jr., and G. T. Powell; Troop 153, Pack 153, St. Mark's Episcopal Church, Paul Carr and James Gibbs; Troop 187, Abney Street Church of God, Arthur Plumley; Troop 200, Pack 200, St. Francis' Catholic Church, Bert Murray and W. H. Wingate; Troop 233, Pack 48, St. Peter's Methodist Church, A. E. Hendricks and Chester Talbot.

Other troops outside of St. Albans participating in the drive will be Troop 164 from Eleanor; Troop 180, Bancroft; Troop 206, Hometown; Troop 162, Poca; and Troop 167, Black Betsy.

Mr. Carl Wright, neighborhood commissioner of Poca, will be in charge of the drive outside of St. Albans.

Many scouts have participated in distribution and collection of Goodwill bags.

THESE SCOUTS MADE THE ANNUAL REPORT TO GOVERNOR JAY ROCKEFELLER ON MAY 8, 1984.

ZACH BONNETT AND TYLER JACKSON OF TROOP 146 COMPETE IN THE SPEED SAW AT THE WINTER CAMPOREE, CAMP ARROWHEAD JANUARY, 2002.

MAY 11 - SCOUT FAIR

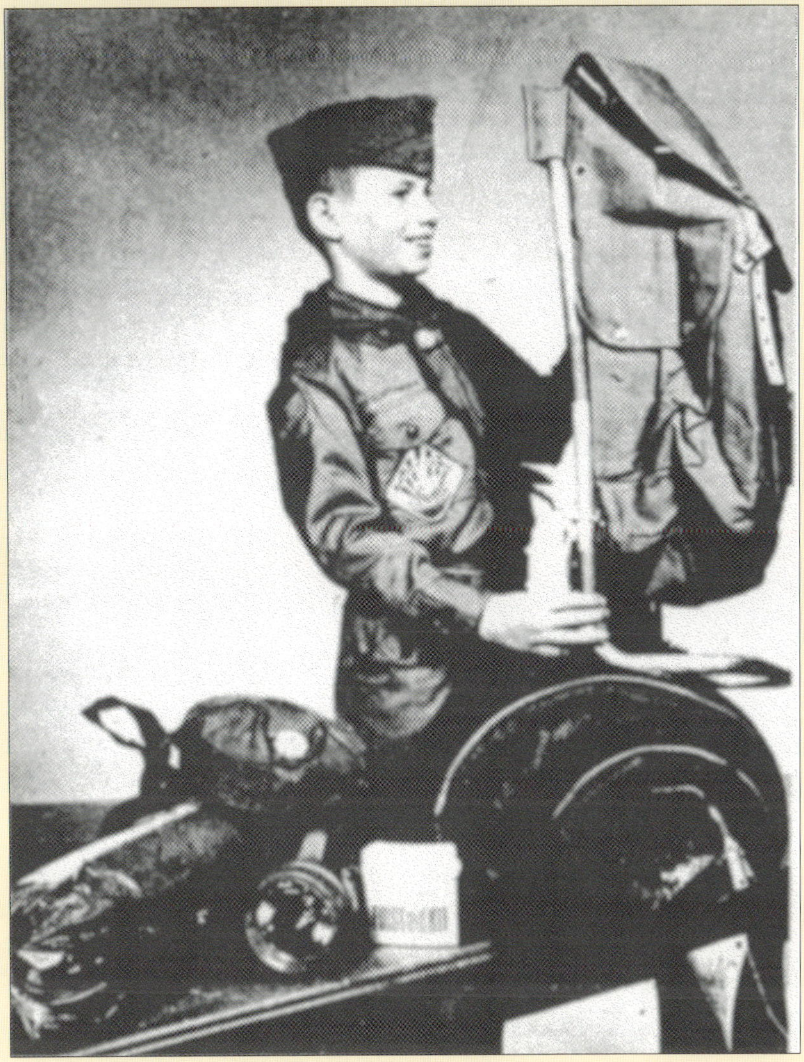

1974 SCOUT FAIR. . . .MEN For Tomorrow. The Scout Fair serving Braxton, Clay, Fayette, Greenbrier, Kanawha, Monroe, Nicholas, Pocahontas, Putnam and Webster Counties will be held May 11 in three locations in West Virginia. At Morris Harvey Soccer Field in Charleston, the State Fair Grounds at Fairlea in Greenbrier County and at Carnifax Ferry State Park, Summersville.

Hours at all Scout Fairs will be from 11 a.m. to 6 p.m. Admission $1. Children under 12 admitted free.

The purpose of Scout Fair '74 is to provide unusual programs for boys in Scouting, to show Scouting to the public, to provice Cubs and Scouts with opportunities for prizes and equipment. Judging will be on quality, originality, informative value, attractiveness and neatness.

More than 150 exhibits will feature booths and demonstrations from a wide selection of Scouting subjects.

A Scout Fair brought the ideals and activities of scouting to members of the community.

SUNDAY, GAZETTE MAIL, OCTOBER 7, 1984.

Photo by CHRIS DORST

Straight Arrow

Scoutmaster John Patterson teaches Jeffrey Galloway, 8, the proper way to shoot a bow and arrow at Saturday's Scout Expo at the South Charleston Community Center.

THIS YOUNGSTER IS DRAWING BEAD ON HIS FUTURE BOY SCOUT CAREER.

Chapter Six

Some Early and Present Troops By the Numbers

When you ask someone what troop he was in, the answer can be confusing. Troop numbers sometimes changed as a troop's charter expired, then was renewed with a new number. That would have happened in an instance in which an expired number was picked up by another troop, perhaps in another town. For example, the original Troop 11 existed in Charleston, but when its charter expired in the late 1980s, that number was picked up by a troop in Delbarton, Mingo County.

It is interesting and informative to look at the locations and activities of a number of troops thought to be representative of Buckskin Council Scouting. When calls for information about troops went out, these responded.

Troop 1

Troop 1 was chartered in 1925 (although it was by no means the first troop to exist in the council). Its sponsoring institution was Boyd Memorial Church in Charleston, West Virginia. But its charter expired in 1931 and the Troop 1 number was picked up by St. Mark's Methodist Church, which is also in Charleston. Later, Troop 1 moved again, simply because the charter had expired at St. Mark's Church. This time Number 1 was given to the troop at Reynolds Memorial United Methodist Church in Marmet, West Virginia. That charter stayed active through 1987 when it expired. At present, Troop 1 is sponsored by the Men of First United Methodist Church, Princeton, West Virginia, in the Mountain Dominion District. Its Scoutmaster is Michael P. Lamothe.

Troop 2

Troop 2 is among the oldest continuously chartered troops in the council. It is sponsored by Sacred Heart Co-Cathedral in Charleston, the Mountain Rifle District. It was originally chartered in 1919. At that time the chairman of the troop committee was the Reverend Father Thomas, pastor of the church. In 1979 a 60th anniversary of the troop was held. Featured on the program that night was John Swint, a longtime area scouter with Troop 2 who was a relative of Dr. B. P. H. Swint, one of the troop's original organizers in 1919 and a member of the troop committee for many years thereafter. The present scoutmaster is Peter J. Dailey.

Troop 3

Troop 3 originated in 1920 at St. Matthew's Episcopal Church in Charleston and its charter was active there for ten years. When its charter expired in 1930 the number lay dormant for several years until it was picked up for one year by Vandalia Methodist Church in Beaumont, West Virginia. Later, other sponsoring institutions included Boyd Memorial Christian Church in Charleston, Hanson Chapel in Charleston,

Troop 2 Scoutmaster John Swint does some map work with an unknown scout.

Troop 2 prepares for a swim at Buckskin Scout Reservation in 1991. Pictured is George Burke, assistant scoutmaster.

Massey Chapel Methodist Church in Big Chimney, and First Baptist Church of Charleston, which held the charter through 1985. Today Troop 3 is located in the town of Beckley, Seneca District, where it is sponsored by Memorial Baptist Church. Its Scoutmaster is Charles H. Carpenter.

Troop 4

Like Troop 2, Troop 4 was chartered in 1919 and remains actively chartered today. It is sponsored by Calvary Baptist Church in Charleston. In the 1920s and 1930s Troop 4 was one of the most active in the council. One of its members was Charles Thom, who was its Senior Patrol Leader in 1927. In 1930 Thom won a national award in signaling. On February 15 of that year he set a record by sending fifty letters by semaphore in only 22.4 seconds. The medal he won that day remains on display in the museum on the lower level of the Council Service Center in Charleston (page 221).

An early photograph of Troop 4, chartered at Calvary Baptist Church, Charleston.

Troop 5

Troop 5 is chartered at First Presbyterian Church in Charleston, where it began in 1914. In the 1950s, 1960s and 1970s, Troop 5 had over 100 scouts registered and more than 40 Eagles were awarded. It was likely the largest troop in the state during those times, with so many scouts that it split into two divisions, holding its meetings on two different nights. Active scoutmasters during those years included Jim Thomas, who was in the coal business, and Herb Miller. From 1975 to 1983 the scoutmaster of Troop 5 was Harvey Gastineau, who produced 29 Eagle Scouts. These included three

This 1946 Parents' night dinner honored Mr. and Mrs. M.H.F. Kinsey as Kinsey was retiring from his long years of service as Buckskin Council Scout Executive. Some of those seated at the table are (left to right): Joe Londeree, Mrs. Kinsey, Sam C. Hill, M.H.F. Kinsey, unknown, unknown, Charles Love.

A Troop 5 scout makes a report to the governor, Arch A. Moore, in 1969.

of his own sons. Tragically, Gastineau died suddenly in 1983. In 1984, Bob Skinner became the scoutmaster and has continued with the troop up to the publication of this book, 20 years. Under Skinner's leadership an additional 48 Eagle Scouts have emerged from Troop 5. Interestingly, Skinner, an oil and gas field sales representative, was never himself a scout but simply wanted to do some community service. That had begun in 1952 when a leader of Troop 13 at Bream Presbyterian Church in Charleston was needed. Although Skinner did not attend that church, he agreed to serve as its scoutmaster, and did so until 1959. At that point Skinner was transferred to another town

Troop 5, 1960s era. Some of those shown include, front row, second from left, Jack Hill; sixth from left, Phil Terrie; to Terrie's left is Bobby Gardner; Brooks McCabe, second from right and John Casto on right. Second row on left is David McCorkle; fourth from right is Nate Casto and to his left is Ted Elden; far right is Charlie Wright. Third row, far left is Jeff Van Olst; eighth from left is Mark Stewart. Fourth row on left is Herb Miller; fourth from left is Steve Davis; third from right is Tony Shepherd. Back row, fifth from left is Bob Elias; to his left is Earl Nestman and to his left is Rob Auld.

The 1980 Pioneer District Winter Camporee featured a dog sled race. Troop 6 of St. Albans pulled hard. In cowboy hat is Mike Stephens. To his left (blue jacket, facing camera) is Shaun Ellis.

A 1980 Winter Camporee was the setting for fire building by Troop 6 (St. Albans) scouts Tim Thompson (standing, left) and Mike De Hart (on ground, back to camera). Others are unidentified.

and was not involved with Charleston area Scouting for several years, until his return and the start of his long involvement with Troop 5.

Troop 6—St. Albans

Troop 6 has long been chartered at the First Presbyterian Church in St. Albans, West Virginia. It had been chartered initially in 1913 as Troop 1, but the charter lapsed, then was renewed. This occurred off and on for several years, each lapse due to a lack of completed paperwork. It has been chartered continuously, as Troop 6, since 1922.

Early scouts of Troop 6 included James Boxley, Clyde Alford (later a coach at St. Albans High School and Mayor of St. Albans), Jordan Hugart, Albert Sharpe, Harry Wheaton, Ralph May (who became a postmaster in St. Albans), Henry Hopkins, Robert Kearns, Hansford Morris,

The other Troop 6: Albert Allen, Jr., presents an Eagle Award in the early 1950s, Beckley, West Virginia.

West Virginia State Archives and Albert Allen, Jr.

THIS 1949 WEEKEND CAMPOUT SHOWS THE SCOUTS OF BECKLEY'S TROOP 6 IN LINE, PERHAPS THEY HAVE BEEN WAITING FOR THEIR DINNER, FROM THE LOOKS ON THEIR FACES. WEST VIRGINIA STATE ARCHIVES AND ALBERT ALLEN, JR.

Herbert Bryan, Charles Kern, Clifford Sutherland, Harry White (later President of the St. Albans Chamber of Commerce), Robert McDermit, Keith Hopkins, Robert Kirk and Ray Kirk.

The troop's first two Eagle scouts earned the award in 1928. They were Arthur Edwards and Carroll Barker. Edwards became a chemist. In World War II he served as a navigator in the Philippines and was captured by the Japanese forces and forced to make the Bataan Death March. He died when an unmarked Japanese prisoner of war ship was sunk by Allied Forces, who thought it was a Japanese supply ship.

Troop 6 has had many distinguished volunteers including the first recipient of the Silver Beaver in the Buckskin Council, C. P. Guice, who was one of its early scoutmasters. Other scoutmasters have included Edgar Delaney, Richard S. Masters, and Donald Ellis, who served as scoutmaster from 1959 to 1986. A longtime assistant scoutmaster of Troop 6 was Robert D. "Bunk" Thompson, from 1961 to 1981, the year of his death. Longtime committee members included Roger Bond and Jim Poindexter.

TROOP 6—BECKLEY

From 1949 to 1991 Beckley's Troop 6 was part of the Appalachian Council and, thus, there was no "number" conflict until that council merged with Buckskin Council. See the photos of "Troops 6."

TROOP 7

Troop 7 was chartered in 1937 at Kanawha Salines Presbyterian Church in Malden, West Virginia. The charter expired after 1951 and was picked up at Wade Chapel Methodist Church in Red House, Putnam County, where the troop was chartered off and on through 1988.

TROOP 8

This troop came into existence in 1948 and was sponsored by the Eleanor Lions Club in Putnam County, West Virginia. Later its charter moved to the Eleanor Presbyterian Church. After that the charter expired and was picked up with Troop 8 emerging in Waneta, West Virginia, sponsored by the Union Mission Church. When the charter expired there it was later picked up for several years by the Imperial Colliery Company

Troop 9 scouts demonstrate old-fashioned artificial respiration at a 1947 Scout Fair.

in Burnwell, West Virginia. It has not been rechartered since 1962.

Troop 9

In 1920 the Young Men's Hebrew Association of Charleston established Troop 9. Later the charter transferred to Jewish Temple of Charleston where it was chartered off and on for many years until 1986.

Troop 10

St. John's Episcopal Church of Charleston established Troop 10 in 1918. The charter was active through 1973 when it expired. No other council troop picked up the number 10 until Teays Valley Ward of Scott Depot, West Virginia, reestablished the troop in 1993 where it remains today.

Troop 11

Troop 11 is another troop that was in existence before the formal organization of the Buckskin Council in 1919. It was established at the First Methodist Episcopal Church in Charleston in 1916. It remained there until 1940 when it was rechartered, essentially without a gap in time, at Christ Church United Methodist where it remained chartered through 1988. At that point the charter was lost and Troop 11 no longer existed. However, the Delbarton, WV (Mingo County, Chief Cornstalk District) Kiwanis Club sought a troop number in 1997 and number 11 being available, they selected it. After one year the troop became defunct but the number 11 was picked up in the year 2000 by the W. A. Conolly Memorial Baptist Church, also of Delbarton. The charter expired there in 2001.

During the 1950s and 1960s when the troop was sponsored by Christ Church United Methodist in Charleston it had a very active outdoor program. The troop averaged about ten camping trips each year. In 1959 Ralph Ross, who was Committee Chairman, and John Howell, a Committeeman, took eight scouts to hike the 32-mile Lincoln Trail located near Hodgenville, Kentucky. The scouts and leaders received medals in recognition of the hike's completion. On their return trip they visited attractions such as the home of Stephen Foster in Bardstown and Calumet Farms which produced racing champion Man O'War.

Troop 12

In 1946 the B'nai B'rith Lodge of Charleston organized Troop 12. In subsequent years the Troop 12 number appeared at Bower Presbyterian Church

These Troop 12 scouts took a five-mile hike one week before Christmas in 1976. The scouts are (left to right) Craig Estep, David Barnette, Jeff Elkins, Mark Klein, Andy Callard, and Jimmy Fiber.

This ceremony took place at Bream Memorial Presybyterian Church in 1949. Troop 13's Scoutmaster was H. "Hike" Hager.

in Charleston, Asbury Methodist Church in Charleston (where the troop was active from 1950 to 1985), and finally at the YWCA Sojourners Homeless Shelter in Charleston from 1992 to 1994. Harold Cook served many years as Scoutmaster while the troop was sponsored by Asbury Methodist Church.

Troop 13

Bream Memorial Presbyterian Church in Charleston was home to Troop 13 for many years, 1919 through 1960. One of its early leaders was Emmett Thaxton who served as scoutmaster from 1921 to 1926. Thaxton was cited by the first Scout Executive, M. H. F. Kinsey, as one of the early influences who helped make the Buckskin Council strong. Over the years scoutmasters included Clarence Mudd, Byron Guthrie, and H.H. "Ike" Hager. In 1952 Bob Skinner became the scoutmaster. He led the troop until 1959. Later Skinner became the longtime scoutmaster of Troop 5. When number 13 was not rechartered at Bream Presbyterian Church in 1960, it was picked up by Boomer, West Virginia's, Boomer Civic Committee. The troop was chartered there through 1977 when the charter expired. Later the number 13 was picked up by the town of Pax, West Virginia, which chartered the troop. From 2001–2004 the Alum Creek Lions Club has been the sponsoring institution for Troop 13.

Troop 14

The South Charleston American Legion Post chartered Troop 14 in 1929. It held the charter through 1947. Later the number 14 appeared at Greenlee Chapel in Charleston, Ivydale Methodist Church in Ivydale, Sattes Presbyterian Church in Nitro, and the Twin City Bible Church in Nitro, West Virginia. The charter expired there in 1986. In 1989 Troop 14 was again chartered, this time at First Christian Church in Bluefield, WV, the Mountain Dominion District. Its present scoutmaster is Wayne Hartley.

Troop 15

This troop was chartered at St. Matthew Protestant Episcopal Church in Charleston in 1934 and the charter remained there through 1983, with the exception of a hiatus in the 1970s. Subsequent to that, the charter expired in 1983 but later was picked up again by St. Matthew Episcopal Church in Charleston in 1998, where it remains chartered today.

Troop 17

Troop 17 was founded in 1991 at the Teays Valley Christian Church, Scott Depot, West Virginia. It previously had been sponsored by Holy Cross Lutheran Church. It is a Pioneer District troop and its present scoutmaster is Gill Rogers.

Troop 19

Troop 19, of the Mountain Rifle District, is sponsored by Aldersgate United Methodist Men, Pocatalico, West Virginia. The troop was founded in 1992. Its present scoutmaster is Dana Burns.

Troop 19 is one of the larger and more active troops in the Mountain Rifle District. It generally has from 22 to 28 boys active. According to its scoutmaster the main objective is for the boys to

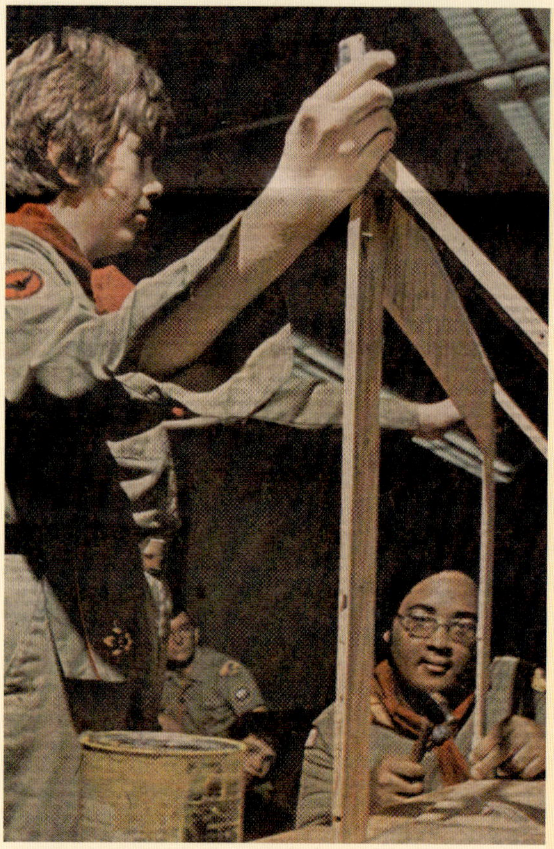

UNIQUE GROUP — Boy Scout Troop 23 is a unique group of boys. The youngsters are all trainable mentally retarded students at Owens Center for Exceptional Children. At left Blaine Hill and Robert Johnson, right, worked on a model stage which will help them earn a theater merit badge. Solemnly reciting the scout oath were Ricky Moore, left, and Gary Harrison. — Daily Mail Photos By Earl Benton.

A Very Special Troop

Owens Boys Enthusiastically Tackle Rigors Of Scouting

By NANYA GADD
Of The Daily Mail Staff

"On my honor I will do my best to do my duty to God and my country...

"...to keep myself physically strong, mentally awake and morally straight..."

Millions of boy scouts have spoken those words, but there was something different about the troop that solemnly recited the pledge yesterday.

Owens Boy Scout Troop 23 has 14 active members. They pay dues, sport green khaki uniforms, and talk excitedly about camping and hiking just like any other scout troop. The difference is all the youngsters are mentally retarded.

Students at Owens Center for Exceptional Children, all the boys are considered trainable. They may eventually lead nearly independent lives but will always need a certain amount of custodial care, according to Troop Leader Janet Vest.

The troop was begun three years ago by a male teacher at the school. When he left there was no man available to lead the boys, so Mrs. Vest volunteered.

"At that time women weren't allowed to be scoutmasters, so the scout office knew me as J. Vest," the teacher said. The profession has since been opened to females, however, and two other teachers, one male, assist Mrs. Vest with the troop.

The boys are able to perform most regular scouting activities; they just move at a slower pace. Merit badges are earned by the whole group since the youngsters are unable to work individually.

For the first time this year, almost the entire troop is outfitted in uniforms. Last Saturday Mrs. Vest took her troop to the Charleston scout office where second-hand uniforms are collected by Goodwill.

"They had a great time down in the basement of the scout office, trying on things and trading pants back and forth," she said.

They also visited Buckskin Council's fall camporee held near Winfield last weekend. Because of the cold rainy weather, the boys at first only huddled and shivered under a shelter.

But they were soon adopted by another group, Troop 57 from the Davis Creek Nazarene Church. The seasoned scouts showed the Owens students around the campsite.

At yesterday's meeting, the troop split into two patrols, the Coyotes and the Roadrunners. After reciting the scout pledge and paying their 10 cent weekly dues, the boys began work on a theater merit badge.

To earn the award, they will perform skits, design and paint sets, and act in a Christmas play. For a skit, they decided to enact a campout in preparation for a trip they may actually get to take.

Sometime this month, Mrs. Vest and the other teachers may take the boys on their first overnight excursion. If they can borrow some camping equipment, they'll go to a farm near Sissonville, she said.

Mrs. Vest believes the boys will gain social skills from being scouts. She called it part of the "normalization" process.

"It helps them learn how to get along in their communities. We really don't like having a separate troop for the retarded. We'd ideally like to see them go into a regular troop," she said.

Itinerant physical education teacher Jack Robertson has been a scoutmaster for several years and helps with the Owens troop when he's at the school.

"These boys can accomplish the same things the others do. We just have to slow the whole program down a bit," Robertson said.

"And they're a lot more enthusiastic," he added.

Troop 23 was established for the special education students at Owens School, Charleston.

learn to be leaders by being active and having fun while learning scouting skills. The troop typically has ten to eleven outings each year and customarily spends a week at Buckskin Reservation in the Apache Campsite. Between 1996 and 2003, twenty-three scouts of Troop 19 earned the rank of Eagle.

TROOP 21

This troop, sponsored by Bland United Methodist Church in Bland, Virginia, of the Mountain Dominion District was founded in October, 1988.

TROOP 31

Troop 31 was founded in May, 1921. It is located at Baptist Temple, Charleston, West Virginia, in the Mountain Rifle District. Its present scoutmaster is James G. Porter.

TROOP 34

Troop 34 is sponsored by St. Andrew Presbyterian Church, Elkview, West Virginia, of the Mountain Rifle District. It was founded in May, 1962, and its present scoutmaster is Edward M. Fox. In the 42 years of the troop's existence, 38 young men have earned the rank of Eagle Scout. Scouts have learned important aspects of our early history by visiting such sites as Williamsburg, Virginia, and the U.S.S. Yorktown. Over the years numerous troop members have been parts of contingents to Philmont and various National Scout Jamborees.

TROOP 36

This troop was founded in 1953 and is sponsored by First Baptist Church in Hurricane, West Virginia, of the Pioneer District. Its present scoutmaster is Steve Caldwell.

TROOP 38

Father Harold and his Eagles

In Troop 38 and his family, the real McCoy

NANYA FRIEND
Daily Mail Editor

HOW do you measure the impact of a human life? In the case of an Abe Lincoln, you might count the generations of students who have memorized the Gettysburg Address.

Or there's Shakespeare, whose words put to paper four centuries ago still are being spoken on modern stages.

For most human beings, impact comes on a much smaller scale. In my family, we're counting Eagle scouts.

My father died almost 18 years ago. Only one grandson had been born. That was my nephew Alex, born in September 1985, only a few months before my father's death.

Two more grandsons soon would come along — my son in July 1986 and Alex's younger brother, Scott, in February 1988.

Almost enough for a scout troop.

Well, my brother and I live far apart, so the boys couldn't be in the same troop. But all three became Boy Scouts, a destiny as certain for them as getting their DPT shots and starting to school.

That's because of a steadfast belief in scouting ingrained in our family psyche by Harold Gadd, longtime scoutmaster of Troop 38.

My dad was a scoutmaster long before my brother was old enough to join. Every Monday night he would put on the khaki green uniform and head down to Humphreys Memorial United Methodist Church on the West Side for the weekly meeting.

On weekends there were hikes and camping trips. Every summer he used a week of precious vacation time to take the troop to the Buckskin Scout Reservation in Pocahontas County.

When it came to scouting, he was hard-nosed. If you wanted a merit badge in knot-tying, you learned square, slip, half-hitch and many more. If you wanted the swimming badge, you mastered every stroke. The same went for hiking, cooking, canoeing, camping, citizenship — there were no shortcuts.

Consequently, his troop produced relatively few Eagles. He disdained what he called the "Eagle mills" that cranked out scouting's top award with predictable ease. A Troop 38 Eagle was the real McCoy.

In making so many adolescent boys work so hard for so long, my father managed to imprint his own children.

We would raise Eagles, too.

Alex received his award last May. Keith's has been approved, and the ceremony is being planned. Scott has met all the requirements and is finishing up his paperwork.

I don't think it's a coincidence that all three made it this far.

Until recently, I didn't know whether my dad had actually been a Boy Scout himself. I asked my brother.

The answer was yes, briefly. He joined a troop but didn't stay in the program as a youth because the family couldn't afford the uniform.

But our grandparents did teach him to be independent and self-sufficient and passed on their love of the woods and outdoors. He built on that knowledge by taking advantage of training opportunities as an adult leader.

My brother told me something else I didn't know.

"You may not remember, but I pinned my Eagle Award on him at his funeral because I thought he absolutely represented what being an Eagle was all about. He's still my guiding light for honor, integrity, love and devotion to family, good citizenship in the community, and doing his duty."

So I'm counting my Eagles. Brother, Eric. Son, Keith. Nephews, Alex and Scott.

And father, Harold.

TROOP 38 WAS REMEMBERED BY *CHARLESTON DAILY MAIL* EDITOR NANYA FRIEND. HER FATHER, HAROLD GADD, WAS TROOP 38'S SCOUTMASTER FOR MANY YEARS. TROOP SPONSOR WAS HUMPHREYS MEMORIAL UNITED METHODIST CHURCH, CHARLESTON.

POST-48 OF SPRING HILL, WEST VIRGINIA, VERY LIKELY SET A NATIONAL RECORD WHEN, IN 1950, AT SPRING HILL BAPTIST CHURCH, A FATHER AND HIS THREE SONS WERE AWARDED THE EAGLE BADGE ON THE VERY SAME DAY. PICTURED, LEFT TO RIGHT, ARE WESLEY DILLON, JAMES DILLON, CLARENCE DILLON AND DONALD DILLON. INTERESTINGLY, DAD WESLEY DILLON WORKED AT UNION CARBIDE AND ALL OF HIS SONS LATER DID SO AS WELL. SONS CLARENCE AND DONALD LATER BECAME MINISTERS IN THE CHURCH OF GOD.

TROOP 46

This Mountain Rifle District Troop was founded in 1949. It is sponsored by First Baptist Church of Dunbar, West Virginia. Its present scoutmaster is Matthew Jones.

TROOP 51

Chief Cornstalk District's troop 51 is located in Logan County. A longtime scoutmaster was Dale Harwood. (See photos on pages 21 and 22.)

Lewisburg, West Virginia's Troop 54 participated in a 1978 Seneca District Scout Fair. In both photos these scouts are working hard in a blindfold competition.

Troop 68

Joel Patten is the scoutmaster of Troop 68, which is sponsored by Cross Lanes United Methodist Church of Cross Lanes, West Virginia, of the Pioneer District. The troop previously was sponsored by Humphrey Memorial Methodist Church. The troop was founded in 1950.

Troop 70

Troop 70 is located in the Wilderness District. Its present scoutmaster is Clifford Baker. The troop is sponsored by Lewisburg United Methodist Church, Lewisburg, West Virginia. Earlier the troop had been sponsored by various groups including the Lewisburg Lions Club, the Rotary Club, the Businessmen's Club and the American Legion, all of the Lewisburg area. It was founded in 1934.

Atomic Round-Up Held for Scouts

LEWISBURG, Jan. 13 (RNS)—Boy Scout Troop No. 70, Lewisburg, held a twin event this past week. Both events were held as a part of the troop's meeting held Wednesday.

One of the events was an Atomic U-235 Round-Up Ceremony, sponsored by the Buckskin Council for Scout Recruitment competition, and the other a Board of Review conducted by Troop 70 committee for three applicants for the rank of second class scout.

Officiating at the U-235 Round-Up Ceremonies was Robie, a robot made by Lewis Detch, a troop member. This robot is equipped with a speaking voice. It is about three feet high, covered with metal foil and is uncanny in its performance of command. This robot has been entered in the robot contest to be judged in Charleston. Winning the competition for the best robot means that eight boys will receive an expense-paid trip to the Oak Ridge Atomic Energy Plant at Oak Ridge, Tenn.

At this Round-Up Ceremony, Brad Stuart, assistant Wolf Patrol Leader, and acting in behalf of the seven "old" troop members, gave a speech of welcome to the 14 scouts recruited since last October. The speech of response was given by Tommy Freeman for the newer members of Scouting. Under the "planning" of the U-235 Round-Up, each of the Scouts from last year had prospected for Uranium (U equals Youth), had "staked a claim" on the new recruits by putting "claim tags" on the newer scouts, and had helped them attain the tenderfoot requirements.

Following this Round-Up ceremony, a Board of Review was conducted for Mike Dawson, Wolf Patrol Leader, and for Herbert Montgomery, who were examined by the board for the second class rank.

Board members present were: Herbert Rothwell, chairman of Troop 70 Committee, E. Wilton Cooper, Hayward L. Hinzman, and Joseph Gerzaffi, who conducted the questioning. Julian Fawcett, senior counselor for the troop, and a former Eagle Scout, prepared the applicants for the board and introduced each boy to the members of the Board of Review.

All three of the troop patrols rose to the occasion with a 100 per cent attendance, and with perfect scores in the merit pointing system designed for Troop 70 by the scoutmaster, Melvin Hickman. The system has been in operation since last October, but this is the first time that the steadily rising scores reached 100 per cent for the whole troop.

Beckley, January 14, 1957

Troop 61

The Citizens for Scouting of Richlands, Virginia, in the Mountain Dominion District sponsor this troop. It was founded in 1975 and its present scoutmaster is Timothy H. Wallace.

Troop 64

Founded in 1937, this troop is sponsored by Emmanuel Baptist Church, Charleston, West Virginia, of the Mountain Rifle District. Its present scoutmaster is Robert Sharp.

Lewisburg, West Virginia's Lions Club sponsored Troop 70. Above: This photo, taken at Camp McClintic, shows Scoutmaster E.V. Wickline as he directs a scout craft project. Left: Troop 70 scouts participated in this 1981 skit.

Troop 71

Troop 71 is sponsored by Wesley United Methodist Church on Charleston's west side. It was one of the earliest troops in Charleston and annually competed in troop competitions, often winning them in the days in which troops competed against each other. Later the troop continued to flourish as troops competed against standards rather than each other. The troop has had many fine leaders, including men such as Sebert H. Brown, Howard Miller and its present Scoutmaster, Woody Hill.

Two early leaders of Troop 71 were Ross Dowler and Don Morrison.

1937

Troop 71 Rally & Jamboree Team.

Rally 625 Points

Jamboree 767 Points [High point Troop for 2nd straight year.]

No. of Points received in Jamboree		Teams
200	★	First Aid – Jr. Bailey, Noble Wyatt, Bill Wyatt and Bill Cherrington (patient).
10	★	Semaphore signalling – Jr. Bailey (sender), Bill Wyatt (receiver)
	★	Wig Wag signalling – Bill Wyatt (sender), Noble Wyatt (receiver)
90		Semaphore, Wig Wag relay – (s) Jr. Bailey, Bill Wyatt (middleman), (w) Noble Wyatt.
24	★	Eight knots on one rope – Noble Wyatt.
24	★	Eight knots on eight ropes – Jr. Bailey.
24	★	Eight knots on eight ropes blindfolded – Jr. Bailey.
32	★	Eight man knot relay – Orville Thomas (clove hitch), Paul Mace (slip), Bill Cherrington (square), Noble Wyatt (bowline), Bruce Chmon (sheetbend), Cornell Jones (timber hitch), Bill Wyatt (sheetbend), and Jr. Bailey (fishermans).
		Lariat Throwing – Noble Wyatt.
	★	Rope Spinning – Noble Wyatt
25		Fire by Friction – Bill Wyatt.
25		Fire by Flint & Steel – Noble Wyatt.
		Fireman's drag & carry – Paul Mace & Bruce Chmon (patient).
48	★	Compass relay – Orville Thomas, Paul Mace, Cornell Jones, Bruce Chmon, Bill Cherrington, Noble Wyatt, Jr. Bailey and Leo Bonhana.

In 1937 Troop 71 of Charleston's west side won its second straight city-wide Jamboree.

Troop 71 Entertains

Members of Boy Scout Troop 71 entertained their parents and friends Friday evening with a banquet at the Wesley M. E. church. An attendance of 78 persons heard Scout Executive M. H. F. Kinsey talk on "The Boy of Today." Mr. Kinsey took the modern scout and contrasted him with the boy of yesterday. Other speakers of the evening included members of the troop committee, J. F. Riggs, E. E. O'Dell and D. L. Morrison.

One of the high points of the program was presentation by the scouts to Scoutmaster Sebert Brown of a scout trophy in appreciation for his work with the troop.

The following scouts were awarded badges: Tenderfoot badges went to Joe Kendall, David Lanham, Frank Wilson, Gene Bailey, John Goad, Keith Coyner, Guy Thomas and Edwin O'Dell. Second class badges went to James Taylor and Jack Grey while Charles Bradley qualified for first class rank.

Guests Attending

Those present were Mrs. Bettie M. Lowe, Mr. and Mrs. D. L. Morrison, Mr. and Mrs. E. E. O'Dell, Mrs. Ethel Coyner, Mrs. George Thomas, Mrs. W. H. Wyatt, Mr. and Mrs. Sebert Brown Mrs. Minnie Jones, Mr. and Mrs. Lant Givens, Mr. and Mrs. Norwood Bonham, Mr. J. Ross Dowler, Mr. and Mrs. C. R. Harmon, Mr. and Mrs. F. A. Wilson, Mr. and Mrs. B. R. Currence, Mr. and Mrs. J. F. Riggs, R. D. Gray, Mr. and Mrs. C. W. Bradley, Mr. and Mrs. J. J. Kendall, Mrs. A. H. Goad, Mr. and Mrs. R. E. Ellis, Mrs. Dan Prouse, Rev. and Mrs. C. S. Thompson, Mr. and Mrs. W. H. Cherrington, Mr. R. I. Davis, Mr. and Mrs. M. H. F. Kinsey, Martha McClure, Doris O'Dell, Callie Jones, Janice Gandee, Pauline O'Dell, Ruby Whited, Phyllis Willard, Jewel Gandee, Mrs. J. K. Gandee, Mrs. H. B. Snodgrass, Mrs. E. T. Hunt, Keith Brown, Jackie Riggs and the following scouts: Billy Wyatt, Charles Harmon, Jr., Joe Kendall, David Lanham, Junior Thompson, Edwin O'Dell, Frank R. Wilson, Billy Ellis, Bobby Ellis, Houston Lowe, Gene Bailey, John Goad, Charles Bradley, Keith Coyner, Guy Thomas, Jack Currence, Cornell Jones, Jack Gray, James Taylor, James Bonham, Billy Cherrington, Charles Davis, Eugene Halstead and Howard Prouse.

This 1930s era clipping shows that Troop 71 entertained parents and its other supporters.

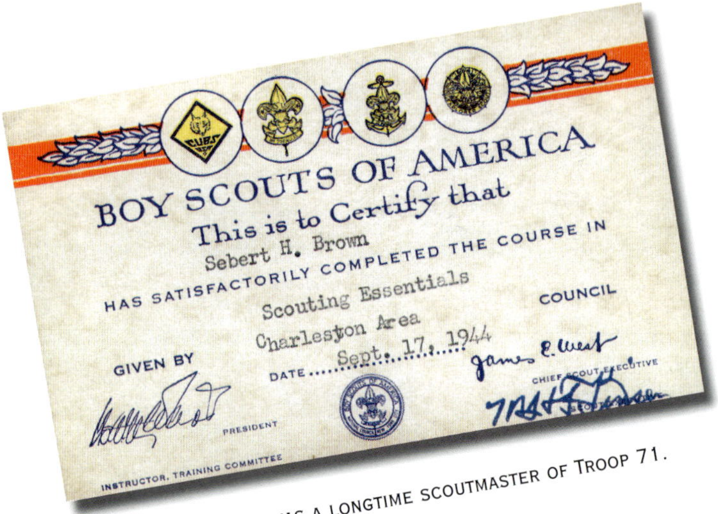

Sebert H. Brown was a longtime scoutmaster of Troop 71.

The highlight of any scout's career is attainment of the Eagle rank. In this 1971 photo Troop 71's Richard Crouser displays the Eagle badge alongside another of the most important awards, the God & Country badge. Troop 71 has long been sponsored by Wesley United Methodist on Charleston's west side.

IS YOUR TROOP OPERATING ON THE TROOP BUDGET PLAN? YES ☒ NO ☐
If not, shall we send you printed information about this Plan? Complete information and copy of the Troop Budget Financial Record Book are available to all Scoutmasters. See your Scout Executive or write to the Registration Service, 2 Park Ave., New York, N. Y.

SCOUT ROSTER

Troop No. (Local) Seventy One of Charleston (City or Town) W. Va. (State)

Council Charleston

NOTE: PLEASE CLASSIFY SCOUTS' NAMES AND LIST SEPARATELY AS INDICATED BELOW

Record in last column only the number of full years of Scouting experience, except for less than 1 year write (-1)
A Scout must be full 12 years of age. No exception can be made. A Sea Scout must be 15.
Indicate Scout's rank as follows: T—Tenderfoot; S—Second Class; F—First Class or higher. Add the letter "a" to indicate Associate.

NOTE: HOW MANY OF THE BOYS ARE—NEGRO [ ]; CHINESE [ ]; JAPANESE [ ]; MEXICAN [ ]; INDIAN [ ].
Population of Town or City if under 100,000 Is Troop in open country How many farm boys

If space is needed for more boys, use a second copy of this same form.

Please arrange names in the following order: 1) Reregistering 2) New 3) New Scouts formerly Cubs 4) Drop'd Returning 5) Transfer

Scout Rank		Family Name	Give Name and Initials	Street	City	Re—Rereg. N—New NC—New Scouts formerly Cubs Dr—Drop'd. Returning T—Transfer	Has Uniform	Age	Number full years in Scouting less than one year write (-1)
F	1	Bailey	Jimmie	Route 5 - Box 150	Charleston	Re	✓		
T	2	"	Gene	" " 150	"	Re	✓	12	
T	3	Bonham	James	" " 152	"	Re			
	4	"	Carl	" " 152	"	N			
F	5	Bradley	Charles	1806 Crescent Rd.	"	Re	✓		
F	6	Currence	Jack	8 Allen Drive	"	Re	✓		
T	7	Coyner	Keith	33 Arlington Ave.	"	Re		14	
T	8	Christian	Joe	Route #5, Box 208	"	Re	✓	13	
	9	Chester	Ernest	1624 Crescent Rd	"	N		13	
T	10	Ellis	William	2005 O'Dell Ave	"	Re	✓	14	
T	11	"	Robert	2005 O'Dell Ave	"	Re	✓	13	
T	12	Goad	John	Route #5, Box 120A	"	Re	✓	13	
S	13	Grey	Jack	General Delivery	"	Re		14	
T	14	~~Halstead~~	~~Eugene~~			Re			
T	15	Harmon	Charles	1819 Bigley Ave	"	Re	✓		
	16	Harkins	Garland		"	N			
F	17	Jones	Cornell	1820½ Bigley Ave	"	Re	✓	17	
T	18	Kendall	Joseph	1827 Crescent Rd	"	Re		12	
	19	Kiser	Dale	Station A	"	N		14	
F	20	Lowe	Huston	224 Cora St	"	Re		17	
T	21	Morris	William	2118 Penn. Ave	"	N		15	
T	22	O'Dell	Carl	1626 Crescent Rd	"	N		12	
T	23	O'Dell	Edwin	2114 Penn. Ave	"	Re	✓	12	
S	24	Riggs	Robert	1805 Bigley Ave	"	Re	✓		
S	25	Taylor	James	Route #5 Box 149	"	Re	✓	13	
T	26	Thomas	Guy	120 Emily St.	"	Re	✓	13	
S	27	Thompson	Charles	320 Alethea St.	"	Re	✓	13	
T	28	Trammell	Bert	2018 Crescent Rd.	"	N	✓	12	
T	29	Willard	Harry	2013 Crescent Rd.	"	N	✓	13	
T	30	Wilson	Frank	1912 Crescent Rd.	"	Re	✓	13	
	31	Withrow	James	Route #5 Box 143	"	N		12	
T	32	Ehman	Bruce	1730 Bigley Ave	"	Re	✓		

PLEASE!—Errors in classification of Scouts are chief source of statistical discrepancies.

PLEASE ENTER TOTALS HERE
Reregistering Scouts........ New Scouts........ New Scouts formerly Cubs........
Dropped Returning Scouts........ Transfer Scouts........

SOMETIMES IT'S INTERESTING TO LOOK AT THE NAMES OF THOSE WHO WERE MEMBERS OF A TROOP FROM LONG AGO. THIS IS AN APPLICATION FOR RENEWAL OF A TROOP CHARTER FOR TROOP 71. THIS APPLICATION WAS FOR THE YEAR 1939. READ THE NAMES. HAVE YOU KNOWN ANY OF THESE FOLKS?

Wolf Head – 100 miles
Pine Tree – 250 "
Indian Head – 500 "
A.T.B. – 750 "
Corsair – 1000 "

Troop 71 Trail Blazers

Miles	Emblems
580	Simon Bailey – Wolf Head, Pine Tree and Indian Head.
	Frank Faulknier – Wolf Head.
	Bernard Hill – Wolf Head.
	Vernon Smith – Wolf Head.
	Stanley Wyatt – Wolf Head, Pine Tree and Indian Head.
400	Noble Wyatt – Wolf Head and Pine Tree.
1029	Bill Wyatt – Wolf Head, Pine Tree, Indian Head, A.T.B. and Corsair.
150	Bill Cherrington – Wolf Head.
	Jackie Currence – Wolf Head, Pine Tree, Indian Head, A.T.B. and Corsair.
	Charles Bradley – Wolf Head, Pine Tree, Indian Head, A.T.B. Corsair
	Howard Prowse – Wolf Head, Pine Tree
	Jackie Gray – Wolf Head, Pine Tree
	Cornell Jones – Wolf Head, Pine Tree, Indian Head
	Joe Kendall – Wolf Head, Pine Tree
	Gene Bailey – Wolf Head, Pine Tree
	Bobby Riggs – Wolf Head,
	Jimmie Taylor – Wolf Head,
	Junior Hughart – Wolf Head.

Numerous members of Troop 71 participated in first Scout Executive M.H.F. Kinsey's Trailblazer's Club. Here is a list of individuals who had achieved several milestones as they worked toward the 1,000-mile hike award.

Troop 71 was proud to display this award, as winner in a 1934 rally.

The scouts of Troop 72, are shown in this 1956 photo, evidently at Camp McClintic. Their scoutmaster is Charles W. McKamey.

On December 11, 1960, Troop 71 held a special event at which scoutmaster Howard Miller (far right) and his son, Howard Miller, Jr. (far left) were both awarded the rank of Eagle Scout. Individuals over 18 are no longer permitted to earn scout rank. Also present in the photograph are Mrs. Miller (mother of Howard Miller, Jr.), Former Scoutmaster Sebert Brown, and Mrs. Minnie Miller, mother of Howard Miller, Sr., and grandmother of Howard Miller, Jr.

Troop 75

This Pioneer District troop has a vibrant history that developed under fine leaders such as Alex Rice and Richard Kronmiller. The latter died tragically in a canoeing accident in Canada where he had taken the troop in the 1960s. The troop is sponsored by Highlawn Presbyterian Church in St. Albans.

Troop 75 seen camping, around 1956–57. Scoutmaster Alex Rice is at left, back row. Son James Rice is seen in the back row, second from right.

Troop 77

Troop 77 was founded in 1955. It is sponsored by the E.K. Perrow Presbyterian Church, Cross Lanes, West Virginia, of the Pioneer District. Its present scoutmaster is John W. Taylor. Earlier the troop had been located in Spencer, West Virginia.

These Troop 77 scouts are shown in front of their tent at Camp McClintic in the 1950s. The troop is located in Spencer, West Virginia. Its scoutmaster shown here is the late Wilmouth Hanna.

Canoeing . . .

Can Sometimes Be A 'Drag'

By JIM PAHL
Of The Daily Mail Staff

As the great comedian W.C. Fields would say, "There we were ... surrounded by the Great Outdoors, dragging our canoes behind us!"

Twenty-three Boy Scouts from Troop 75 in St. Albans (and one Irish Setter named Pete) HIKED a canoe trip on the Greenbrier River last weekend. Miniscule rainfall had reduced much of the swift water to a four-inch deep trickle.

PAHL

"We've left enough aluminum on these rocks that they can be recycled." said leader Randy Melton, 19, of 711 Holley St.

The scouts began their trek at dawn Saturday after camping at Ronceverte. The novice paddlers weaved from bank to bank. Some even travelled in cirlces.

"Of course, we're falling behind. We're going twice as far as everyone else," shouted Joe Henderson, 11, of 502 Edgehill Dr. "Why don't you learn to steer this thing."

After hours of pushing and paddling in the 85-degree heat, some of the younger scouts began to lose their enthusiasim for canoeing.

"Come on, Danny, paddle," pleaded J.B. Kessler, 61, of 811 Greenbrier St., an employe of the Charleston Sanitation Board.

"I am," replied Danny Nester, a 12-year-old Tenderfoot scout.

"Well, you've got to put your paddle in the water first," Kessler said.

But the real trouble came with the whitewater.

Picking a water route through the shallow rapids became a sporting event. The convoy waited in the deep water while a few canoes gambled to find a passage. When the vanguard agreed on a location, the ordeal began:

"Paddle hard! Now draw to the left. More! Now paddle on the right. The right! After this next rock sweep to the left. Now! Paddle hard..."

Just when it seemed the canoe had made it...CRUUNNCH! The deck buckled. The bow surged into the air. Th stern filled with gushing water.

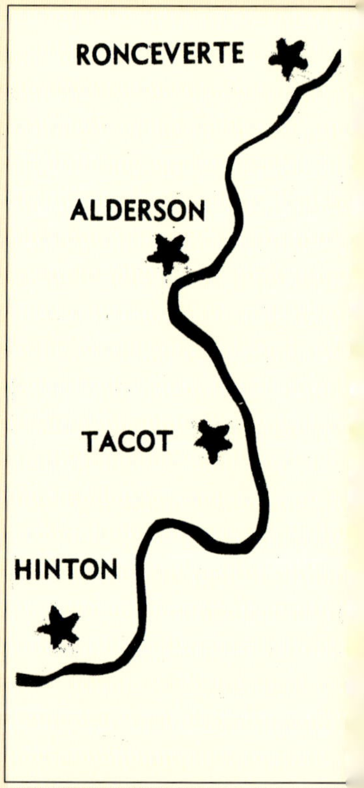

STRANDED!!

With the first hint of success, th others began their race through th rocky maze.

"Hurry, go to the left. Yell when yo see a rock."

"Watch out!"

"What?"

BANG!!

"Get out of my way."

SCRAPE!!

"Why don't you watch where you'r going."

THUD!!

"I told you to yell when you saw rock."

"Coming up on your left."

CRASH!!

"Why don't you get out and push!"

"Somebody grab my paddle."

(Turn to Pg. 8A, Col. 3)

SHALLOW — Whoever said still waters run deep would have a hard time convincing Mark Busch, Bruce Elswick, Joe Henderson, Rusty Hall, Guy Smith, and Jim Perksas they walked their canoes along the shallow Greenbrier River last weekend. — Daily Mail Photo By Jim Pahl.

Continued From Page One

By the time the scouts pitched the first camp at Alderson, the river had taken its toll. "I don't know which hurts more: my back or my sunburn," said John Smithson, 26, of 13 Orchard Dr. "There's nothing worse than having to put on wet shorts," said Rusty Hall, 16, of 940 Lee St. "There a dead fish in my knapsack," exclaimed Marck Busch, 13, of 2042 Benedict Circle.

Dinner was a high-protein mixture of macaroni and cheese, tuna, and mushrooms. Afterwards, the scouts and the adults squared-off in a football game which was postponed due to darkness. (The adults were leading 5-0.)

The paddling, tugging, wading, stumbling, and retrieving continued through the second day. While most canoes carried two scouts, their personal gear, and troop equipment, Scoutmaster John Meadows, 26, an employe of Rish Equipment, had to carry Pete.

"Sit down, you stupid dog," Meadows yelled. However, Pete decided the fish were more interesting, and overturned the canoe more than once while pawing at the trout.

Because of the low water, the scouts decided to go over (rather than around) Bacon Falls. This proved to be a most disasterous mistake.

Riding in whitewater down the side of the cascade, four canoes overturned or swamped before they reached safe water, including the film for this story's illustraions. Another canoe flooded before it even started down.

Swirling waters at the bottom made recovering the disabled canoes a tedious and time-consuming chore. After an 30 minutes of lifting and pulling, the voayage resumed.

At day's end, the exhausted scouts made camp at Talcott and relaxed around a campfire. "This kind of high adventure is good for the boys," said. Asst. Scoutmaster Bill Kessler, 26, a diesel mechanic for Rish equipment. "Some of these kids don't know what it means to hurt, to give that second effort."

But a third effort was required Monday morning to complete the trip. Eight miles, seven wadings, four shoals, three canoe spills and two whitewater runs later, the waterlogged scouts beached their canoes at Hinton for the last time.

"Although it wasn't much of a canoe trip, we can certainly chalk this one up to experience," Meadows said.

And it was agreed W.C. Fields was right. There we were dragging our canoes behind us.

TROOP 75 IS SPONSORED BY HIGHLAWN PRESBYTERIAN CHURCH, ST. ALBANS, WEST VIRGINIA.

BENJAMIN TOLLIVER, JR., WAS THE SCOUTMASTER OF TROOP 93 AT SIMPSON MEMORIAL CHURCH IN CHARLESTON. SEVERAL OF THE SCOUTS PICTURED HERE INCLUDE PETE PORTER, LESTER GORE, TOM BANDY, AND MARVIN STARDER. THE OTHERS ARE UNIDENTIFIED.

TROOP 80

This Beckley, West Virginia, troop is sponsored by the United Methodist Temple. It is a Seneca District Troop and was founded in 1969. Its present scoutmaster is Daniel R. Shorts.

TROOP 103

Another Seneca District Troop is Troop 103, sponsored presently by the First Baptist Church of Prosperity, West Virginia. The troop was founded in 1949 and previously was sponsored by the Bluestone Baptist Church. Its present scoutmaster is Arnold Bolen.

TROOP 107

Summersville Baptist Church of Summersville, West Virginia sponsors Troop 107. In earlier times the troop had been sponsored by the Summersville Lions Club. This Wilderness District troop was originally founded in November, 1941. Its present scoutmaster is Timothy G. Larrick.

TROOP 135

The Wilderness District Troop, whose present Scoutmaster is William D. Given, was founded in 1992 with Braxton County Memorial Hospital as its sponsor. Presently, however, it is sponsored by Gassaway United Methodist Church, Gassaway, West Virginia.

TROOP 146

Troop 146 was established in 1939 by the Christian Board of Education at St. Andrew United Methodist Church in St. Albans, West Virginia. Its first scoutmaster was William "Brownie" Dunlap. The first assistant scoutmaster was Buford C. Green. The troop started with a dozen scouts including James Atkins, David Carrel, Russell Grass, William Hawley, Gail Harbour, George Hopkins, William Hopkins, Gordon Berriage, Charles Sparkes, Victor Taylor, and Richard Terry.

The troop's first Eagle Scout Award went to Jack Lanier in 1949. Over the years about five dozen others have attained the Eagle rank. Lanier recalled an incident that occurred in the summer before his senior year at St. Albans High School where he was a frontline member of the football team. While working on the Camp McClintic staff, Lanier learned of a scout canoe trip to be held during the last two weeks of the summer, a time when he would be expected to attend daily football practice in preparation for the season's first game. The scout canoe trip was to be from Charleston to Cincinnati, and Lanier was doubtful that his football coach, Richard Sidebottom, would excuse him from practices.

TROOP 146 HAS BEEN CHARTERED AT ST. ANDREW UNITED METHODIST CHURCH IN ST. ALBANS FOR MORE THAN 50 YEARS. ITS FIRST EAGLE SCOUT WAS JACK LANIER, WHO WAS AWARDED THE EAGLE RANK IN 1950.

THIS 1960 CAMPOREE TRIP BY TROOP 146 FEATURED MEMBERS OF THE WARRIOR PATROL. THEY ARE (LEFT TO RIGHT): ROLLAND (BUTCH) WILLIAMSON, JAMES ALBERT, C.W. EAKER, JOE WYATT, STEVE HOPKINS, MIKE POTTER, AND BARRY CLARK.

At the 1964 St. Albans Town Fair, scout David Brucker demonstrated rope spinning.

In July 1963 while on a day trip to Green Bank National Astronomy Observatory from the Buckskin Scout Reservation, these Troop 146 scouts were joined by two scouts from other units as they toured the observatory. Left to right are Baine Shafer, Troop 146 Committee Chairman; Rick Gilbert, Troop 146; Pat O'Neal, Troop 25 and Camp Staff; James Tucker Johnson, Troop 146; Phil Johnson (in hat), Troop 75; and Jay Cottrell, Troop 146, Assistant Scoutmaster.

Discouraged, Lanier had no solution to his dilemma and, thus, put the matter aside. But quite fortuitously Lanier found himself in a Lewisburg restaurant on his weekly evening off from his duties at Camp McClintic. In walked the coach, who was in the area on a fishing trip. Seizing the opportunity, Lanier approached his coach who was glad to see him. After some small talk about scout camp and football, Lanier broached the subject of the canoe trip. The coach thought about the unusual request from one of his star players, then said, "Jack, after paddling a canoe from Charleston to Cincinnati you'll be in better shape than you would after two weeks of football practice. So go ahead." And Lanier made the trip.

In 1945 Dunlap gave the troop over to its new scoutmaster, John Hawkins. After about two years William H. "Bill" Wyatt began a 21-year stint as scoutmaster, which continued until 1969. Thereafter followed Charles Evans from 1969 to 1973, Roger Rasmussen from 1973 to 1988, Steve Niday from 1988 to 1999, and Newt Harmon from 1999 to the present.

Troop 146 has been involved in scrap metal drives, town fair exhibits, Goodwill drives, home

In 1959 Troop 146 camped for a week at Carter Caves State Park in Kentucky. This photo shows scout Michael Vogel posing before his tent. Vogel went on to be a scoutmaster for many years in the Midwest.

In the mid 1950s Troop 146 camped at Droop Mountain State Park. Those pictured are (left to right): Tony Delbart, Joe Cottrell, Carl Heck (assistant scoutmaster), Steve Freese, Phil Shafer, Rhodes McClelland and Joe Wyatt.

In 1990 Troop 146 held a reunion at the 50 year anniversary of its original charter. The author of this book, Joe Wyatt, is left of center in the gray coat with red tie.

show activities, church events, parades, missing person searches, track meets, troop summer camps, district camporees and jamborees and has camped at Camp Clifton McClintic, Buckskin Reservation, and each of the National and World Jamborees since the 1950s.

The next several paragraphs depart from the tone of the rest of his book in that they are much more personal to the author. The author grew up in Troop 146 and has much more knowledge of the history of its leaders and scouts than of any other unit's history. Other Buckskin Council troops have produced as many outstanding citizens as Troop 146 and may be equally proud. What follows is a look at some of the former scouts of Troop 146. This overview is intended as but a single demonstration of scouting's influence on young lives, influences that have been, and continue to be, repeated in troops throughout the Buckskin Council.

The troop's scouts have often gone on to careers in numerous distinguished positions. There are many examples and just a few will be listed here. They include Robert Barnett who later became Chief of Police in St. Albans and then Chief of Police at Yeager Airport; David Brucker, an industrial products company controller; Bruton Peterson, who is involved with the motion picture industry in Hollywood; Barry Clark, Charles W. Aker, David Vande Lind, and the author, who became college professors; Ben Edwards, Joe Meadows, John Vaughn, and Scott Wallace who became physicians; Tom Johnson who became a veterinarian; Ron Colby, Bob Cunningham, John Hall, and Robert Tissue, all of whom became certified public accountants.

Other Troop 146 alums went on to distinguished careers with the government, law enforcement and military service. These included Charles Callihan who became a State of Georgia pharmacy analyst, David Gilbert who served as a special agent for the Bureau of Alcohol, Tobacco and Firearms; Fred Heim who pursued a career in the United States Air Force; Jack Lanier (the troop's first Eagle Scout) whose career was with the Department of Defense; George Pride, Jr., also a special agent with the Drug Enforcement Administration; and Jerry Webster who spent his career with the Immigration and Naturalization Service. Others entered areas of the health field other than medicine. They include Eric Quillen who became an orthodontist; registered nurses such as Max Crouch; Bill Deel who became a respiratory therapist; and Robert Farley, a pharmacist. Others went into the teaching profession, including Ronald "Tags" Meredith, William Snyder, and Roy White, III. Attorneys to come out of Troop 146 include Mike Potter, Mike Funk, Robert McClelland and Larry Arnold.

Many others have become successful in the private sector, business and industry. These include ex-scouts who have gone on to careers as project managers, sales representatives, computer specialists and more. Some of these are Douglas Baier, Bill Bryan, James Cottrell, Ted Danford, Bill Endicott, II, Bill Evans, Allen Ferrell, Steve Ferrell, Nathan Hall, III, Earl Heim, Philip Heim, William Hensley, Jr., Tom Hickerson, Bill Hopkins, George Hopkins, Steve Hopkins, Terry Johnson, James Tucker Johnson, Rich Mallory, Robert Moore, Pat Mullins, Jim Phelps, Ralph Ranson, Ted Robinette (an engineer for E. I. Dupont), William Robinette, Jr. (a physicist and manager for T.R.W.), Gene Thompson, John Thompson, Mike Vogel, Moffett Warren, Roy White, Thomas W. White, Stanley D. Wyatt, Richard McClellan (a mechanical engineer attached to the United States Army); David Danford (a civil engineer with the Tennessee Valley Authority), Steve Niday, Steve Kraft, Tim Priddy (a civil engineer), and Patrick McBrayer, a training development specialist for the State of West Virginia.

Again, Troop 146 is not unique in producing so many outstanding citizens. Many troops of the Buckskin Council have done as well at developing boys into men.

Troop 162

This troop was founded in 1955 in the Pioneer District. It is sponsored by Poca United Methodist Church, Poca, West Virginia. Its scoutmaster is David W. Good.

TROOP 117 OF OAK HILL, WEST VIRGINIA, WAS LOOKING SHARP IN THIS GROUP PICTURE TAKEN AT CAMP MCCLINTIC IN THE 1950S.

TROOP 124 WAS SPONSORED BY STARCHER BAPTIST CHURCH IN CHARLESTON. THIS PHOTO WAS TAKEN AROUND 1940. THE SCOUTMASTER (ON RIGHT) WAS W. ERSKINE MARTIN.

TROOP 170

Another active troop is the Seneca District's Troop 170, sponsored by the Meadow Bridge Kiwanis Club of Meadow Bridge, West Virginia. Its present scoutmaster is Jeff Diehl.

TROOP 177

This troop previously was sponsored by Holy Family Church of Richwood, West Virginia, but presently is sponsored by Morris Memorial United Methodist Church in Charleston, West Virginia. The Mountain Rifle District Troop was founded in 1956. Its present scoutmaster is J. Michael Reynolds.

Sutton, West Virginia's Troop 136 poses outside one of the Camp McClintic buildings in the 1950s.

Kenneth Robbins was the longtime scoutmaster of Troop 141 in Charlton Heights. In the photo above Robbins has just received his Twenty Year Veterans Award by the Boy Scouts of America. Also pictured are (left to right): Jeanne Robbins, a senior girl scout with nine years experience; Mrs. Francis Robbins, a den mother and girl scout board member of the Mountain Laurel Girl Scout Council totaling seventeen years service; and Curtis Robbins, a Bear Cub Scout with two years experience. Additionally, the Robbins family included two others with a great deal of scout experience. They are Kay Robbins, who had 16 years with the girl scouts, as scout and leader, and Jimmy Robbins, who in his 12 years of scouting achieved the Eagle Scout rank. The photo is from 1965.

Troop 195

Troop 195 was founded in 1952. In 1955 Carroll Barker became its scoutmaster and a total of 25 boys were registered at that time. Membership in the troop rose over the years, reaching a total of 76 in 1970. The troop camps as frequently as once a month. Other outings have included winter camping, 50 mile hikes, canoe trips, family camping trips, and backpacking in the Cranberry Wilderness Area. The troop annually completes a number of community service projects and spends a week camping at Buckskin Reservation. In September, 2002 the troop celebrated its fiftieth year with a week of activities, many of which were held at the South Charleston mound. Its sponsor is the Methodist Men of the First United Methodist Church of South Charleston, West Virginia. Its scoutmaster is George Soltis.

The Scouts and Explorers of Troop-Post 147 of Garten and Gatewood, near Fayetteville, shown above, have pledged themselves to the theme, "Jamboree or Bust." These boys, left to right, Charles Campbell, Billy Riner, Jerry Keffer and Douglas Tygrett, are eagerly awaiting the rich experience of a week of camping with 50,000 boys at the Fourth National Scouting Jamboree at Valley Forge, Pa., July 12-18.

(Frank Mauritz Studio)

★ ★ ★ ★ ★ ★ ★ ★ ★ ★ ★ ★

Four Fayette County Scouts To Attend National Jamboree

OAK HILL (RNS) — Four boys including two Scouts and two Explorers, will be representing Troop-Post 147 at the National Boy Scout Jamboree, July 12-18 at Valley Forge, Pa.

Troop-Post 147 is community wide including Garten and Gatewood near Fayetteville. It is sponsored by the Pleasant View Church of the Brethren.

Scoutmaster Lewis Baldry, New River and Pocahontas store manager at Kaymoor, announces that the Scouts from Troop 147 who will be attending the jamboree include Jerry Keffer and Billy Riner.

Jamboree - bound Explorers from Post 147 include Charles Campbell and Douglas Tygrett, according to Explorer Advisor Ballard Pennington, an employe of the NR&P mine at Kaymoor.

Parents of the boys have formed a Jamboree Parents Auxiliary.

LOCAL NEWSPAPERS TYPICALLY PROVIDE COVERAGE OF SCOUTING EVENTS. NONE GENERATE MORE INTEREST THAN LOCAL SCOUTS WHO ATTEND A NATIONAL JAMBOREE.

Troop 217 toured the USS Yorktown.

Logan County's Troop 217 is chartered at Justice, West Virginia, Christian Church. They are seen here at Carver's Gap as they hike the Appalachian Trail in May 2003. First row, left to right, are Colvin Morgan, Mark Davis, Thomas Knowles, Nathan Kelly, Bill McDonald, Eric Snyder, Joey Justice, Jonathan McKenzie. Second row, left to right, are Joe Justice, John Skidmore, Tristan Morgan, and Eugene Snyder.

Signaling aids in communications over long distances and all Boy Scouts know its usefulness. Scoutmaster Edgar Patton and scouts Henry Henson, Bobbie Carpenter, Harry Pote, Harold Myres and Donald Mines from Troop 166, backed by Pleasant View Church of God, discuss this subject with the assistance of Ashby Spratley (holding signal flag), scoutmaster of Troop 51, St. Paul's Methodist Church, Nitro.

Area Boy Scouts Hold Camparee At Teays Valley

Tents against a forest background, with the American flags and troop flags proudly displayed by each troop, were an inspiring sight last Friday, Saturday, and Sunday, as the St. Albans, - Nitro - Putnam District, Buckskin Council, Inc. Boy Scouts of American, held its annual Fall Camporee.

Over 150 boys and their scoutmasters assembled Friday evening in a large clearing surround- by beautiful wooded hills on the property of Homer West in Teays Valley. Sixteen scout troops, from St. Albans, Nitro, Hometown, Poca, Eleanor, Hurricane, and Teays Valley attended, out of a possible thirty-one troops in the District.

The theme of the Camporee was "Adventure Trail."

Friday evening was devoted to camp organization, with unit camp fires and leader co-ordination.

The "Adventure Trail" began Saturday morning at 9:30 with twenty-three stations set up around the clearing. Each station presented one phase of scout work, such as Nature Study, First Aid, Cooking, Signalling, Rope Work, Demonstration Camp, Ax Handling, Survival, Compass and Map Reading, etc., and was supervised by a man skilled in the subject. The station supervisor gave each troop a project and scored the boys on their knowledge and proficiency. Each troop set at a station and on signal progressed to the next station.

Saturday evening, everyone assembled around a large camp fire to join in fellowship. Noble Wyatt, of Kanawha City, led group singing and stunts, and entertained with magic and stories.

Church services were held at 8:00 a.m., Sunday morning in the clearing. Rev. Wade Austin, Abney Street Church of God, who served as Camp Chaplain, conducted the services. This brought out the most important scout law, "A Scout is Reverent."

SEMAPHORE WAS THE TOPIC AT THIS 1950S ERA CAMPOREE IN PUTNAM COUNTY. PARAGRAPH ONE DESCRIBES THE AREA AS THE "ST. ALBANS–NITRO–PUTNAM" DISTRICT. TODAY IS IS KNOWN AS THE PIONEER DISTRICT.

THE SENECA DISTRICT'S TROOP 225 WAS FOR MANY YEARS LED BY THE LATE WARREN DUBEE. PICTURED ABOVE ARE THE INSIGNIA, INCLUDING THE 1960 JUBILEE PATCH, FROM DUBEE'S UNIFORM. (DUBEE IS PICTURED ON PAGE 133.)

TROOPS 236 AND 36 OF THE PIONEER DISTRICT WERE SPONSORED BY FORREST BURDETTE UNITED METHODIST CHURCH AND THE FIRST BAPTIST CHURCH, BOTH OF HURRICANE. THE TWO TROOPS PRODUCED A TOTAL OF FOUR EAGLE SCOUTS FROM ONE FAMILY. PICTURED IN THIS MID 1990S PHOTO ARE ERIC HAYSLETT, FRONT, WHO LATER RECEIVED HIS EAGLE BADGE IN 1999; BACK ROW, LEFT TO RIGHT, TIM, ROGER AND JAMIE HAYSLETT, EAGLES ALL.

1974 Scout Fair A Success

SCOUTS OF TROOP 220 of Glade Creek. Their display of lashings won them First Place in Class B at the 1974 Scout Fair.

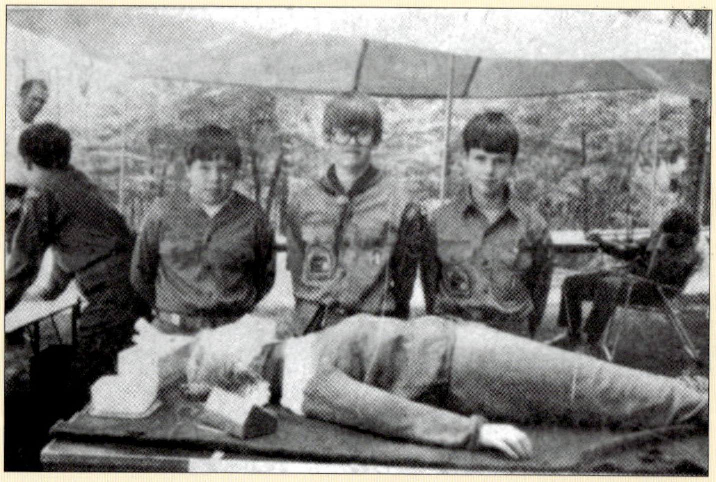

The 1974 Scout Fair is now history. Looking back there are many people who deserve a hearty 'Thanks.' Howard Blankenship did a fine job as Fair Chairman and put in a great deal of time in making it such a great success. Phil Conley served as Ticket Chairman and also did a fine job in corresponding with the outlying units. Farrell Johnson and WVAR gave us invaluable help in promoting this years fair. It should be said here that Nine Rivers District led all of Buckskin Council in ticket sales. We also had more units participating in the Fair than any other District. Our biggest 'Thanks' goes to the people of Nicholas, Braxton, and Webster counties who supported the Scouts in the three county area. Without your attendance and support, the success enjoyed would not have been possible.

There were 4 Cub Scout Packs entered in this year's Fair which was only the second one ever held in Nine Rivers District, and all the boys did a fine job. Pack 269 of Richwood won the President's Award. There were 9 Scout Troops entered in the Fair with Troop 35 of Summersville winning the overall Award.

As we look to next year there are some improvements to be made but in the months to come, I think that the parents and the Scouts can look back to this year's success and plan for next year's and make it even better.

THE SUMMERSVILLE AREA HAS A HISTORY OF MANY ACTIVE PROGRAMS.

Troop 220

Summersville, West Virginia, is the home of Troop 220, which is sponsored by Summersville Presbyterian Church. An earlier sponsor was the Muddlety Glade Creek Rotarian Club. This Wilderness District Troop was founded in 2002 and its present scoutmaster is Gary L. Ashby.

Troop 236

This troop is sponsored by Forrest Burdette Memorial United Methodist Church in Hurricane, West Virginia, of the Pioneer District. Its present scoutmaster is Troy E. Beaver.

GOOD SCOUTS—Former Governor Arch A. Moore Jr. presented Eagle Scout awards to five members of Troop 236 of the Pioneer District in Hurricane last night. Receiving the highest award Boy Scouting offers are Greg Edwards, Greg Hoff, Eric Sheets, David Graham and Scott Guthrie. Daily Mail photo by Adrian Gwin.

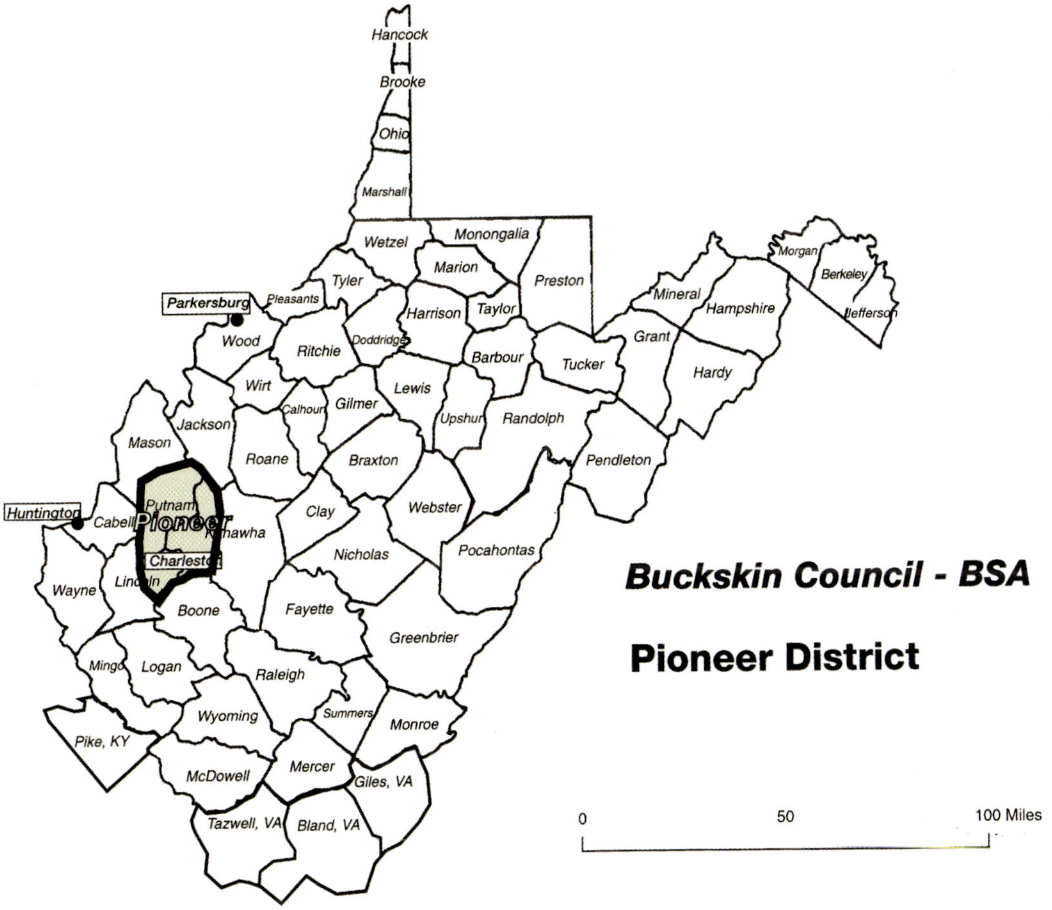

FRI., JULY 5, 1974 Charleston Daily Mail 13A

RECALLS SCOUTING SERVICE

Banker Says No Hero

By ADRIAN GWIN
Daily Mail Roving Reporter

A 57-year-old Boy Scout membership, a 60-year Masonic affiliation and a bank which has increased its assets by $3 million since the beginning of this year just about sums up the life, times and beliefs of L. L. Wilson.

Wilson is a short man who bounces around like a 35-year-old bank messenger. He is president and chairman of the board of the Putnam County Bank at Hurricane, and has 65 years service there. He's been head of the bank since 1930.

But the thing of which he is probably the proudest is his old registration card as Scoutmaster of Troop 1, Hurricane. It is dated June, 1917.

"I organized that troop, the first here, and we had some fine times together. One of my boys at that time is now a retired city editor of the Huntington Advertiser. Another is a retired Dunn and Bradstreet executive. Another, is still living here in town, Elmer Billups, a retired schoolteacher.

"That first summer the boys wanted to go swimming. We caught the train down to Scary on the Kanawha River, and we swam and boated all that Saturday. We camped overnight, and the boys wanted to hike back the next day. I said all right, and we did. But I tell you I could hardly walk for three days!"

Today, he is a sustaining member of the Buckskin Council.

He was wearing a tiny Masonic pin, and I asked him when he became a Mason. "Let me see. It was about 10 years ago that I got my 50-year pin," he said.

"They are two great organizations, the Boy Scouts and the Masons," he said. "Gives a man a chance to help others and himself. No better goals in life than improving yourself while helping others.

"That's our belief at the bank," he said. "When you come in here for a loan, we try to make you comfortable. There's no reason for anyone to apologize for borrowing money. We want to help our people better themselves.

"When I came here in 1909, this bank had assets of less than $100,000. As of December 31, 1973, we had assets of $25,296,176.57. And on May 3, 1974, our assets amounted to $28,346,165.68.

"We have a completely computerized operation, employ 16 young women and 4 young men — and to think that I used to do it all myself!"

At the age of 84, L. L. Wilson looks and thinks like a young man. The bank has moved to newer quarters once, enlarged twice, is expected to enlarge again in the near future, added drive-in windows and the computerization very recently, and all the while it has retained the old-time flavor of a small-town bank where the people working behind the desks are neighbors and home folks to the customers.

Mr. and Mrs. Wilson have three daughters and three sons, and the youngest son Jack, is vice president and cashier of the bank. "He is the best banker in the business," said the father of the son.

Why doesn't he retire?

"We're just working-class people," Wilson said, "so I'll work. There was a dear old friend of mine in here the other day, Mrs. Blanche Dick — she's nearly 90, you know — and she sat there where you're sitting and in her own hand she wrote this for me."

The slip of paper was inscribed "Heroism is endurance one moment longer."

The twinkle-eyed bank president said, "Now I don't want to be a hero, but I think I'll endure a moment longer."

DURABLE — Still putting in a full day at the Putnam County Bank after 65 years there, L. L. Wilson is president and chairman of the board. "Helping others" is his credo, and one of his proudest possessions is his registration card as first Scoutmaster of Troop 1, Hurricane Boy Scouts, dated June 1917.—Daily Mail Photo by Adrian Gwin.

For a time another Troop 1 was located in Hurricane, West Virginia. Its first Scoutmaster and organizer was L.L. Wilson, who became president of Putnam County Bank. Wilson organized the troop in 1917, prior to the formal establishment of the Buckskin Council in 1919.

Troop 250's Assistant Scoutmaster in 1994 was Bob Wilson.

At the spring 1990 camporee Steve Torman of Troop 250 tried to cross this log.

Troop 250's Paul Nestor made his own bow, July 1991.

In March 1993 Troop 250 showed how to construct an emergency shelter.

Troop 250

The first scoutmaster was Bob Wiblin who served only three months. He was followed by Randall Trowbridge, Carl Cobb, Leonard Taylor, Robert Rife, Jan Hacker, William Price, Eric Fletcher and the present scoutmaster, John E. Thompson, Jr. The Pioneer District Troop was founded in October, 1957 and is sponsored by Riverlawn Presbyterian Church in St. Albans, West Virginia. A major project for the troop involved planting hundreds of dogwood trees in an effort to upgrade the beauty of the St. Albans area. Other projects have included the cleanup of the Marlinton Presbyterian Church and three private homes in Marlinton, West Virginia, after a devastating flood in 1955. The troop annually is involved in a highway litter pickup activity, along with projects such as clearing snow from around fire hydrants to help firefighters find them quickly. The troop has attended summer camp at Buckskin Reservation every year since the camp opened. As with many other troops, a number of former scouts from Troop 250 have continued in

Troop 225 of Falls View, West Virginia, is hard at work building a signal tower.

scouting as scoutmasters, cub masters, den leaders, and committee persons. The troop's former scouts are contributing significantly in many professions including optometry, medicine, law, government, foreign service, and the military.

Troop 271

This Logan County troop has produced dozens of Eagle Scouts. It was led for 31 years by Logan attorney Douglas Witten.

Troop 295

Perry Memorial United Methodist Church of Shady Spring, West Virginia is the sponsor of this Seneca District Troop. The troop was founded in 1970 and previously was sponsored by First Baptist Church of Shady Spring, West Virginia. Its present scoutmaster is Walter M. Winant.

Troop 164, Eleanor, First Baptist Church. Left to right, first row, are Wayne McClanahan and Larry Smith. Second row, Bob Anthony, Gary Pickens, Paul Hescht, Dale Hescht and Larry Westbrook. Third row, Jim Gibson - Assistant Scoutmaster, Denny Jividen, Bill Walters, Eddie Anthony, Franklin McClanahan, Johnny Hopkins, Jim Hager - Explorer Advisor and Roy McClain -Scoutmaster.

A 1950s era photo captures scouts of Troop 164 from the government-planned town of Eleanor, West Virginia.

LEADERS OF THE SENECA DISTRICT'S TROOPS 141 AND 225 LED SCOUTS ON A WILDERNESS CANOE TRIP IN 1972. THOSE LEADERS WERE (BACK ROW, LEFT) WARREN DUBEE AND (BACK ROW, SECOND FROM RIGHT) KENNETH ROBBINS. OTHERS PICTURED HERE INCLUDE (FRONT ROW, LEFT TO RIGHT) CHUCK WILSON, DAVID HUNT, KENNY JUDY, DAVID DAVIS. MIDDLE ROW: SCOTT YON, _____ JOHNSON, MIKE SMITH, KENNY NUTTALL. BACK ROW: DUBEE, CURTIS ROBBINS, ROBBINS, AND KEN COURTEAU.

TROOP 302

Phelps Church of Christ in Phelps, Kentucky, of the Chief Cornstalk District, sponsors Troop 302. Its present scoutmaster is David W. Stratton. The troop was inaugurated in 2002.

TROOP 321

Belfry United Methodist Church in Belfry, Kentucky, of the Chief Cornstalk District, sponsors Troop 321. The troop, which was founded in 1990, is presently led by scoutmaster Paul D. Reed.

TROOP 384

Kenton W. Dilly is the scoutmaster of Troop 384 which was founded in 1984. The troop is located in the Mountain Dominion District and sponsored by Concord United Methodist Church of Athens, West Virginia.

TROOP 392

This troop is sponsored by Olive Baptist Church of Julia, West Virginia in the Chief Cornstalk District. It had earlier been sponsored by

ABOVE: A VERY EARLY MEMBER OF THE BOY SCOUTS (POSSIBLY THE FIRST) IN FAYETTE COUNTY WAS RUSSELL E. WALKER WHO WAS BORN IN 1902. IN THIS PHOTO WALKER IS PICTURED A YEAR OR TWO BEFORE HE JOINED THE SCOUTS IN FRONT OF HIS HOME IN MOUNT HOPE. AS HIS MOTHER LOOKS ON, HE AND HIS SIBLINGS APPEAR TO BE DRESSED FOR A SPECIAL EVENT. COULD IT HAVE BEEN A HALLOWEEN PARTY?

TROOP 217'S TRISTAN MORGAN HIKES THE APPALACHIAN TRAIL, AUGUST 2003.

Troop 206, Hometown, Wilkinson Memorial Methodist Church. Lef to right are Walter Woods - Troop Chairman, Paul Casto, Bill Brown, Carl Persinger, Jerry Hedrick, Robert Wilkinson, Denz Barnett - Assistant Scoutmaster. Second row, Bob Cottrill, Pro Hanna, Kent Hill, Arnie Persinger, Larry Ray Cottrill, Bi Whittington. Third row, Wayne Null, Larry Wilkinson, Russel Reed, Brent Payne, Francis Casto, Danny Harris and Leslie Nul

HOMETOWN IS LOCATED IN PUTNAM COUNTY.

Pinnacle Church. It was founded in 1993 and its scoutmaster at present is Randall F. Kirby.

TROOP 1250

This troop is located in Beckley, West Virginia, and is sponsored by the Roger Grocery Store. The Seneca District Troop is led by scoutmaster Robert G. Wilson. It was founded in 1992.

TROOP 2000

Troop 2000 is located at Red House, West Virginia, and is sponsored by Wade Chapel Church. The Pioneer District Troop was founded in 1997 and its present scoutmaster is Franklin W. Flowers.

TROOP 187 OF ZELA, did a fantastic job in making the log cabin shown above with a few of the Scouts in the foreground. Working for the past couple of months on the cabin, the Zela Troop narrowly missed first place. Their Scoutmaster, Howard Blankenship, was the Scout Fair Chairman.

A PROJECT SUCH AS THIS CABIN PROVIDES SCOUTS WITH OUTSTANDING EXPERIENCE IN WORKING AS A TEAM.

Big Boy Scout Parade Saturday

Nicholas-Rimfire District Cubs Scouts Explorers March

This weekend belongs to youth in Richwood! Saturday morning, led by the Big Orange and Black Richwood High School Band, from 150 to 200 Boy Scouts from Craigsville, Richwood, Fenwick, La Frank, Muddlety, Summersville and some perhaps from Webster and Fayette counties, will have a big parade over Oakford Avenue and Main Streets, beginning at 10:00 a. m.

The Civil Air Patrol sponsored, Squadron 2, will be hosts for the big event. Cub Scouts and older Scouts are collaborating in the weekend annual Boy Scout Rally Day. There is to be bicycle demonstrations, tent demonstrations, knot tieing and fire building, woodcraft, nature and trail sign demonstrations, games, first aid problems and all that goes into a well organized day of Boy Scout activities.

The parade will start at Richwood High School and return there, where demonstrations will be held on the Athletic Field or what is left of it after the Lumberjack - Bulldog gridiron fray Friday night. Cubs, Boy Scouts and Explorers will all participate in the program plan-

The Wilderness District has been known by other names, as this announcement shows.

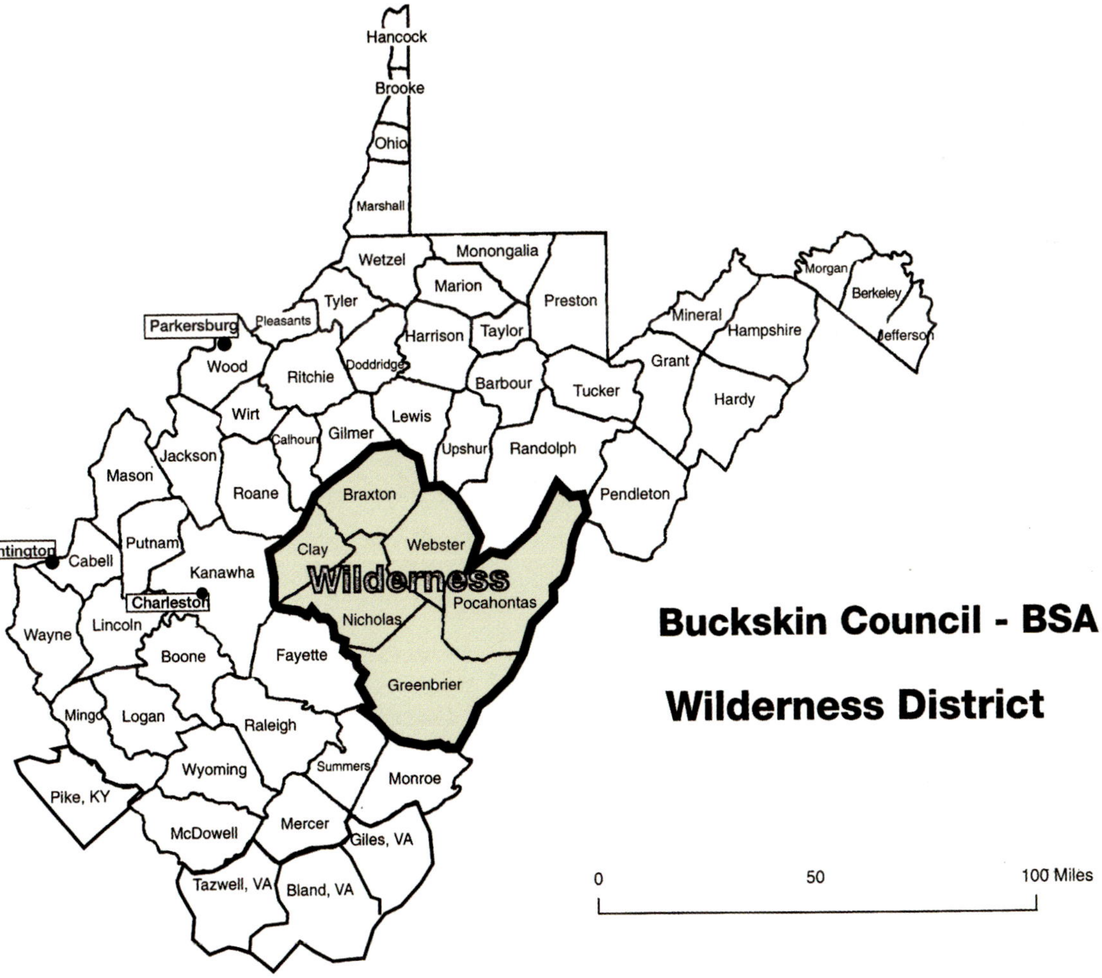

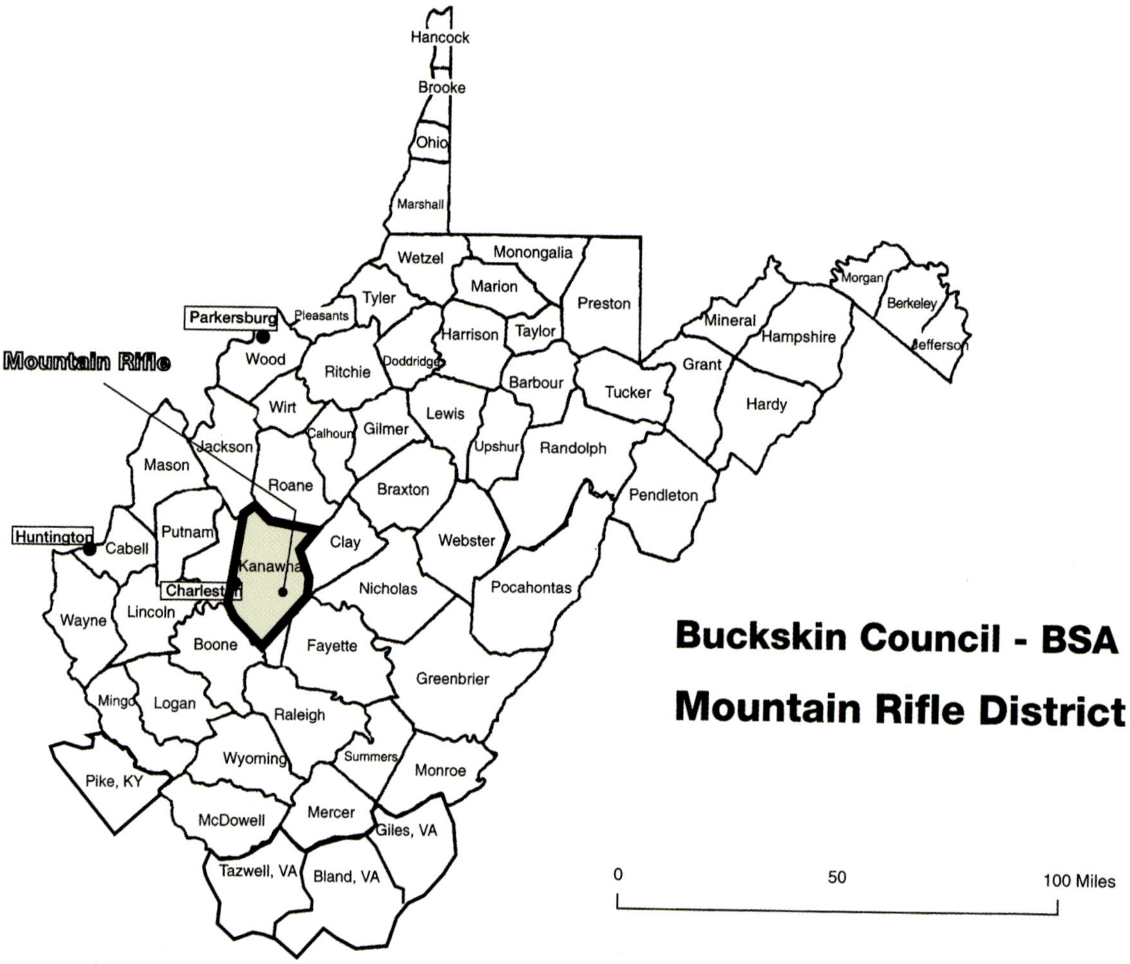

Several of the scouts, troops, and events pictured on the preceding pages come from the eastern two-thirds of Kanawha County, shown here. This is known today as the Mountain Rifle District.

Chapter Seven

Exploring at Sea and on Land

This was the Charleston Sea Scout ship (troop) in 1936. Left to right they are as follows, front: Doug Venable, Bill Newlon. First row: E. Von Woglum (mate), Bill Cline, Bill Wray, Grant Fletcher, Bill Wyatt, George Martin (skipper). Second row: John Morris, Bill Strong, Ellsworth Clark, Will Miller. Third row: Dick Eggleton, ________ McIlwain, Dewitt Blunden, ________. Fourth row: Louie Miller, ________, Warren Point. Fifth row: Jim McCabe, Jack Slaughter, Froud Casey, Richard Perkins. Sixth row: Jack Wilson, Lanny Thompson, Sid Drasnin, Bob Martens. Seventh row: Harold Kantor, Donally Morris, ________, Homer Hix, Frank Higganbottom, Pelly Johnson, Herman Nash. Back: Z.T. Phillips.

Sea Scouts

Sea Scouting was developed as a branch of Explorer Scouts. It was an activity for boys in the 14 to 18 age group. The Buckskin Council has had Sea Scouting at various times dating back to the 1930s.

One of the successful early groups was Sea Scout Ship Number 1 (Troop No. 1). It was sponsored by the Knights of Pythias and met at their lodge hall on Kanawha Street (now Kanawha Boulevard). The boys were allowed to make a "land ship" in the meeting room.

The leaders of the ship (troop) were George Martin, Ben Walkup, and Eathen VonWoglum. Martin was the skipper; Walkup and VonWoglum were the mates. E. C. Richardson, Hereford Egleton and Joe Londeree were among the committeemen.

George Martin was a former Navy man and he operated the ship with strict discipline. Scouts were taught close order drill and marching drill. The boys were invited to march in many parades because of their smart appearance. The membership was limited to 40 scouts.

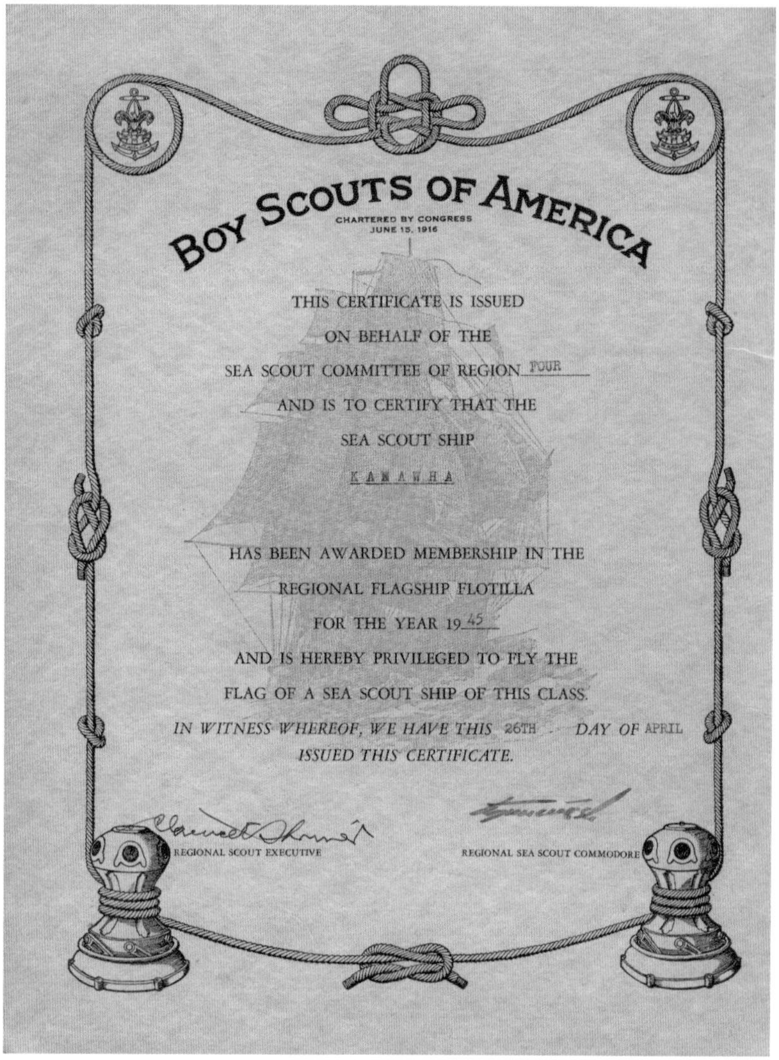

BOY SCOUTS OF AMERICA

CHARTERED BY CONGRESS JUNE 15, 1916

THIS CERTIFICATE IS ISSUED
ON BEHALF OF THE
SEA SCOUT COMMITTEE OF REGION FOUR
AND IS TO CERTIFY THAT THE
SEA SCOUT SHIP
KANAWHA
HAS BEEN AWARDED MEMBERSHIP IN THE
REGIONAL FLAGSHIP FLOTILLA
FOR THE YEAR 1945
AND IS HEREBY PRIVILEGED TO FLY THE
FLAG OF A SEA SCOUT SHIP OF THIS CLASS.

IN WITNESS WHEREOF, WE HAVE THIS 26TH *DAY OF* APRIL *ISSUED THIS CERTIFICATE.*

REGIONAL SCOUT EXECUTIVE

REGIONAL SEA SCOUT COMMODORE

The Sea Scout "ship" Kanawha's 1945 Charter.

In 1937 there was major flooding in the Ohio River Valley and the Sea Scouts took action. Thousands of people were homeless and communication with the town of Point Pleasant had been completely cut off.

The scouts collected clothing and other supplies. The superintendent of schools gave blanket permission for every scout in Charleston to be excused in order to help collect the supplies, another example of the mobilization effort and what could be done on short notice. By noon of the first day of the call for help, 500 boys had assembled on a vacant lot opposite the public library, the building in which the Scout Headquarters was located. The boys were quickly organized and they went from house to house collecting whatever could be used to help the flood refugees in the Point Pleasant areas and beyond. Trucks drove down the middle of the street and scouts helped fill the trucks with donations. By 6:00 p.m. one building had been completely filled with flood relief items.

Then the Sea Scouts took over. Using a boat that had been donated and refurbished, they took the supplies to Point Pleasant.

On their way down the Kanawha River they stopped at communities such as Buffalo, Leon, and others to help the people of those communities, many of whose homes were floating off their foun-

Two views of the Trojan III (later renamed the Albatross).

dations. In time the ship made it to Point Pleasant with the much needed supplies.

The expedition was described by one of the scouts who made the trip, Bill Wyatt. While still in high school he wrote about the experience:

SSS Kanawha
Flood Relief Trip to
Point Pleasant, West Virginia
During Ohio Valley Flood of 1937

The purpose of the trip was to take radio equipment to Point Pleasant as all means of communication were broken down, and to do flood duty.

The officers in charge of the SSS Trojan III were Mr. George Martin, Skipper; Mr. Eathen VonWoglum, First Mate; and Mr. Ben Walkup, Second Mate. Mr. John Kramer was radio operator. The crew members were as follows: Douglas Venable, Richard Perkins, Warren Point, Langston Thompson, and Bill Wyatt. Doug Venable acted as engineer's helper and doctor; Wyatt and Thompson served as cooks, and Perkins as handyman.

The boat was loaded at the lock at South Charleston, West Virginia. Equipment included a generator for batteries, seventeen storage batteries, two batteries for the boat engine and fifteen for radio power, a search light, a hundred fifty gallons of gasoline, oil, a shortwave radio set for sending and receiving, a stove, food, water, and crew members' equipment including the complete sea scout winter uniform, heavy shoes, overshoes, two blankets, soap and towels and etc., and a heavy sweater and mackinaw.

The boat was all steel cabin type with an eight cylinder grey marine engine. It weighed eight or nine tons. The props, it so happened on this trip, were too small for the engine, causing a slower speed.

We left South Charleston at 8:00 o'clock, Tuesday evening. We proceeded down the river to the Winfield Dam before making a stop. This stop was to get a man to let us through the dam. From there we went to Lock Nine. Each member of the crew stood lookout on the bow of the boat to keep us in the river channel. The water was high at lock nine. All of the homes were nearly under water. There was only one man there and he was the lock keeper. The crew took different turns at the wheel in order to relieve first mate VonWoglum who was doing most of the steering. The search light was in almost constant use as the river channel was hard to find because the water was so high. The Kanawha River was now from one hill to the other. The only channel markers were the trees on the banks of the river. Mr. Kramer contacted a man in Nitro by radio.

We next stopped at Buffalo. The people in the town were pretty bad off. Some of the people had nothing to sleep on at all. We gave them our mattresses (five) from our bunks. Bill Wyatt fell overboard while trying to shove the boat from a large tree. We left Buffalo about 2:00 a.m. The weather was cold enough to be uncomfortable.

From here we had our greatest trouble keeping the channel. One time we knocked the tops from two haystacks sticking out of the water. We had a narrow escape from hitting high tension electrical wires. We were about 25 feet from them before they could be seen. The engine was thrown into reverse and the rudder kicked around to the left causing us to miss them by about three feet. We arrived at the little town of Leon about 4:30 a.m.

THE SHIP'S "COOKIE" BILL WYATT AND "MESS" LANGSTON THOMPSON

CHIEF ENGINEER B.F. WALKUP

At Leon, Mr. Kramer connected his radio to an electric line and sent messages to Charleston. After getting warm, I (Bill Wyatt) had a man to take me around the town in a rowboat. I counted about 25 houses floating up off the foundations. We had breakfast at an old storeroom and was that food good after that cold trip. We left Leon about 8:00 a.m. taking with us ten men who were to do work at Point Pleasant. It was much warmer now and we proceeded to Point Pleasant without any further happenings. The water here was all around as far as you could see, from hill to hill.

When we arrived in Point Pleasant (11:00 o'clock a.m. Wednesday) we were not able to take the boat down the street as the water was too near the wires. The streetlights were touching in the water. We made fast to a tree near the battle monument and Wyatt and Thompson prepared a meal. The radio set was taken to the courthouse which was under water up to the second floor, where the set was connected to electricity.

Entire crew was taken to a schoolhouse in a motorboat for supper. We were then taken to the K of P Hall where we spent the night. Some of us slept two on a little steel cot without any mattress. The next morning we went to the boat to go back to Leon and home. We left Point Pleasant about noon (Thurs). Mr. Kramer stayed to operate the radio set which we had left at the courthouse. We arrived at Leon about 3:00 p.m. We gave the people there about 50 gallons of gasoline and took four men aboard who were to go as far as Buffalo with us. About 5:00 p.m. our engine broke down and it was dark before it was fixed. While fixing the engine the boat had drifted and we found ourselves at one time on the state highway which was covered with water. We ran aground here but finally pulled the boat off with a block and tackle which we had hooked to a nearby telephone pole. We had to turn back at one point because gas lines had busted and were throwing water high in the air. We finally arrived at Buffalo about midnight. Here we tied up and spent the night on the boat. The trip home was started about 8:00 a.m. (Friday). The trip was uneventful the rest of the way home. Mr. Martin was put ashore at St. Albans. The boat was tied up at Spring Street and unloaded. We arrived at home about 12:30 a.m.

The battle monument at Point Pleasant as seen in 1937 flood.

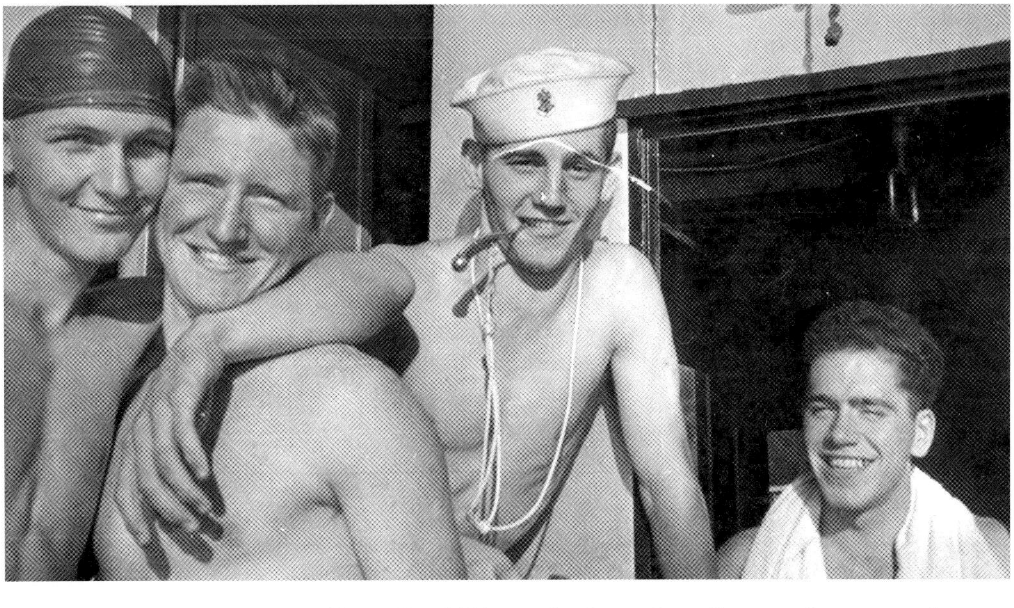

Several members of the crew of the Trojan III in 1941 were Sea Scouts Crow, Matthews, Sweeney, and Andrews.

Sea Scouts Entertain At Dance in Elks' Ballroom

Anniversary Party Is Given; Kent Warner's Orchestra Provides Music for Social Affair

The Sea Scouts of Charleston gave an anniversary dance, Friday evening, in the ballroom of the Elks' club. Kent Warner's orchestra provided music for the occasion.

Those attending were:

Mr. and Mrs. Evan L. Harriss, Jr., Mr. and Mrs. Hereford Eggleton, Mr. and Mrs. Dick Laidley, Mr. and Mrs. L. E. Von Woglom, Mr. and Mrs. George T. Martin, Mr. and Mrs. R. A. Perkins, Mr. and Mrs. Leon MacDonald, Mr. and Mrs. G. J. Gluesenkamp, Miss Ruth Fink, Miss Dorothy Waite, Miss Virginia Rohr.

Miss Ruth Byrd, Miss Nancy Hudson, Miss Mary Agnes Imhoff, Miss Peggy Meredith, Miss Martha Histed, Miss Emma Carrier, Miss Norma Leftwich, Miss Claudine Harris, Miss Mary Eleanor Mulholland, Miss Phyllis Bevis, Miss Virginia Finney, Miss Alva Smoak, Miss Yvonne Sturm, Miss Elaine G. Dye.

Miss Ronice Sias, Miss Juanita Casper, Miss Margaret Nicholas, Miss Sallie Jane Sias, Miss Elizabeth Fay MacDonald, Miss Caroline Truslow, Miss Betty Brought, Miss Myran McKee, Miss Elaine Jackson, Miss Joan Simms, Miss Winifred Belcher, Miss Audrey Slaughter, Miss Manning Frazer, Miss Ruth Lynn, Miss Virginia Green.

Miss Gladys Eastwood, Miss Maxine Goeller, Miss Jane Richmond Vest, Miss Wilda Hall, Miss Marian Gall, Mrs. Butler, Mrs. Jane Vest, Mrs. Ruth Elizabeth Eggleton, Mr. H. Jimmie Hontz, Mr. Alfred Morgan, Mr. John Moore, Mr. Bob Washington, Mr. Richard Perkins, Mr. Robert Adams.

Mr. Raymond F. Rowan, Mr. Jack Curry, Mr. Bill Wyatt, Mr. Leon Neff, Mr. Carl Heindl, Jr., Mr. George Kent, Mr. William Mason, Mr. John Davis, Mr. Joe Popp, Mr. Marion Du Bois, Mr. Jim McLean, Mr. Doug Venable, Mr. John Pauley, Mr. Ira Lee Bostic.

Mr. Bill Cline, Mr. Carl Freeman, Mr. Samuel Ross Reed, Mr. P. Giles, Mr. Carl Haan, Jr., Mr. Gordon Keatley, Mr. Langston Thompson, Mr. Donnally Morris, Mr. Jack Holsclaw, Mr. Morris Flournoy, Mr. Leon MacDonald, Mr. Ed Dalton, Mr. Johnnie Walker, Mr. M. V. Gardner, Jr.

Mr. Don Crumbaker, Mr. John Thompson, Mr. John Hackney, Mr. Guy Belcher, Jr., Mr. William Gentry, Mr. Will Miller, Mr. Steve Stalnaker, Mr. Richard Eggleton, Mr. Orville Kuhn, Mr. Frank Hostetler, Jr., Mr. Warren Point, Mr. Jim Bobbitt, Mr. Dick Denning, Mr. Nelson Gregg, Mr. J. Slaughter, Mr. Robert Simms, Mr. R. W. Amick, Mr. Walter Thurman, Mr. Nathan Baker and Mr. Jimmy Couch.

(C-O-P-Y)

SEA SCOUT SHIP "KANAWHA"

ATTENDENCE RECORD

MONTH OF DECEMBER 1937

	DECEMBER 1	8	15	22	29
1 Guy Belcher	P	P	P	P	A
2 William Dodd	P	P	P	P	P
3 Sidney Drasnin	P	P	P	P	P
4 William Gentry	P	P	P	P	A
5 Donally Morris,Jr.	P	P	P	P	A
6 Richard Perkins	P	P	P	P	P
7 Jack Slaughter	P	P	P	P	P
8 Douglas Venable	P	P	P	P	P
9 Billy Wyatt	P	P	P	A	P
10 Ray Smith	P	P	P	P	P
11 Thornton Wise	P	P	P	P	A
12 Carl Haan	P	P	P	P	A
13 James Harless	P	P	P	P	P
14 Dallas De Vinney	P	P		P	A
15 Bill Cherrington	P	P	P	A	P
16 Will Miller	P	P	A	A	P
17 Gordon Sherwood	P	P	A	P	P
18 Jack Schofield	P	P	P	P	P
19 Cornell Jones	P	P	P	P	P
20 Jimmy Scott	New - Starting in January 1938				
21 Joe Winkler	New - Starting in January 1938				

Charleston Sea Scouts Are Sponsors of Bridge Party

Benefit Event Held to Raise Funds for Repairing the Scout Cruiser; Large Group Attends

Sea Scouts of the Charleston area entertained with a benefit bridge party in the recreation hall of the Appalachian Electric Power company, Tuesday evening. Proceeds will be used to pay for repairing the Sea Scout cruiser, which has been put to such good use taking relief supplies to Huntington during the last few days.

Scores were won by Mrs. J. E. Settle, Miss Hallie Hall, Mrs. O. J. Murer, Mrs. Hayes Picklesimer, Mr. J. L. McLane, Mr. O. J. Murer, Mr. D. M. Cavender and Mr. E. D. Richardson.

Others present were:

Mr. and Mrs. Charles H. Gorby, Mr. and Mrs. J. W. Londeree, Mr. and Mrs. G. Paul Londeree, Mr. and Mrs. Thomas B. Pringle, Mr. and Mrs. M. C. Nelms, Mr. and Mrs. B. T. Montague, Mr. and Mrs. Donnelly H. Morris, Mr. and Mrs. R. H. Counts, Mrs. S. E. Bradley, Mrs. Park Allen, Mrs. E. O. Byrd, Mrs. C. G. Adams, Mrs. H. B. Mearns, Mrs. Robert D. Londeree, Mrs. Roy O. Bowles, Mrs. D. M. Cavender, Mrs. W. R. Harris, Jr., Mrs. J. H. Gaines, Jr., Mrs. T. L. Embleton, Mrs. J. L. McLane, Mrs. A. E. Farley, Mrs. J. A. Bornman, Mrs. H. Webb Angell, Mrs. W. R. Gentry, Mrs. R. S. Good, Mrs. T. Wallen Scales, Mrs. E. M. McGaw, Mrs. C. S. Duffield, Mrs. B. H. Marshall, Mrs. Lucille Slack, Mrs. E. C. Richardson, Mrs. Earl Morton, Miss Clara French, Miss Mildred Griffis, Miss Sada Parsons, Mrs. H. R. Eggleton, Miss Kathleen Guthrie, Miss Mary J. Blagg, Miss Jannis Kirby, Miss Lussie Meyer, Mr. John A. Parsons and Mr. L. Ingram.

THE SEA SCOUTS ENJOYED EVENTS OTHER THAN SAILING, TOO.

Hundreds Join in Memorial Day Program

GAZETTE PHOTO

Military, civic and patriotic organizations joined in the parade and ceremonies commemorating the dead yesterday in front of the Kanawha county public library building, where Philip M. Conley was the orator. A new feature in the parade was the recently organized Sea Scouts, who are shown in their white sailor suits.

By the 1930s when this Memorial Day photo was taken, the Kanawha County Public Library was located in what had been the old State Capitol Annex on Lee Street. This day the Sea Scouts appeared in force.

Vice Commodore Inspects Sea Scout Troop

Dr. W. A. Mudge, of Huntington, vice commodore of region 4 of Sea Scouts, was photographed in the top picture, Wednesday evening as he inspected the group of Sea Scouts. The officer shown in the group is Skipper George T. Martin. Inspection was made on the deck of S. S. S. Kanawha, at 817 1-2 Kanawha street. Members of the inspection committee are, left to right, Dr. Mudge; Dr. J. Ross Hunter, local commodore; M. H. F. Kinsey, scout executive; and G. F. Walker, scout executive at Huntington.

The lower photograph shows members of the ship committee, the officers and the crew. Committee members include:

Mr. Kinsey, Dr. Hunter, Hereford Eggleton, E. C. Richardson, R. A. Roller, Fred A. Bloomberg, J. W. Londeree and E. H. Sutherland.

Officers and crew members include Mr. Martin; L. Ethan Von Woglom, first mate; Ben Walkup, second mate; Guy Belcher, James Cockrell, William Dodd, William C. Drysdale, Sidney Drasnin, Richard Eggleton, William Gentry, Carl Heindl, Carl Haan, Donally Morris, Robert Morris, Will Miller, Robert Mathis, Leon McDonald, Leon Neff, Herman Nash, Warren Point, Richard Perkins, Jack Slaughter, Langston Thompson, Douglas Venable and Billy Wyatt.

Members of the Sea Scouts will sponsor a dance Friday night from 10 until 1 o'clock at the Elks ballroom. Proceeds will be used to send some of the scouts to the national jamboree in Washington, from June 30 to July 9.

THE SEA SCOUTS OF THE 1930S AND 1940S DREW THE ATTENTION OF VARIOUS OFFICIALS AS THE SCOUTS STOOD FOR SPIT-N'-POLISH INSPECTIONS.

Sea Exploring

Scouts Will Hit The River In Salvaged Craft

By ADRIAN GWIN
Of The Daily Mail Staff

Anchors aweigh for The Trojan!

Next Monday will be christening and baptism for a brand new adventure for Kanwaha Valley youth.

Sea Scouting will return to the river.

They call it "Sea Exploring" today, and the "new" ship of Explorer Post 2525 is a 14 by 38-foot steel-hulled cabin cruiser with an entire Navy and the U.S. Coast Guard behind it.

The Trojan will be back in the river at the city boat ramp near the C&P Telephone Co. Monday at 4 p.m., with a lot of dignitaries watching.

But watching most closely will be the 14 members of the crew — boys and girls of 14 to 20 years age who have spent three months of land duty helping recondition and outfit the inboard-diesel-powered cruiser.

It will be the first actual Sea Explorer ship to take to the water in Buckskin Council, Boy Scouts of America, in many years.

The Explorer ship was the idea of two men who are now the ship's officers, Jerry Mollohan, skipper, and Billy Walker, mate. Both are members of the Coast Guard auxiliary, and both are members of the Great Kanawha River Navy. And both those organizations are sponsors of the Scouting venture on the river.

"We talked last year of organizing something to let young people get on the river, not just the old men who could afford a boat of their own," said Mollohan.

"This Sea Explorer Ship was the outcome of many months of talk, planning and work. We got sponsorship and formed the crew with a few youth. We got our charter from the Boy Scouts, and we hunted for a possible craft to obtain.

"Dick Venable of Trojan Steel had built this boat 15 years ago, used it, and 'lost' it when it sunk against the bank in falling high water. It had been sunk for quite a while," he said.

Venable agreed enthusiastically to help salvage the old craft and help recondition it for the Sea Explorer Scouts.

Work was started early this year, on the Trojan Steel fabricating yards near the Patrick Street Bridge.

Now the craft is ready for the water and Ship 2525 will be christened the SES Trojan at the Monday ceremonies.

The crew members are boys and girls of the Kanawha Valley, from Cedar Grove to Nitro, with a variety of experience.

"We hope to have at least 100 on the ship's roster in the future," Mollohan said. "It's for all boys and girls up and down the valley, any of 'em who want to get on the river and would like to be a part of this ship. They can get information for joining from the Boy Scout Service Center."

Their enthusiasm for the water and boating is boundless. The boys and girls have worked like the Trojans they are for months to get the ship ready.

They're planning an overnight cruise upriver to Montgomery before school starts. They'll be in the Sternwheel Regatta river parade and other festivities, with flags flying.

They'll have their twice-monthly meeting of ship's crew aboard the boat. It will be berthed at the Kanawha City docks of the Charleston Boat Club — another sponsor of the organization.

Present members of the crew are Gary Pritchard, boatswain; Bobbie Ruby, purser; Scott Buckley, Jon Cooper, Eric Dennis, Jeff Fields, Robin Robinson, David and James Hash, Don Dickson, Wes Curry, Glen Roark, Steve Bradbury and Greg Kirk.

Ship's committee includes David Haines, Dr. Kenneth MacDonald, R.C. Long, Phil Primozic, Mollohan and Walker.

The boys and girls designed their own "uniform" — a blue T-shirt with appropriates, but this will be their first real boat — and they will run it.

With the Coast Guard auxiliary and the Great Kanawha River Navy behind them for experience and guidance, they're in for a great adventure in exploring the wonders of the world of water.

The 1970s to 1990s saw a revival of interest in the Sea Scouts, often minus the sailor uniforms.

SEA SCOUTS IN MARMET TOOK RESTORED CABIN CRUISER 'THE TROJAN' OUT ON ITS MAIDEN VOYAGE RECENTLY

Photo for the Daily Mail by John McCoy

Teens Restore Boat

Sea Scouts Enjoy Cruising The Kanawha

By JOHN McCOY
For The Daily Mail

With practiced assurance, the young helmsman settles behind the cabin cruiser's wheel.

Deftly, he flicks a couple of switches, and smiles faintly as the diesel engine comes to life with a muffled roar. Nonchalantly, he eases the craft back from its mooring. The Sea Scouts of Explorer Post 525 are under way again.

Sea Scouts? In Marmet, West Virginia? Three hundred miles from the nearest ocean?

Yes. Yes. And Yes. And the members of Post 525 don't mind one bit that they're far removed from sea breezes and salt spray. They're having too much fun to notice, especially when they're afloat on "The Trojan," the 28-year-old cabin cruiser they're restoring.

Actually, rebuilding would be a better word. Last September, when they got the boat, they took stock of what appeared to be a grim situation. The boat had been sunk three times, its engine had been filled with water, its hull was rusty and its fittings were shot.

In October, not exactly the peak of the boatbuilding season, Post 525 rolled up its collective sleeves and went to work.

While the post's adult advisors were out drumming up support for the scouts' efforts, 16 determined young men and women began the backbreaking task of rebuilding the rusty old hulk. They stripped the hull to the bare steel, inside and out. Youngsters who had never worked with metal before found themselves grinding, welding and cutting away the old and replacing it with the new.

In the meantime, the teen-agers found there were a lot of grown-ups willing to help a worthwhile project. A local rebuild shop overhauled the waterlogged engine. A chemical company donated a new exhaust system. A manufacturer chipped in the materials for a new flying bridge, and a rubber goods supplier donated the hoses for a brand-new hydraulic steering system.

In all, local corporations have put about $12,000 into the boat that Post Skipper Rusty Snodgrass said he "wouldn't have given a plugged nickel for" before the restoration.

Now, "The Trojan" is the pride of Marmet. The scouts took it out on its maiden voyage a few weeks ago, and now split their meeting times with cruises on the Kanawha River and continuing the half-completed refurbishing work.

Much still remains. Almost everything below deck still needs restoring. The cabin, galley, and sleeping quarters await the scouts' skilled attentions. The scouts, who have fallen in love with the old boat, seem more than willing to oblige.

In fact, some of the youths spend most of their spare time at the swampy piece of riverbank they helped transform into a tidy little five-slip marina. The post's Bos'n, Greg Cantley of Marmet, explained the appeal.

"Where else do you get the opportunity to learn to operate a boat and learn boating safety while you're still a teen-ager?" he asked.

Michael Pilbeam, another member, added, "I think the best part of it is having a place to be with your friends and have fun working together." Pilbeam may someday turn this pasttime into a career. He's talking with U.S. Navy recruiters right now.

The scouts' hard work hasn't escaped the attention of Marmet's adults, who have supported the gaggle of 15- to 21-year-olds with donations of time, food and money. The young people think the grownups are pretty special.

Obviously, the grownups think young people are pretty neat, too.

CHARLESTON DAILY MAIL, JULY 23, 1987

Explorer Program

Exploring in the Buckskin Council has had an up and down history. The explorer program is for scouts who are 14 to 18 years of age. In some ways Exploring has not been unlike Scouting. For example, at times older scouts entered Exploring while remaining in their scout troops. That was often the case when there was no local post in which the boy could enroll. Explorers simply wore the forest green Explorer uniform while continuing with their scout troop's activities.

By the 1960s it was becoming more difficult to recruit and retain Explorer Scouts, so a decision was made at the national level to admit girls. The first local post to admit girls did so in 1970. It was chartered at Thomas Memorial Hospital and its focus was on introducing Explorers to the medical professions.

A few years earlier, in the 1960s, another decision at the national level had been to encourage posts to focus upon a special interest, typically related to a specific career. Various posts in the council followed that trend.

By 1974 Council Executive B. Robin Meadows announced that thirteen area businesses and organizations would sponsor Explorer Posts. These included: St. Francis Hospital; Charleston-Kanawha Emergency Services; IBM; South Charleston Fire Department; American Motors; West Virginia State College; Equipment Distributor of Nitro; Columbia Gas Company; West Virginia's Department of Natural Resources; Union Boiler Company; Mountaineer Euclid; West Virginia Air National Guard; and Monsanto Corporation.

Although the focus upon careers did fairly well, many Explorer Scouts continued to possess interest in the traditional outdoor activities. The High Adventure Posts served them well. As an example, Post 5, which is sponsored by the First Presbyterian Church in Charleston, developed an active, co-ed High Adventure Post. The Post had been

Explorer Scouting program set up at meeting here

An Explorer Planning Conference met Friday at the St. Andrew Methodist Church and planned for four explorer Scout events for the year 1957-58. These events are for all Explorer Scouts of the St. Albans, Nitro, Putnam District.

The first event will be a vocational exploration field trip on Saturday morning, Oct. 12. This includes a sightseeing trip of the area and equipment of the local Air National Guard unit concluding with a flight in one of their twin-engined planes.

Knute Samples, Explorer advisor of Post 150, sponsored by the Highlawn Baptist Church, will be the adult counsellor and Bill Hazzelrigg, Explorer of Post 150, will be the director of the event.

A father and son hunting event is being planned for Nov. 22-24. The Adult Counsellor is Romie C. Hughart, Explorer advisor of Post 24, sponsored by the First Baptist Church of Nitro, and Buck Double, Explorer of Post 83, sponsored by the Mt. Vernon Baptist Church, will be the event director.

A hayride is being planned for March 7, 1958, for the Explorer Scouts of the district. Henry E. Ennis, Scoutmaster of Troop 187, sponsored by the Abney Street Church of God, is the adult counsellor and Explorer Scout Paul Ennis of Troop 187 is the director of the event.

A Message Relay project is being planned for May 2-4, 1958. John Dulgos, committee chairman of Troop 200, sponsored by the Catholic War Veterans of the St. Francis Catholic Church, St. Albans, is the adult counselor and Explorer Scout Stephen Freese, Nitro, of Troop 146, sponsored by the St. Andrew Methodist Church, St. Albans, is the event director.

Fifteen Explorer Scouts and six Explorer advisors were present for the meeting "Uncle Bill" Graham, A. D. C.

(Continued on Page 2)

By the 1950s Explorer Scouting was burgeoning in the Buckskin Council.

THE CHARLESTON DAILY MAIL, MAY 13, 1953

Dunbar Scout First Of Eagle Rank There In 8 Years

The first Eagle Scout award made to a Dunbar boy in eight years went last week to Stanley Eugene Eppert, son of Mr. and Mrs. C. H. Eppert, Jr., picture above with the proud Eagle. Mrs. Eppert is the Dunbar Correspondent for the Daily Mail.

Stanley is a member of Troop 46, sponsored by the First Baptist church. The last Eagle badges awarded to Dunbar scouts were in 1945, when Harold Crickenberger, Jack Wilson and Jack Hoffman all received their awards at the same court of honor.

Young Eppert is a member of the explorer unit of the troop, but the post has not been activated as yet, the explorers remaining under the troop leadership for the time being.

He is a ninth-grader at Dunbar high school, on the B honor roll, and has been in Scouting for four years.

ABOVE IS SHOWN A COMMON SITUATION. THE EXPLORER SCOUT CONTINUES TO FUNCTION WITH HIS BOY SCOUT TROOP. THE CAPTION MAKES IT CLEAR, THOUGH, THAT EXPLORER SCOUT EPPERT WOULD SOON HAVE HIS POST.

active since its inception in 1950 when Post Advisor Joe R. Groves had registered 15 boys. By 1960 a succession of advisors had overseen the post and 18 Explorers had attained Eagle rank.

By the early 1970s the post was continuing a steady registration of 10 to 15 boys every year. But in 1972 Post 5 opened its doors to girls and 30 of them were registered that year, along with 26 boys. By 1975 Post 5 had 45 boys and 67 girls registered, a high water mark that demonstrated youths' interest in both traditional outdoor activities and in each other.

During the 1970s Post 5 was led by people such as Donald Willard, Barbara Mitchell, and Ed Lewis. The post hiked and camped at Philmont, boated in Bimini, skied at Canaan Valley, and camped at Buckskin Scout Reservation and Camp Dawson. Admission of girls, although opposed by some old-timers, seemed to have revitalized Exploring.

EAGLE SCOUT ranks were increased by one recently when Terry Hudson received the coveted award at services held in Christ Church Methodist. That is his mother, Mrs. Dick Hudson, pinning the Eagle badge on his uniform. Others are (from left) Scoutmaster George Pullen; Terry's father, Dick Hudson, Daily Mail sports editor; Dr. Truman Potter, pastor of the church and M. L. Johnson, Scout executive of the Buckskin Council. Young Hudson is an Explorer Scout in Troop 11, a senior patrol leader in his troop and holds the God and Country award.

Because they were older, Explorers often achieved the Eagle Scout rank, as these photos show.

Other posts throughout the council camped as well, though perhaps not as often as the High Adventure Posts, and they all were involved in other activities. These included an Air Guard "fly-over" of Kanawha County, state conventions, a December dance and banquet, and an unusual look at Kanawha Valley "night life." The last of these involved an all-night trek (by automobile) to ten locations that enabled the Explorers to learn what happens at night in a police station, a hotel laundry, a chemical plant, a hospital, Yeager (then Kanawha) Airport and other locations.

An enterprising post in Shrewsbury revived the Sea Scouts in 1971 as they refurbished an old boat which they named "Winkeydink." The boat was donated by the Coast Guard. It was 36 feet long, and in August, 1971, the Explorers of Ships (Posts) 404 and 118 successfully launched the boat. Bill Walker served as advisor.

By 1979 another boat, the Sea Explorer Ship Trojan, a 38-foot cruiser, had been launched by

Walter Sampson, Jr. center, was presented the Eagle Scout Award, Monday, January 14, by Judge Dennis R. Knapp, of Common Pleas Court. His mother Mrs. Walter Sampson watches as Judge Knapp congratulates the Eagle Scout. Mrs. Sampson received a pin similar to her sons, presented to Eagle mothers.

Boy Scouts and Explorers who replaced the members of the city government Saturday, as part of Scout Civic Day are shown before the days activities began. Seated, left to right, are Porter West, as acting mayor and Dick Sibley, city recorder. In the second row, replacing regular councilmen are: Brent Cooke, Tom Westlund, Charles Bayless, Walter Sampson, Jack Westlund, and Mike Walker. David Carper was absent when picture was taken.

IN MANY COMMUNITIES SCOUTS TAKE OVER CITY GOVERNMENT ONE DAY A YEAR.

Ship (Post) 2525. Jerry Mollohan and Bill Walker served as Skipper and Mate (Post Advisor and Assistant Post Advisor), respectively. Richard Venable of the Trojan Steel Company had built the boat 15 years before, but it had been sunk for some years. He helped salvage the craft and make it seaworthy. The boat later again fell into disuse until, in 1987, another group, Post 525 of Marmet, again put the vessel into seaworthy shape and the Trojan sailed again. Its identification number 2525 remained on her forehull, this time under direction of Skipper Rusty Snodgrass.

Over the years, exploring has seen many changes and has continued to serve older youth in a wide variety of activities within the council. A look at the activities for 2003 shows three ski trips, a white water rafting trip, a spelunking trip, a road rally and a "night on the town" tour of businesses that operate at night. By 2004 the Charleston area alone had 16 chartered crews (posts) in the outdoor/high adventure domain, and a dozen career-oriented posts.

REPRESENTING THE BUCKSKIN COUNCIL Exploring program at the national rally to be held in Detroit this Fall are Sherry Epperly from Post 502 and Steve Kraft from Post 509. Sherry is also president of her post which is an environmental group sponsored by our Institute Plant. The annual road rally competition is just one of the many varied experiences offered high school students in this special interest program. Other career posts active include communications, engineering and chemistry, mining engineering, construction, medical, law enforcement and military. These posts will be starting up in the near future and students interested who have not filled out interest forms at their schools should contact the Buckskin Council Service Center in Charleston.

THE CARBIDER, SEPTEMBER 14, 1973

S. CHARLESTON, DUNBAR 'OFFICIALS'

Boy Scout "mayors" of South Charleston and Dunbar and elected "officials" of the two communities posed for this picture. They will take over the city offices Feb. 9, during National Boy Scout Week. Standing are Richard Casto, South Charleston police judge; Charles Vaughan, South Charleston recorder, and Bill Young, Dunbar City Clerk. Seated are "Mayor" Phil Morgan of Dunbar and "Mayor" Bill Cody of South Charleston. The boys elected must appoint all other "city officials" to represent their real-life counterparts, such as street commissioners, park commissioners and police chiefs.

These explorer scouts are putting on a demonstration at a scout exposition at St. Albans Junior High School, April 16, 1955. They are (left to right) Joe Heck, Norman Parsons, Bob Gilbert, Jerry Schneider, Robert Warren, Jerry Webster, and Jay Cottrell.

Buckskin Council To Take Summer Cruise

THE BUCKSKIN Council Explorers have filled 90 billets aboard two U. S. Navy ships for a cruise this summer.

They will leave Charleston 12:05 a.m. E.D.S.T. June 22 by bus and go to Norfolk, Virginia Navy Base where they will board the U.S.S. Rankin and U.S.S. Kleinsmith for seven days. They will cruise the Norfolk area.

Dr. W. B. Goff of Dunbar, will head the Rankin group while Charles Andrews of Ronceverte, will head the Kleinsmith group.

The Explorers will return home sometime June 30.

Buckskin's Explorer Scouts are always involved in interesting activities.

CHARLESTON DAILY MAIL, OCTOBER 15, 1970

Boy Scout Explorer Post Goes Coed

Members Study Hospital Procedure

Boy Scouting made nationa history about a year ago when it decided that young women could become members of Explorer posts—the senior division of Scouts.

And the newly organized post at Thomas Memorial Hospital in South Charleston has made local history by becoming the first in the valley to have an active coed membership.

Post members all have their eyes on careers in some phase of the medical profession—their "special interest." With the help of the staff and administrators of the hospital, they spend hours each week studying the many facets of life in their chosen field.

When Exploring went "specialized" several years ago, posts with special interests became increasingly numerous.

Leaders in the chosen special interest fields sponsor the posts and assist them in continuing programs which help the youths of both sexes decide their life's work.

At Thomas Hospital, the youths assist in many hospital chores, attend instruction sessions in the use of equipment and attend as student monitors many events of the hospital's everyday operation.

Other Special Interest Explorer posts include a communications specialty sponsored by the C&P Telephone Co.; a legal specialty sponsored by the Kanawha County Bar Association; a finance post by the Charleston National Bank, and an engineering post by the United Fuel Gas Co.

"It's a sort of career counseling with practical applications," said Joseph Kofira, advisor of the Thomas Hospital post.

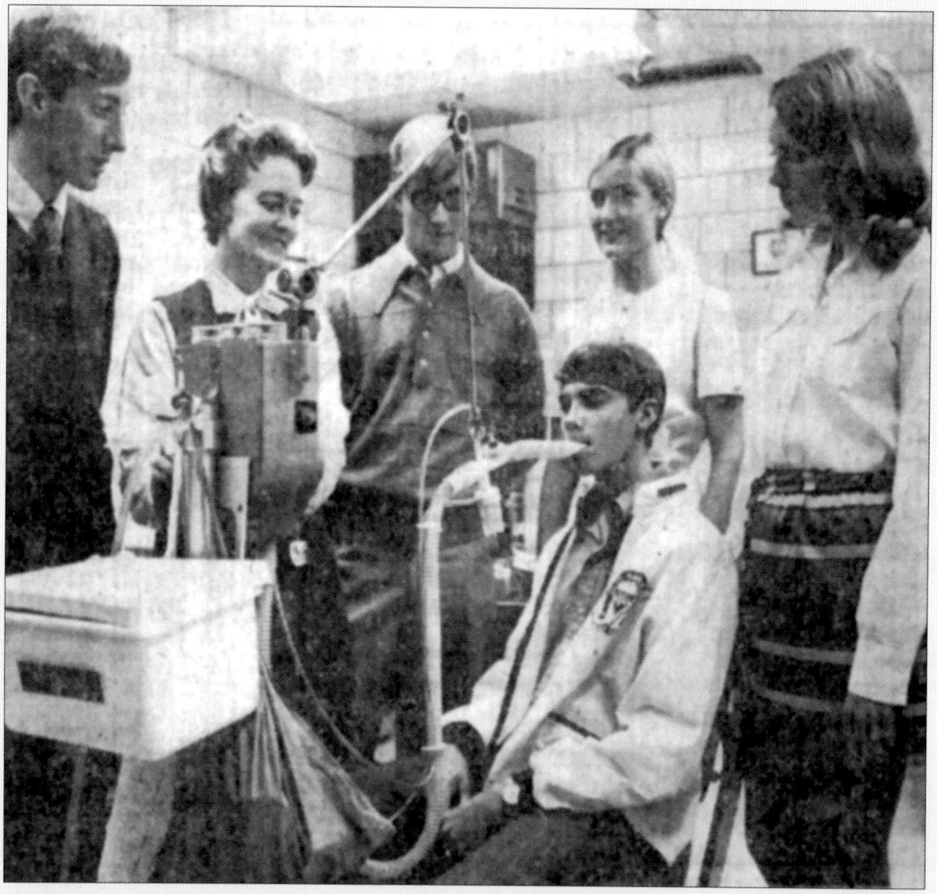

SPECIAL INTEREST SCOUTING—Boy Scouting was never like this when Dad was young! These are members of a new Explorer post with a special interest in medical matters. It is the first Explorer post in the Kanawha Valley to admit young women as regular members. Left to right are Joe Kofira, one of the organizers of the post; Mrs. Ruth Racer, chief inhalation therapist at Thomas Memorial Hospital in South Charleston, which sponsors the senior Scouting division group; and members Tom Fleetwood, Sherry Canterbury and Nancy Hawkins. Steve Bower, seated, is the "patient" for an inhalation demonstration.—Daily Mail Photo by Tom Hodges.

IN THE 1970S, EXPLORING WENT CO-ED NATIONWIDE.

Charleston Daily Mail, April 3, 1976

EXPLORER SCOUTS *from West Virginia were taken on a tour of the national capitol by Congressman Ken Hechler. They are, from left, Debbie Ours of St. Albans, Rebecca Bizik of Beckley, Shari Potter and Jeannine Weese of Charleston, Lucy Wang of St. Albans and Kathy Akers of Beckley.*

In the 1970s one of the most active posts was Post 5. During this time the admission of girls to exploring boosted membership. Pictured here are the Post 5 members at one of their many outings. Those pictured are as follows: (kneeling) Cindy McCartney, Laura Wise, and Terry Bennett; others in general order of left to right include Andi Mitchell, Betsy Peterson, Anna Tassan, John Mitchell, Ted Williams, Don Willard, Lynn Mendaloff, Jo Sydenstricker, Julie Wood, Rank Dawson, Mary Ann Peterson, (unknown), Debbie Divers, Rob Schulz, Mary Lou Weise, Andy Osborne, Marilyn Carpenter, Tom Andreas, Jim Mitchell, Terry Schulz, and (in back) Ann Ullum, Bill Stump, Bruce McVey.

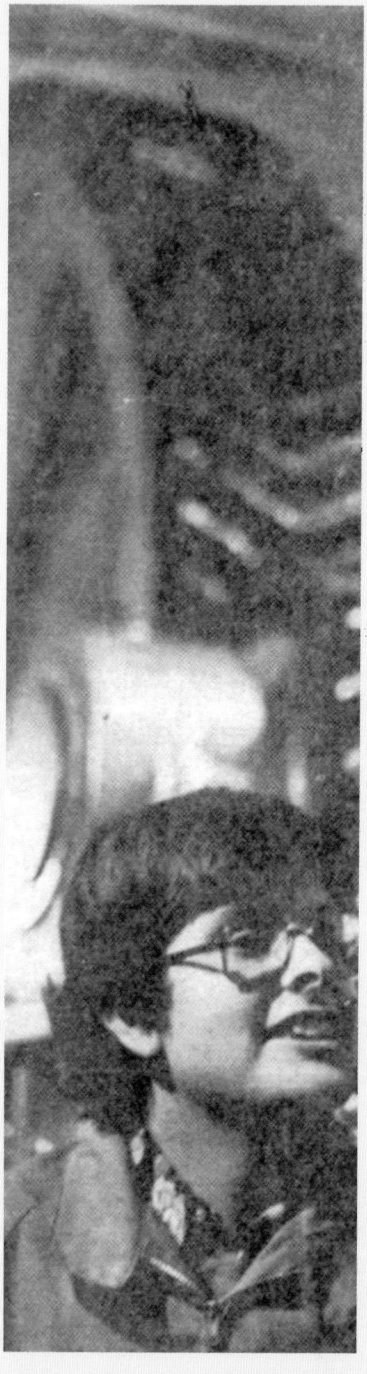

CHARLESTON DAILY MAIL, MARCH 28, 1977

Exploring After Dark . . .

Scouts Get Unusual Look At Area 'Night-Life'

By ADRIAN GWIN
Of The Daily Mail Staff

It beat a drug trip by a metric mile.

Truly mind-expanding, almost unbelievable.

After the moon, what's left to explore?

The fantastic world of the Kanawha Valley at night! The kalidescope of ever-changing, high-pressure, mind-boggling space-age hustle and bustle of the all-night shift of complicated technical and computerized operations that keep the Kanawha Valley churning along at a furious pace.

Forty young men and women, 16 to 19 years old, went on the trip this weekend — exploring.

It was the first of its kind here — an all-night Adventure Trip of the Exploring Division, Buckskin Council, Boy Scouts of America.

Months in the planning, the fast-paced trip took in 10 of the Kanawha Valley's busiest commercial, governmental and industrial enterprises — from the police department to the water company, from a hospital to the DuPont plant, from the Marmet Locks to the telephone company.

Young men and women (girls are part of the Exploring Division of Buckskin Council as much as boys) from six Explorer Posts gathered at The Athens Restaurant at 9 p.m.

They parked their cars there, and in two animated groups, headed out on foot to explore the world at night — the working world, not the world of the night-club set.

They toured the all-night operations of the Kanawha Valley Bank where thousands of banking accounts are "posted" and computerized long after the customers are in bed; they walked to the Chesapeake and Potomac Telephone Company, where they learned that nearly 75,000 calls are completed daily;; they hiked on to the Heart O Town Motor Hotel where they saw a mountain of 3,000 sheets, one day's change of linen, being washed.

Then they went to Charleston General Hospital to walk through the emergency room and laboratories at midnight while 460 patients slept. They toured the Charleston Police communications center, the "brain" of the department.

After a chartered bus ride to Kanawha Airport, they found out about the weather from the official weathermen — the forecast office of the National Oceanic and Atmospheric Administration — where satellite pictures taken from 24,000 miles above the earth help forecasters determine whether tomorrow will be sunny or rainy.

At the West Virginia Water Co.'s Charleston plant the young Explorers saw the processing of drinking water from the river. And after a bus ride up the road, they donned hard hats and protective goggles to tour the DuPont plant at Belle — where tons of ammonia are made daily from hydrogen and nitrogen.

At the Smith Transfer trucking company terminal in Belle they saw the all-night unloading operations of 100 semi-trailers backed up to a 500-yard-long loading dock, where 150 to 200 of the highway monsters arrive and depart daily.

(Turn to Pg. 2A, Col. 1)

EXPLORING — A young Explorer of Buckskin Council, Boy Scouts of America, gets a glimpse of what makes the Kanawha River Locks and Dams effective. He is Kevin Phillips of Post 505, Richwood, in the tower of Pier 3, Marmet Locks, with a 10-foot cog wheel raising the roller in the dam 90 feet below him. At right a group of Explorers get an explanation of the C&P Telephone Co. operations from Mrs. Cathy Greenleaf, crew chief operator. — Daily Mail Photos by Adrian Gwin.

THE AFTER DARK EXPERIENCE PROVED AN EYE-OPENER.

Lee Domotrovich and Carol Blair were active with Post 5.

Businesses Sponsor Explorer Programs

Thirteen area businesses and organizations have signed as sponsors for Explorer programs ot the Explorer Division of the Buckskin Council, Boy Scouts of America.

Students entering the program, which begins in September, will work at one of the following places: St. Francis Hospital, Charleston-Kanawha Emergency Services, IBM, South Charleston Fire Department, American Motors Corporation, West Virginia State COLLEGE, Equipment Distrubtor of Nitro, Columbia Gas Co., W. Va. Department of Natural Resources, Union Boiler Co., Mountaineer Euclid Inc., W. Va. Air National Guard, and Monsanto.

B. Robin Meadows, scout executive, said the explorer program is designed to give young people, aged 15 to 21, the opportunity for experience in such career fields as medicine, automotive mechanics, law, engineering, advertising, and conservation.

No previous association with the Boy Scouts or Girl Scouts is necessary for participation in the Explorer program because it is a separate division of the Buckskin Council.

Charleston Daily Mail, June 19, 1974

Barbara Mitchell and Ed Lewis led Post 5. Here they are seen in a 1980 photo.

CREW #	INSTITUTION	CONTACT PERSON	PHONE	INTEREST
2268	CROSS LANES UNITED METHODIST	MARY BETH MURPHY	776-8373	HIGH ADVENTURE
66	WINFIELD BAPTIST CHURCH	ED PLONA	937-3302	HIGH ADVENTURE
007	TRI-COUNTY YMCA	TOM DRENNAN	757-0016	HIGH ADVENTURE
1444	CHARLESTON MOOSE	MIKE RICHARDSON	345-8379	OUTDOOR/ COMMUNITY SERVICE
111	CROSS LANES UNITED METHODIST	LESLIE RAWLINGS	776-8484	HIGH ADVENTURE
777	CAPITAL HIGH SCHOOL JROTC	COL. NEELEY	348-6500	HIGH ADVENTURE & COMMUNITY SERVICE
333	ST. MATTHEWS EPISCOPAL CHURCH	KAY COOPER	345-6051	HIGH ADVENTURE & COMMUNITY SERVICE
441	CHARLESTON FIRST CHURCH OF THE NAZARENE	RODGER KRATZ	344-4719	HIGH ADVENTURE
522	GEORGE WASHINGTON HIGH SCHOOL JROTC	JIM GOOCH	343-8129	OUTDOORS
412	FREEDOM CHRISTIAN CENTER	RICHARD CLINE	722-9468	HIGH ADVENTURE
900	TRI-STATE SEARCH & RESCUE	LOUIE ROBINSON	372-8897	HIGH ADVENTURE & SEARCH & RESCUE
324	ALTERNATIVE YOUTH	KENNY WILLIAMS	382-0858	HIGH ADVENTURE
511	NATURAL HIGH SO. CHARLESTON HIGH SCHOOL	CONI MEADOWS	766-0649	HIGH ADVENTURE
617	BUCKSKIN SCOUT RESERVATION	JOHN KIRLUK	346-7718	HIGH ADVENTURE
911	NITRO CITY FIRE DEPT.	BOB FARLEY	727-2419	HIGH ADVENTURE
510	NATURAL HIGH SEA SHIP SO. CHARLESTON HIGH SCHOOL	GLEN TOLER	766-0649	HIGH ADVENTURE

Present High Adventure Posts.

EXPLORING POSTS POST #	INSTITUTION	CONTACT PERSON	PHONE	INTEREST
012	CAPITOL HIGH SCHOOL	STAN WHITE	348-6500	CAREER AWARENESS
615	WV SERVICE LEARNING INSTITUTE	LISA CIRCLE	347-6914	COMMUNITY SERVICE
529	CHARLESTON AREA MEDICAL CENTER	ANDREW WEBER	388-7375	MEDICAL
951	AIR FORCE JROTC	FRED CHANCE	766-0633	MILITARY/ OUTDOORS
100	CHARLES RYAN ASSOCIATES	KEVIN HARLESS	556-9108	PUBLIC RELATIONS/ ADVERTISING
311	MARQUEE CINEMAS	CASEY CROUCH	746-9900	FILM PRODUCTION/ THEATER OPERATIONS
110	KANAWHA BLVD. ANIMAL HOSPITAL	DR. ERIC LEE	343-3261	VETERINARIAN MEDICINE
010	GATEWAY COUNTRY COMPUTERS	JON SYNER	746-7718	COMPUTER TECHNOLOGY
024	STEPTOE & JOHNSON	STEVEN MCGOWAN	353-8114	LAW
555	ST. FRANCIS HOSPITAL	DAN LAUFFER	347-6633	MEDICAL
300	CHARLESTON MARRIOTT	STEVE NICHOLS	353-3610	CULINARY ARTS
1320	WV SCHOOL EMPLOYEES FEDERAL CREDIT UNION	JACKIE CHAPMAN	348-7727 x125	BUSINESS/ FINANCE

Present career posts.

Above: Megan Smith of Venture Scout Crew 2268 of Cross Lanes is sailing at Camp Oyo in Ohio, July 2002.

Left: Venture Crew 2268's Brandon Chambers and Patrick Murphy are shown participating in the Kanawha River Cleanup, September 2002.

Crew 2268 held an overnight sleepover on the sternwheeler "Spirit of South Charleston" in May 2004. Pictured (left to right) are crew members Brandon Chambers, Patrick Murphy, Megan Smith, Erin Murphy, Mary Beth Murphy (adult advisor) and John Gaines (rear).

Chapter Eight

Honor Camper Organizations

In the Boy Scouts there have been various honor groups in different parts of the country. In the Buckskin Council the first honor group was called The Scouts of the Mountain.

In the Scouts of the Mountain, new members were selected by the camp staff during each week of summer camp. Scouts had a short duty to perform before being officially accepted into the group. They were given a large green "W" emblem as a sign of membership. The "W" stood for Walhonde, which was the council's summer camp, on Alum Creek, from the mid 1920s until the mid 1940s. The Scouts of the Mountain had begun at Walhonde. Later the "W" was replaced by a round patch which was awarded to scouts who became members.

In time, the Order of the Arrow, which is a national honor camper organization recognized by the National Boy Scout Council, replaced the Scouts of the Mountain. The Order of the Arrow became the official honor camper organization of the Buckskin Council on January 1, 1952.

In this group the scout is elected by his local troop. Each troop may elect a number of scouts according to the numbers of their membership. After being elected by his troop, the scout must go through an "ordeal" before becoming a full member of the group.

The Order of the Arrow in the Buckskin Council is designed not just to honor scouts, but also to accomplish service projects for the benefit of the council and the community. The original name of the Buckskin lodge was Wachu Menatopolis. The original lodge number was 475.

The Order of the Arrow has long been an important honor camper organization within the Buckskin Council. Prior to its adoption, the Buckskin Council's honor campers joined the Scouts of the Mountain.

With the merger of the Appalachian and Chief Cornstalk Councils into the Buckskin Council, a

THIS 1969 PHOTO SHOWS SEVERAL NEW MEMBERS OF THE ORDER OF THE ARROW INCLUDING (LEFT TO RIGHT) HUGH KRAFT, STEVE KRAFT, TIM PRIDDY, AND KEN PRIDDY. THE SETTING IS BUCKSKIN SCOUT RESERVATION.

new lodge was formed of all three old lodges. The new lodge is now called Chi-Hoota-Wei. The lodges of the former merged councils had been known as Hy-tone and Ajudimo.

One of the precepts of the Order of the Arrow is to honor and follow the principles of brotherhood of Native Americans. This has been accomplished in a number of ways, one of which is the Wachu Dancers.

AT THE BUCKSKIN SCOUT RESERVATION THIS 1980 PHOTO SHOWS A "TAP-OUT" CEREMONY ABOUT TO TAKE PLACE. IN RED IS ROBERT TISSUE.

In 1965 Peter Howell, formerly a member of Troop 11 and Post 111, organized a number of his scouting friends into a group whose interest was in putting on exhibitions of Indian regalia and dancing as a way to promote both scouting and the Order of the Arrow. The idea grew rapidly. The scouts came from all areas of Kanawha County and, among others, included economically disadvantaged boys who were in need of mentoring and role models.

At its height in the 1970s there were about 20 regular members. Peter Howell, by this time the adult advisor, had spent some of his time in college learning how to make Indian style beadwork suitable for enhancing costumes. Thus, he was a natural leader and coach for the dance group. Around 1975 when Howell was retiring from the group, an adult group of dance team members came into existence. It included individuals such as Pat O'Neal, Andy Waddell, Earl Heim, and Jay Parkins. The team continued to grow well into the 1980s.

During the 1970s, and later, the Order of the Arrow Dance Team won numerous awards. This 1972 edition of the team includes (left to right), front: John Preston, Jim Porter, Ron Colby, Steve Gorham, Jay Arceneaux, Bill Shropshire, Rick Perdue. Back row: Joe Ong, Peter Howell, Bob Murray, Dean Litz, Andy Waddell, James Crace, John O'Donnell, Steve Cook, Jeff Reinhart, and Steve Starkey. This photo was taken at the dining hall at Camp Chief Logan.

Another honor scout organization is the National Eagle Scout Association. The Eagle Scout Association came to be known as the Knights of Dunimas.

Over the years the team won numerous recognitions and awards, including four times the award for best overall dance team in Area 4F, which included most of West Virginia and parts of Virginia, Ohio, and Kentucky. The Wachu Dancers would go on to win 12 consecutive American Indian awards in area competition. The team also won second place during the national competition at the National Order of the Arrow Conference held at Miami University (OH) in 1975.

The dancers performed at many grade schools throughout West Virginia and Ohio and performed weekly at Buckskin Reservation during the camping season. The team made trips to national conferences in Bloomington, Indiana and to southern California. They made trips to many Native American festivals and Pow-Wows.

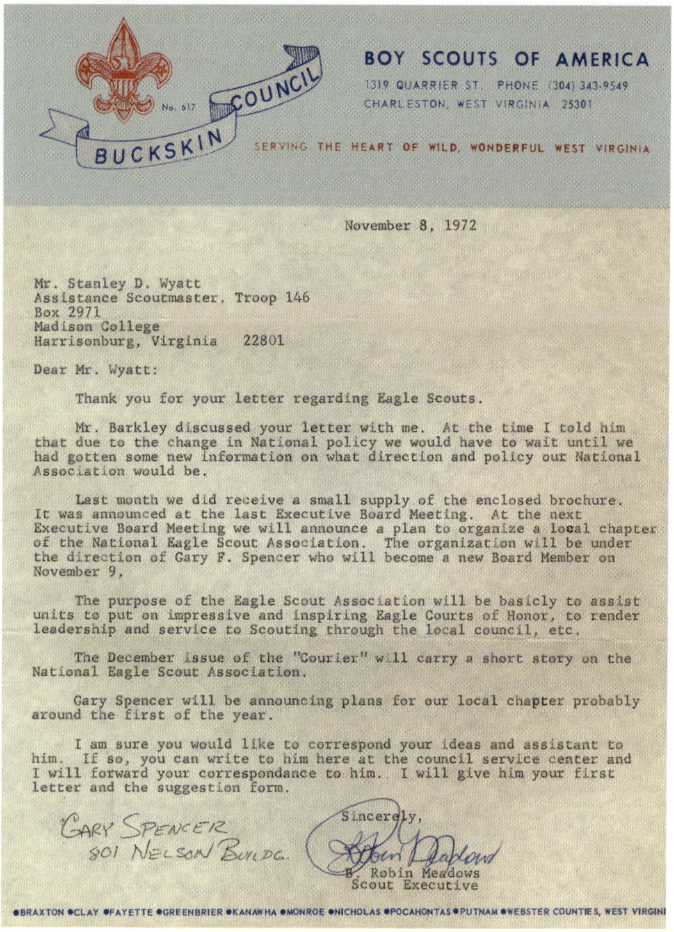

BOY SCOUTS OF AMERICA
1319 QUARRIER ST. PHONE (304) 343-9549
CHARLESTON, WEST VIRGINIA 25301

BUCKSKIN COUNCIL No. 617

SERVING THE HEART OF WILD, WONDERFUL WEST VIRGINIA

November 8, 1972

Mr. Stanley D. Wyatt
Assistance Scoutmaster, Troop 146
Box 2971
Madison College
Harrisonburg, Virginia 22801

Dear Mr. Wyatt:

Thank you for your letter regarding Eagle Scouts.

Mr. Barkley discussed your letter with me. At the time I told him that due to the change in National policy we would have to wait until we had gotten some new information on what direction and policy our National Association would be.

Last month we did receive a small supply of the enclosed brochure. It was announced at the last Executive Board Meeting. At the next Executive Board Meeting we will announce a plan to organize a local chapter of the National Eagle Scout Association. The organization will be under the direction of Gary F. Spencer who will become a new Board Member on November 9,

The purpose of the Eagle Scout Association will be basicly to assist units to put on impressive and inspiring Eagle Courts of Honor, to render leadership and service to Scouting through the local council, etc.

The December issue of the "Courier" will carry a short story on the National Eagle Scout Association.

Gary Spencer will be announcing plans for our local chapter probably around the first of the year.

I am sure you would like to correspond your ideas and assistant to him. If so, you can write to him here at the council service center and I will forward your correspondance to him. I will give him your first letter and the suggestion form.

Gary Spencer
801 Nelson Buildg.

Sincerely,

B. Robin Meadows
Scout Executive

•BRAXTON •CLAY •FAYETTE •GREENBRIER •KANAWHA •MONROE •NICHOLAS •POCAHONTAS •PUTNAM •WEBSTER COUNTIES, WEST VIRGINI

CLAY "SQUIRREL" HANNA OF TROOP 146 BUILDS A FIRE BY FRICTION AT THE FALL 1996 OA FELLOWSHIP WEEKEND. THE EVENT TOOK PLACE AT THE RECONSTRUCTED WOLF CREEK INDIAN VILLAGE, BASTAIN, VIRIGNIA.

Because materials for equipment and travel were expensive, Jim Waybright hired the group to wash dishes at many of his catered events. Waybright was a local restauranteur. It was required that team members work in the kitchen to raise funds, and usually the team raised about $4,500.

At the printing of this book, the extended family of the Wachu dance team remains close, with many of the old members pursuing their professional careers and maintaining their scouting values and principles.

Charleston Daily Mail MON., JAN. 19, 1970

KNIGHTS OF DUNIMAS ELECT

New Officers of West Virginia's only chapter of the Knights of Dunimas, national Eagle Scout service association founded in California in 1925 are Bill Johnson, counselor; Stan Wyatt, commander, and Robert Logan, treasurer, all from Charleston. They were installed Sunday at a meeting at the Church of The Good Shepherd in Kanawha City. The Buckskin Chapter was organized in Charleston last May, with more than 20 Eagle Scout members from the nine-county council.

THE KNIGHTS OF DUNIMAS PROVIDES A VENUE FOR CONTINUED PARTICIPATION OF OLDER SCOUTS WHO HAVE ATTAINED THE RANK OF EAGLE SCOUT.

Chapter Nine

Leadership Training

The first local Woodbadge Leader Training Course took place at Buckskin Scout Reservation in 1968. Pictured here are members of the "Eagle Patrol." They are (front row, left to right): Tom Brannan, Ken Robbins, Bob Frey, and Bill Briton. Back row (left to right) are Bill Wyatt, Jim Malone, D.C. Wingate, and Otto Brown.

Woodbadge

Woodbadge is sometimes termed the "Ph.D. of scout leader training." It is a training course undertaken only by those adults with exceptional interest in the role of Scoutmaster or Assistant Scoutmaster.

Rigorous standards of knowledge and performance of scouting's leader requirements must be met in order to earn one's Woodbadge Beads. Teamwork and completion of various skill-related projects during a week of dawn-to-dusk training are required. Detailed write-ups of one's successes and shortcomings during the week are reviewed by staff. Later a much more detailed overview of the experience must be written.

Many Buckskin leaders have earned the beads. Those who wear them can say that they have become the finest leaders of scouts.

Brownsea 22 Junior Leaders' Training

Brownsea 22 is steeped in tradition. The program closely parallels the first Scout camp conducted by Baden-Powell, founder of Scouting, on Brownsea Island in Poole Harbor, England in 1907. The Patrol names and colors are the same ones used on that course. The Brownsea Junior Leader Training course is a 7-day outdoor experience for Senior Patrol Leaders, Asst. Senior Patrol Leaders and Patrol Leaders who will be supporting the Scoutmaster in running the troop activities. Brownsea is intended to teach the scout various leadership skills and how to use them in his home troop. The course is the next step in training Junior Leaders after they have had the basic Junior Leaders training course. Brownsea is conducted by the Council Leadership Training Committee based on an outline approved by the National Council, Boy Scouts of America.

Brownsea participants are in a troop leadership position or ready to assume a troop leadership position: Senior Patrol Leader, Assistant Senior Patrol Leader, Patrol Leader, Assistant Patrol Leader. In Brownsea 22, it is taken for granted that the scouts are all camp-skilled. They are therefore thrown directly into performing the skills in vigorous games and patrol competition. In Brownsea 22 it is taken for granted that the Scouts have demonstrated certain leadership abilities by the fact that they have followers who have elected them as their leaders in their home troops. They are therefore given the challenge to perform by assuming leadership of the Brownsea patrols and they are expected to learn how to run their home troops.

Over the years many scouts have learned valuable leadership skills during their week of Brownsea 22 training at Buckskin Reservation. The most recent Brownsea course was conducted in 1999. Many fine leaders have given their time so that scouts, and later their home troops, would benefit from the advanced training. Bill Wyatt served as scoutmaster for the first six courses. He was followed by Dick Master (four courses), Ed Deitz (one course), and Jan Hacker (nine courses). Matt Blackwood was scoutmaster in 1999.

For twenty years Leonard Taylor served as the Brownsea Program Director. He described an episode that typifies the old saying: "Boys will be boys." One evening a scout came to Taylor's first aid tent complaining of an upset stomach. Taylor found the scout had no fever or other observable problem. He

The 1995 Brownsea staff shown here include, front row (left to right) Mark Fredrick, Jan Hacker, Bob McCloy, Matt Blackwood, Mike Richardson and Dale Casewell. Back row (left to right) are Bill Wyatt, John Howell, Carl Johnson, Leonard Taylor, Steve Hardman, C.J. Price, Chuck Kittinger and Josh Phoenix.

Mark Fredricks and Carl Johnson discuss training at Brownsea 1995.

THE BULL PATROL AT BROWNSEA 1995 INCLUDED (NOT IN ORDER) RYAN MORGAN, JARED WELLS, JARED TAYLOR, KYLE WHEELER, ERIC ANDERSON, BO BROWN, JONATHAN LEE MOORE, AND CRAIG WHITE.

MONKEY BRIDGE AT BROWNSEA 1993.

gave the scout a can of pop to help settle his stomach and had the boy lie down. In a while the scout was feeling better and went on his way.

Later, a second, then a third scout came to Taylor with the same complaint, and Taylor provided the same treatment. Then came several others and Taylor began to wonder if the cooks had poisoned everyone. Then he figured out the cause of all the "illness." The word was out. Pop was available at sick bay.

Taylor devised a "cure." He posted an old skull in front of the tent. He had acquired the skull while in medical school. Only one other case of stomachache appeared, and it was soon "cured."

Chapter Ten

National Jamborees

Buckskin Council scouts and leaders have attended every National Jamboree, starting with the first which was held on the National Mall in Washington, D.C., in 1937.

These photos will bring back many memories of swapping patches and pins, seeing Presidents, traveling to far places and meeting scouts from every state and many foreign countries.

The neckerchiefs of Jamborees from 1935 (cancelled due to a polio epidemic) to more recent years serve as powerful reminders of Jamboree experiences.

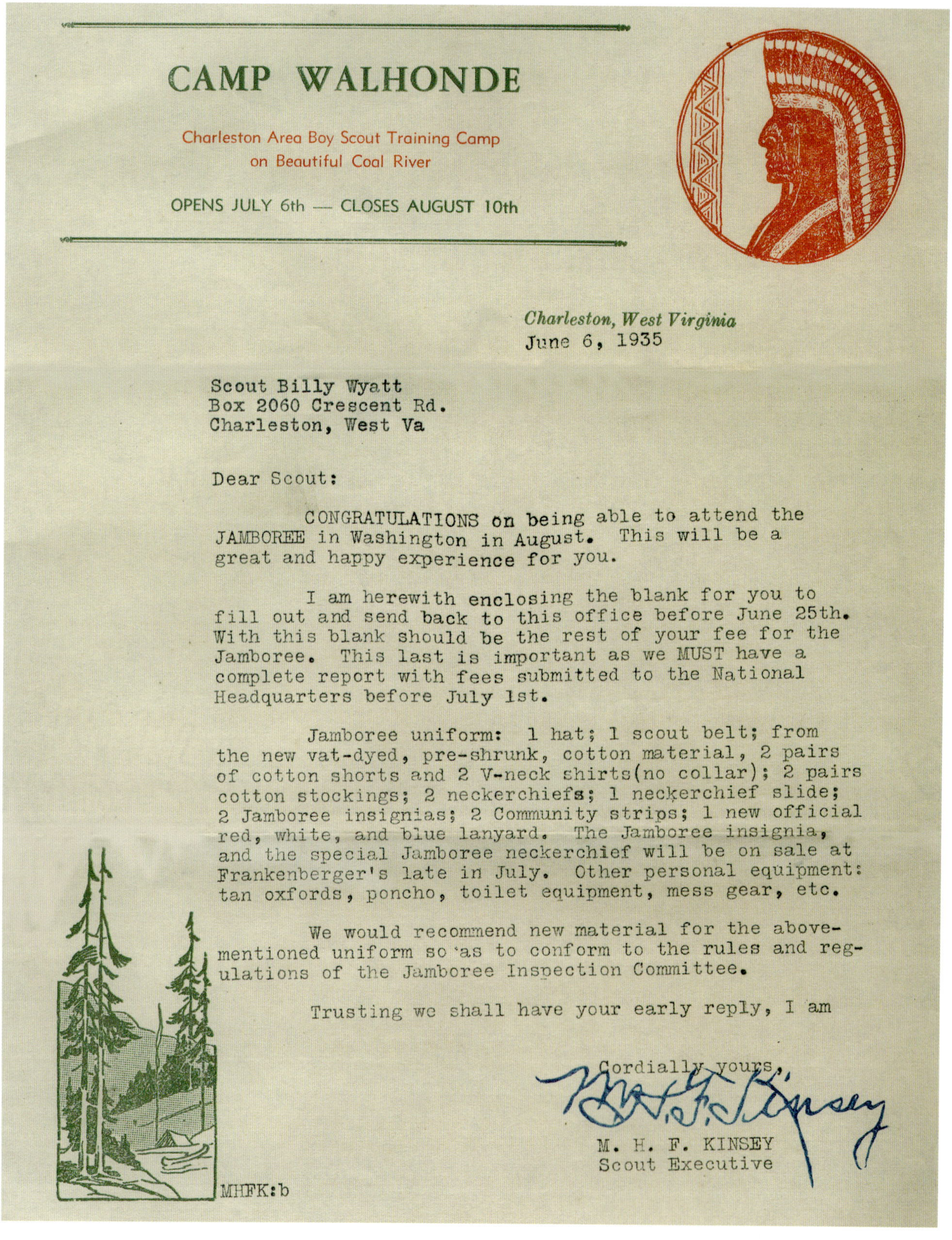

CAMP WALHONDE

Charleston Area Boy Scout Training Camp
on Beautiful Coal River

OPENS JULY 6th — CLOSES AUGUST 10th

Charleston, West Virginia
June 6, 1935

Scout Billy Wyatt
Box 2060 Crescent Rd.
Charleston, West Va

Dear Scout:

CONGRATULATIONS on being able to attend the JAMBOREE in Washington in August. This will be a great and happy experience for you.

I am herewith enclosing the blank for you to fill out and send back to this office before June 25th. With this blank should be the rest of your fee for the Jamboree. This last is important as we MUST have a complete report with fees submitted to the National Headquarters before July 1st.

Jamboree uniform: 1 hat; 1 scout belt; from the new vat-dyed, pre-shrunk, cotton material, 2 pairs of cotton shorts and 2 V-neck shirts(no collar); 2 pairs cotton stockings; 2 neckerchiefs; 1 neckerchief slide; 2 Jamboree insignias; 2 Community strips; 1 new official red, white, and blue lanyard. The Jamboree insignia, and the special Jamboree neckerchief will be on sale at Frankenberger's late in July. Other personal equipment: tan oxfords, poncho, toilet equipment, mess gear, etc.

We would recommend new material for the above-mentioned uniform so as to conform to the rules and regulations of the Jamboree Inspection Committee.

Trusting we shall have your early reply, I am

Cordially yours,

M. H. F. Kinsey

M. H. F. KINSEY
Scout Executive

MHFK:b

Letter to Scout Billy Wyatt from M.H.F. Kinsey detailing his uniform, fees, etc., confirming the scout's registration for the first National Jamboree in 1935. Unfortunately, a polio epidemic caused cancellation of the Jamboree just days prior to its start.

This was the cover of a 1950 Jamboree booklet. The jamboree was the first of several held at Valley Forge, Pennsylvania.

This is thought to be a photograph of the 1937 Buckskin Jamboree Troop.

THRONG OF 75,000 SCOUTS AND V

PRESIDENT TRUMAN SPOKE TO THE SCOUTS ASSEMBLED AT VALLEY FORGE, PENNSYLVANIA, IN 1950.

President Exalts Peace Aims at Scout Jamboree

Fight World Hate, He Urges 75,000 At Valley Forge

Text of President Truman's address on page 4.

By JOHN C. O'BRIEN

President Truman called upon the Boy Scouts of America last night to help spread their ideal of human brotherhood to nations where youth are being regimented for racial hatred and war.

Mr. Truman cautioned some 50,000 Scouts and 25,000 guests at the Boy Scout Jamboree at Valley Forge not to return the hate which youth in the Communist-dominated countries are being taught to feel toward the United States.

"We must realize," he said, "that they are the victims of a cynical group of leaders. We must make it clear to them that we believe in the fellowship of human beings, in the possibility of cooperative human action, and in peace based on mutual understanding. We must show them over and over again that fellowship is possible between men of different nations, different colors and different creeds."

FIERCE BELIEF IN FREEDOM'

The President insisted on keeping an engagement made many weeks ago to speak to the Boy Scouts, despite the Korean crisis which has monopolized his time in the last few days. He journeyed to Valley Forge by special train, leaving Washington at 4:40 P. M. After the speech he returned to Philadelphia, where he boarded the yacht Williamsburg at the Navy Yard for a week-end cruise down the Delaware River, through Chesapeake Bay and up the Potomac River to Washington.

The President departed from the text of his speech only to remind the Scouts how fortunate they were to be well clothed and well fed, in contrast to the patriots who suffered here in 1777.

"You should be very thankful to your country," the President said.

AT VALLEY FORGE LISTENS AS PRESIDENT TRUMAN DELIVERS ADDRESS

Boy Scouts pass in parade. More than 47,000 are participating in the second national jamboree in Valley Forge.

The mass of scouting humanity is evident in these 1950 National Jamboree photos.

The cover of the 1953 Jamboree commemorative booklet provides some idea of the scope of a "Jamboree City." The photo shows the encampment at Irvine Ranch, California.

The 1953 National Jamboree contingent prepares to depart from the Charleston Depot. Front row, sixth from right is Ed Hacala who provided this rare photo. Standing, far left is Jack Lewis, Buckskin Council Representative, and to his left is Asst. Scoutmaster Ray Trimble. Quartermaster Stan Cohen is on Trimble's left. Standing, far right is Scoutmaster Bill Waytt. Kneeling, far right is Asst. Scoutmaster Charlie Daniels.

Prior to each National Jamboree a weekend practice camp is held. Here plans are discussed for the 1953 Jamboree by, left to right, kneeling: Jack Lewis, Eddie Hacala, Bill Miller, Charles Bartels, John Vaughn, John Murrell and Charlie Daniels. Standing are Don Krisher, Pat Mullins, R.M. Thomas, (unidentified), and Bill Wyatt. Looking from tent is Frank Tuckwiller.

The "West Virginia Rebels" troop at Coonskin Park prior to leaving for the 1953 Jamboree. Left to right: Bill Miller, Jon Young, Larry Berman, Stan Cohen ("Buckskin Boys" publisher), John Reynolds, Walter Walker, Ted McClure, Walter Witchey. All are from Charleston except Young and McClure who are from Marlinton.

Our Place on the Map Today

THE 1953 NATIONAL JAMBOREE WAS BIG NEWS.

REUNION—Norman Rockwell, famed artist, chats with First Class Scout Wayne Riblett, 14, and Army Private Dick Tyler, 20 (left), who three years ago posed for a picture by Rockwell that became the official Boy Scout calendar for 1952.

—Los Angeles Examiner photo.

Buckskin Scouts Attend Services

Marching files of Buckskin council Boy Scouts are seen at left parading to church services at "Jamboree City," Newport Beach, Calif., where the young Charlestonians are among 50,000 scouts attending the national jamboree.

In the photo at right another column steps snappily through the "Buckskin Council" archway which marks their camping area.

A Typical Day in Bustling Jamboree City

Examiner Staff Cartoonist Karl Hubenthal Scouts the Scouts

'TRADE' DEALS OCCUPY BOYS

'Men of Tomorrow' Prove Good Merchants of Today

JAMBOREE CITY, Newport Harbor, July 16.—Rub any two Boy Scouts together and you've kindled a red-hot "deal."

And they are rubbing together by the thousands, day and night, in the big circus-style "swapping tents" at each of the trading posts.

At night, each tent resembles a convention of midget-sized pitch men.

They spread their wares on the picnic-style tables.

They mill and jostle from table to table, raising such a constant dust cloud even the banks of bright lights above appear dimmed.

Visitor Lauds Organization

French Executive in Trip to Camp Site

JAMBOREE CITY, Newport Harbor, July 16.—High praise for the organization of the Third National Jamboree came today from Marc Cambana, French scout executive, who is visiting the Jamboree site.

Cambana, veteran of 15 years in the French scout movement, has charge of 17 troops in his home town, Wissous, near Paris.

For his visit to the Jamboree, he changed his French Merchant Marine officer's uniform for a scout shirt, bright neckerchief and black leather pants.

His ship, La Coubre, is docked at Los Angeles Harbor.

"I read about the Jamboree in the Examiner and I didn't want to miss the chance to see what is going on," he said.

L. A. GREETED BY MARYLAND

Baltimore Scouts Bring Word From Mayor and Governor

Greetings from the Mayor of Baltimore and the Governor of Maryland were brought to Los Angeles yesterday by Robert Patterson, 12, representing 105 Boy Scouts from Baltimore.

The boys are here to attend the Third Annual National Scout Jamboree.

The greetings were presented to City Council President John S. Gibson Jr., acting Mayor of Los Angeles.

They were from Arthur B. Price, ex-officio Mayor of Baltimore, and Theodore R. McKeldin, Governor of Maryland.

(Additional Jamboree news on Page 16).

Local newspapers provide coverage. At top is a Los Angeles newspaper cartoonist's "take." Several stories appeared daily in 1953 (bottom).

'MOUNTAIN' LIKE ANT HILL

10,000 Cheer Rogers Rodeo From Slopes Above Campfire

JAMBOREE CITY, Newport Harbor, July 18.—Ten thousand Boy Scouts turned a "mountain" into a seething ant hill today as they jammed the slopes above Campfire Area Two to cheer Roy (King of the Cowboys) Rogers and his rodeo show.

That was the high point of this energetic day that saw the first huge crowd of visitors—so many even the inter-camp bus system could not handle them all—hiking over every area of the vast site right along with the Scouts.

Bands blared everywhere while beach-bound thousands spilled waves of music in the wake of their buses with the singing of songs which usually boasted of home.

"Beautiful Ohio" was in competition with "Oklahoma!" and "My Maryland."

MYRIAD TRA LS—

And those not otherwise occupied proved Scouts know the shortest distance between two points as their feet tramped out myriad trails up, down and around every knob of land in this nearly five square miles of camp sites, cross-hatching it like a jumble of king-sized tic-tac-toe games.

At the rodeo site in Big Canyon, repeated roars of delight came from the boys, who, generally, were seeing real Western movie stars and a band of cowhands for the first time.

Saturday was the fitting time for them to see the people they share their fancy with in darkness of neighborhood movies on Saturdays back home—Roy, Dale Evans, his "queen of the Golden West"; Trigger, Bullet, Pat Brady, Iron Eyes Cody, the Five Whipperwills and the Black Brothers.

TRIGGER FANS—

For two hours they soaked up the thrill of seeing Trigger go through his paces, seeing Bullet perform, so they can go back home after this Jamboree tell their less fortunate buddies:

"They REALLY can do all those things!"

Manny Harmon and his orchestra were on hand, too, to furnish musical background for Roy's and Dale's singing, and there were other entertainers, too—Juggler Frank Faylen and Douglas Wyckoff.

Roy wasn't far from the truth, either, when he sang "The Kid With a Rip in His Pants," since fully half of the thousands before him had skittered down hill on the seats of their own to reach chosen vantage points.

Dignitaries Visit Scouts At Jamboree

VALLEY FORGE, Pa., July 15 (AP)—Army brass and high-up civilians, from Washington and from many Eastern states, today joined the unending flow of lesser known visitors to the Boy Scouts' Jamboree City.

It was a special day for nearby Region 3 — Pennsylvania, Delaware, Maryland, Virginia and the District of Columbia.

* * *

THIS LARGE contingent, which includes the host delegation, held an impressive ceremony high on a hill under an archway the scouts themselves built at the entrance to their huge camping area.

Several hundred boys gathered in a crescent to watch the presentation of awards to top officials of scouting and to the heads of state from their home areas. An outstanding scout from each section was chosen to hand over the awards and after a brief speech a band played a passage from the state anthem.

Gov. J. Caleb Boggs received citation for Delaware. Others were Maj. Gen. Anthony J. Drexel Biddle, head of the Pennsylvania National Guard; Maryland Secretary of State Claude B. Hellman; N. W. Kelley of Roanoke, Va., and Robert E. McLaughlin, commissioner of the District of Columbia.

The awards were presented also to Kenneth K. Bechtel, National Council president of the scouts; Henry B. Grandin, chairman of the jamboree committee, and Dr. Arthur A. Schuck, chief scout executive.

The visiting dignitaries lunched with the scouts from their home territories and later made the rounds of their camp sites.

* * *

ANOTHER illustrious visitor was four star Gen. Willard G. Wyman of Ft. Monroe, Va., who heads the U.S. Continental Army Command.

Late in the afternoon excitement hit a high pitch when five Air Force jet fighters streaked over the historic area with a thunderous clap each time they broke the sound barrier. The famed five-man team of Thunderbird pilots was making a reconnaisance of the area over which they will formally perform Wednesday for the scouts.

Roy Rogers and Dale Evans visited the 1953 National Jamboree (above). "Army brass and high-up civilians" visited scouts at the 1957 National Jamboree held at Valley Forge, Pennsylvania (right).

The 1957 National Jamboree was held at Valley Forge, Pennsylvania, as was the 1950 Jamboree. We have identified more than half of these scouts. Front row, fifth from left, Steve Gillespie and eighth from left is Mike Funk. Second row, left to right, Bob Farley, unidentified, Richard Carte, Arnold Moore, unidentified, Pat O'Neal, Bob Moore, Jim Rice, Lansing Skidmore, unidentified, Hugh Denny, unidentified. Back row, left to right, Asst. Scoutmaster Ralph Moore, Jerry Webster, Raymond Moore, unidentified, Joe Meadows, unidentified, Gene Thompson, unidentified, Bob Bland, ____ Jones, David Vande Linde, Bob Warren, unidentified, Scoutmaster Dick Kronmiller.

Scout Troop 31 shown ready to leave for Valley Forge, in 1957.

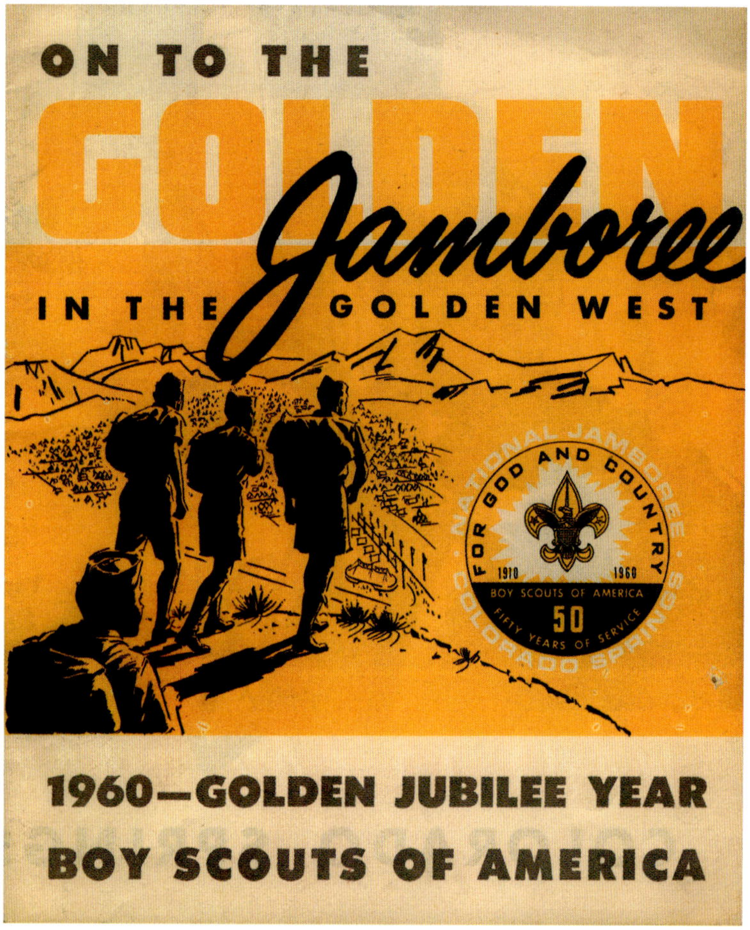

The amphitheater at the 1960 National Jamboree, Colorado Springs. Note Pike's Peak in the background. This photograph was taken during a religious service.

President Eisenhower visited the 1960 National Jamboree in Colorado Springs.

This was Troop 1, comprised of scouts and leaders from the Chief Cornstalk District, at the 1964 Jamboree. Several of those whom we have identified include Dale Harwood (third from left on the back row), Tom White (sixth from left), Dick White (seventh), Scoutmaster Harry White (eighth), Harry White, Jr. (ninth). On the back row, extreme right is Asst. Scoutmaster Duffy Mays.

Scouts who attended the 1964 Jamboree took a side trip to the New York World's Fair. Above: scouts pictured here are Rob Pennington (with jacket) and J.D. Robinette. Left: Another scene from the World's Fair.

Troop 76 of the Buckskin Council attended the 1964 National Jamboree. Scoutmaster was Paul Cleek. Harvey Herbert and Ray Bail were Assistant Scoutmasters.

Above: Lowell Cosby of Troop 51 in the Chief Cornstalk District tried his hand at the barrel at the 1964 Jamboree.

Left: These Chief Cornstalk scouts are climbing the wall, generally regarded as the toughest part of the obstacle course at each jamboree.

SCOUT TROOP 45 OF BECKLEY AT THE 1969 NATIONAL JAMBOREE AT FARRAGUT PARK, IDAHO. WEST VIRGINIA STATE ARCHIVES, ALBERT R. ALLEN JR. COLLECTION

THIS WAS TROOP 47 OF THE BUCKSKIN COUNCIL AT FARRAGUT PARK, IDAHO. PAUL CLEEK WAS SCOUTMASTER. WILLIAM HARRINGTON AND CHARLES EVANS WERE ASSISTANT SCOUTMASTERS.

JAMBOREE TROOP ROSTER 1973 Jamboree East

JAMBOREE TROOP NO. 146
SCOUTS 21
LEADERS 2
TOTAL PARTICIPANTS 23

Council Name Buckskin Number 617
Council City Charleston State W. Va.

1973

Please list everybody in your jamboree troop alphabetically, including leaders. Put an "L" in the leader column beside each leader's name. Bring this roster to the jamboree because you will need it for checking in at your camp. Make it out in triplicate - copy for jamboree - copy for council - copy for troop leader.

PLEASE PRINT OR TYPE

	Ldr.	Last Name	First Name	Street Address	City
1		Baier	Douglas	195 Monterey Dr	St. Albans
2		Colby	Ronald	703 Chestnut st.	" "
3		Rasmussen	Karl	2519 Winter St	" "
4		Robinette	Ted	2529 ParkView Dr.	" "
5		Johnson	Robert	304 Robinson Rd	" "
6		Johnson	Phillip	" " "	" "
7		Heim	Earl	418 Holley St	" "
8		Heim	Fred	" " "	" "
9		Morgan	Michael	937 Lexington Ave	" "
10		Martin	Andrew	1001 Elm St	" "
11		Niday	Stephen	1100 Summitt Dr.	" "
12		Wallace	Scott	937 Lotus Rd.	" "
13		Ellis	Larry	905 Sutherland Dr	" "
14		Cook	Michael	1014 Ellis Rd.	" "
15		Ours	Weldon	333 Scenic Dr	" "
16		Cleary	Stephen	913 Hughes Dr	" "
17		Melton	Randy	711 Holley St	" "
18		Kimble	Cecil	202 Rocky Step Rd	Scott Depot
19		Mabe	Gale	4818 Spring Hill Ave	South Charleston
20		Taylor	Robert	210 Sun Valley Dr	St. Albans
21		Santee	David	2609 Hollister Dr.	Charleston
22	L	Rasmussen	Roger	2519 Winter St	St. Albans
23	L	Brucker	David	1515 Kanawha Terr.	" "

THE 1973 JAMBOREE WAS HELD IN TWO LOCATIONS. THESE WERE CALLED JAMBOREE EAST AND WEST. THE JAMBOREE EAST WAS HELD AT MORAINE STATE PARK IN PENNSYLVANIA. TROOPS WITH ENOUGH SCOUTS WERE ALLOWED TO ATTEND AS A GROUP, RATHER THAN BEING SPLIT UP AND CONSOLIDATED INTO CONTINGENT GROUPS.

DOUG BAIER AND BANE SHAFFER ARE PICTURED IN THIS 1973 NATIONAL JAMBOREE (EAST) PHOTO.

SCOUTS BOARD BUS FOR NATIONAL JAMBOREE AFTER SAYING GOODBYES
Inset Shows Commemorative Jamboree Patches Worn By Campers

— Daily Mail Photo By Chet Hawes.

'Boy' Scout Heads For Jamboree

By ADRIAN GWIN
Of The Daily Mail Staff

Forty years is a long time, and I know I'm going to feel foolish.

Particularly in a red beret.

Well, maybe not. With 40,000 others wearing them, maybe I'll feel right at home. But a red beret isn't quite like the old Boy Scout hat.

Oh? Sorry, I'm getting ahead of myself.

I'm off to the National Boy Scout Jamboree, being held for a week in the Moraine State Park, Pennsylvania.

This is the 9th national jamboree, and I haven't attended one of them since the first one 40 years ago.

I was a man-sized Boy Scout then, back there in 1937, when that first jamboree was held in Washington. Today you could call me a boy-sized man-scout, I guess.

They're changed a lot of the rules since then. Then, I was a "boy" — a patrol leader, even if I was 20 years old. Today's "boys" have to be under 18, or they go as men, as an assistant Scoutmaster or other leader.

This time I'm joining 36 Scouts and their leaders from Buckskin Council, and I'm going as correspondent to write about what the boys of "Jamboree Troop 165" are doing each day.

OUR MAN GWIN

I'll try to remember what fun it was for me and find some scout from our troop who is seeing this for the first time, and write about him and his adventures.

There will be bronze, silver and gold medals for scout competitions like tent-pitching and fire-building, and there will be demonstrations by Scouts from all over the country — like bull-whip cracking by the Oklahomans, and deer-skinning by the "Mountain Men" Scouts of Utah or Colorado — things like that.

I remember the Oklahomans in 1937 had a 60-foot bullwhip, too heavy for a boy to heft, that they laid out on the ground. Then a scout would take the handle, give it a fast whip-like motion up and down, and the whip would ripple like a running blacksnake, and if he'd done it right, the end would rise up and crack like a rifleshot. I tried it, and my ripple didn't even get to the end of the whip!

We'll camp around Lake Arthur in Moraine State Park, 40 miles north of Pittsburgh, just off Interstate 79, all 40,000 of us.

We'll live in tents, camping by patrols of eight boys, four patrols or more to a troop camp, with troops of each state and region camping together.

There will be International Scouts there, too, a few patrols or individuals from other countries visiting, and our boys will find that their emblem, the "Universal Scout Emblem" and the scout sign, made with the right hand upraised, thumb over the nail of the little finger, is indeed a universal sign among Scouts.

(I remember flashing that sign to a Dutchman near the German border in World War II, me a bearded GI Joe, greeting a total stranger with the scout sign, and being instantly recognized as a Boy Scout and friend. He took four American soldiers to his home for dinner because of that.)

1977 marked 40 years since the first National Jamboree.

OUR MAN GWIN AND 1937 JAMBOREE-MATES AT 1977 EVENT

MEMORIES

Scouting Veterans Recall First Jamboree 40 Years Ago

By ADRIAN GWIN
Of The Daily Mail Staff

MORAINE STATE PARK, Pa.— Each one was one in a thousand.

They were the Old Men of the 1977 Jamboree — the 24 of us who are here for the ninth National Jamboree.

We are the 24 out of the 28,000 who attended the first jamboree in Washington, D.C., 40 years ago, who are still at it today — attending the jamboree.

At the only Jamboree reunion ever held, we gathered the other night at the pavillion tent to swap lies and yarns about our experience.

The eldest is Wes H. Klusman of California, at 79 an aide on the national staff here, assisting the jamboree director.

If experience counts, he's the deacon.

He joined the Boy Scouts in 1911, dropped out a year later to go to work, returned to Scouting later and now has 57 years as a Scouter.

He was Troop leader for the Los Angeles Council to the first jamboree in 1937, and was Scoutmaster of the American troop which went to the World Jamboree that year.

He has been to all nine national and three world jamborees and has no intention of dropping out of Scouting at age 79.

The youngest was a boy of 12 in 1937.

They came from Washington state, Oregon, North Carolina, Louisiana, West Virginia, Pennsylvania, California, Connecticut, New York and points in between. Most of the 24 are Eagle Scouts, most of them hold the top council honor, the Silver Beaver. A few hold the Silver Antelope, regional honor for Scouters. Many are on the national staff of Scouting, most are on regional of council staffs in some capacity, and most now have sons who have been Boy Scouts.

We remember that the 1937 jamboree was a hungry time, no food ever wasted, someone always ready to eat an extra portion or two if anything was left over. We remembered the hot long walks in to Washington, with everyone in full uniforms. We remembered the mud ankle deep when it rained, and the security patrols who wouldn't let you out of the area if you didn't have the right color neckerchief on.

We signed a roster in keeping of Walt Morgan of Brookings, South Dakota, who "organized" the reunion. Walt was a scout from Connecticut in 1937, a boy of 15, has since taught genetics and biology at universities for years.

We sat around for an hour remembering this and that and interrupting each other to recall one or another incident, and then Walt said we'd about squeezed the water out of the rag and let's get back to this jamboree and the boys, and we broke it up, not promising to get together again in another 40 years or anything.

And we headed back to our respective jobs here at the 1977 Jamboree where the boys still have several days to go on THEIR big adventure, quite unmindful that perhaps 40 years from now THEY will be the ones — maybe 24 of them, — who have made another jamboree possible or another batch of Boy Scouts of America.

Our Buckskin boys were at a Friendship Campfire program in our own camping area, and that will be a highlight of their national jamboree — remember that first campfire we had over in the woods — and the guys who put on that skit about . . . and the kid who did alll the imitations . . . and . . . and . . .

Remember?

Columnist Adrian Gwin had attended the first National Jamboree in 1937. Forty years later he met up with others who had been at the initial Jamboree. Their reunion was at Moraine State Park, Pennsylvania.

A Charleston Daily Mail SAT., JULY 25, 1981

71 Boy Scouts Jamboree Bound

y ADRIAN GWIN
The Daily Mail Staff

With packs strapped down for a 10-day stay, 71 Boy Scouts and eir leaders left this morning for the National Jamboree.

The boys are all from Buckskin Council's 10-county Southern est Virginia area.

This year's gathering — they've been held every four years since 937 — is at Fort A.P. Hill near Fredericksburg, Va.

About 30,000 Scouts and leaders from every state and a scatterg of foreign countries will converge on the vast military reservaon Sunday, for the 10-day stay.

Buckskin Council's two Jamboree trips are under the leadership f Dean Parkins of Charleston and John Meadows of St. Albans, veteran Scouting leaders.

Chartered buses will take the boys to Colonial Williamsburg for a unday visit and the nearby Busch Gardens before the Jamboree officially opens Monday.

At the Jamboree, the Scouts will camp in tents and live in the couting tradition with others, demonstrating Scouting skills, visitg with Scouts from other parts of the country, and enjoying enterinment in the grand arenas.

"It's just a big social get-together of Scouts from all over," said lbert "El" Aspinall, Buckskin executive.

"And it's a chance for the boys to compete with other Scouts in ames and skills of all kinds while they're enjoying their big advenire of the Jamboree with other boys from every state."

Buses will return the boys to the Buckskin Service Center at Danel Boone Roadside Park on Aug. 5, Aspinall said.

PRATT'S RONALD LEE COTTRELL IS ALL PACKED

SCOTT DEPOT'S ASHLEY COWDER IMPATIENTLY AWAITS DEPARTURE

Daily Mail Photos by Chet Hawes

In 1981 the National Jamboree was held at Fort A.P. Hill, near Fredricksburg, Virginia, for the first time.

These Buckskin scouts are seen at the 1989 National Jamboree, again at Fort A.P. Hill.

1989's Jamboree saw groups from Buckskin and (then) Chief Logan Council, in this troop.

The 1993 West Virginia leaders and support staff are pictured.
By the 1990s all National Jamborees were being held at Fort A.P. Hill in Virginia.

These two groups of Buckskin men and boys attended the 1993 National Jamboree.

Left to right are Steven Brucker, Marty Maret, and Nathan Kelly shown at the 1997 National Jamboree at Fort A.P. Hill in Virginia.

Marty Maret and Clay "Squirrel" Hanna are pictured here at the 1997 National Jamboree.

The Water Bucket Brigade was practiced at the National Jamboree in 1997.

Many scouts bring home souvenirs from jamborees. The patches (below) and neckerchief (top) represent items from various eras. The neckerchief is from the 13th World Jamboree. The compasses are from the collection owned by Robert Skinner.

Two Buckskin Scouters To Attend Baden-Powell Jamboree in England

It's across the Atlantic for two Buckskin Council Scouts to the Baden-Powell Jubilee Jamboree at Sutton Park, Warwickshirt, England, August 1-17, 1957.

They are Richard McCollum of Kanawha City and James Rice of St. Albans.

The Baden-Powell Jubilee is being held to celebrate the 100th birthday of Lord Baden-Powell, founder of the Boy Scout movement and the 50th Anniversary of Scouting in the world.

McCollum and Rice will attend the National Jamboree of the Boy Scouts of America at Valley Forge, Pennsylvania, before joining the 1,500 other Scouts for the trip by steam ship to England.

At the conclusion of the Jubilee, they will take an American Express tour of France, Belgium, Holland and Germany before returning to the United States late in August.

Richard is the son of Mr. and Mrs. H. A. McCollum of 5509 Staunton Ave., S.E. He is a member of the ninth grade class at Horace Mann Junior High School, where he is a member of the National Junior Honor Society, School Band, Glee Club and Book Club. He is a member of the Morris Memorial Methodist Church where he has earned the God and Country Award.

James is the son of Mr. and Mrs. Alex Rice Jr. of Kanawha Terrace, St. Albans. James is an active member of Troop 75 and the Highlawn Presbyterian Church, a student at St. Albans Junior High School, a paper route carrier, and the Order of the Arrow National Camping Honor Fraternity.

Both boys hold the Life Scout Rank, and will have qualified for the Eagle Rank before leaving for the Jubilee Jamboree.

Pictured here are Richard McCollum and James Rice.

Many Buckskin scouts have attended World Jamborees. This tells of two local scouts, Richard McCollum of Charleston and James Rice of St. Albans, who would attend the World Jamboree in England in 1957, the 100th birthday of Scouting's founder, Robert Baden-Powell.

Chapter Eleven

Cub Scouting

The Cub Scout program is for boys who are too young to become Boy Scouts. Originally cubs had to be eight years of age. Now boys can become Tiger Cubs at six years of age, or when they are in the first grade in school.

Cubbing today has a large number of young boys in the council program. Most of the program is under the leadership of den leaders. In the beginning, nearly all den leaders were mothers of the scouts. Now a den leader may be male or female. Most weekly den meetings are held in the home of the leader. Monthly pack meetings, in which all of the dens in the pack come together, are usually held at the sponsoring institution.

The program involves the weekly den meetings, monthly pack meetings, day camps, powwows, Webeleos weekends, and more.

In the Buckskin Council, cubbing has generally been highly successful. Buckskin cubs often join the Boy Scouts in outdoor activities such as Expos, Fairs, Scout-O-Ramas, various good turns, reports to the governors and the like.

In October 1973 these cub scouts of Pack 95 in Rainelle, West Virginia, won an award for their float in a local parade. Their den mother was Virginia Thompson.

SCOUT-O-RAMA TO OPEN AT O-I GYM

Cub Scouts, Boy Scouts and Explorers have joined to demonstrate their skills and crafts in the "Scout-O-Rama," which will open tonight at 7 o'clock at the gymnasium of the Owens-Illinois Glass Co. Jack Allman, general chairman, said two other shows will be given Saturday from 2 to 5 p. m. and 7 to 9:30 p. m. The event is sponsored by the Shawnee and Long Rifle districts of Buckskin Council. Shown, left to right, with some of the prizes to be given to participants, are Mrs. Dorothy James, den mother of Pack 11; Cub Scouts John Matthews, Bruce McHaul, Ernie James and Williams Fenwick and Boy Scout Ken Haas.

CUBS OFTEN JOIN THE OLDER SCOUTS FOR ACTIVITIES.

IN 1952 THE BOYS OF DEN 2, PACK 25 OF SOUTH CHARLESTON PRESBYTERIAN CHURCH WERE EXCITED ABOUT CUBBING. THEY ARE (LEFT TO RIGHT): DALE GUNNO, MELTON DORSEY, CORKY PROSSER, PETER HOWELL, RICHARD LALANCE AND DEN CHIEF JOHN HOWELL.

Cub Scout Packs Formed In Scarbro and Carlisle

OAK HILL (RNS) — Denzil Skinner, Fayette District Scout executive, today announced the formation of new Cub Scout Packs at Scarbro and Carlisle.

The pack at Scarbro, sponsored by the Scarbro Fellowship Committee, has 14 charter members. Carlisle's pack will be sponsored by the Carlisle First Church of God and has approximately 18 boys as charter members.

The Rev. O. C. Landrum, Presbyterian minister, will serve as stitutional representative and c mittee chairman for the Scar group. Cubmaster will be Ca Foster and committee men clude C. R. Weatherford, W. Craft and Kenton Thompson.

Scarbro Den Mothers incl Mrs. Lawrence Gravely, M Elick Bozo and Mrs. William Pr

John Toney will serve as C master for Carlisle. He will assisted by James Bailes. Rev. C. C. Bays, pastor of sponsoring institution, will be institutional representative, and T. Riser will serve as commi chairman.

Carlisle's committeemen incl Fred Seltyn and Jennings Ri Den Mothers include Mrs. Jar Bailes, Mrs. R. T. Riser, M Lewis Fernandez and Mrs. F Seltyn. Serving as assistant I Mothers will be Mrs. John To and Mrs. Roger Rains.

Local Scout Selected One Of Top Six In Nation

Jimmy McKenzie of Rainelle flashed this big smile after reading a letter from Dr. Jack Stark, chairman, Regional Cub Scout Committee, East Central Region - Boy Scouts of America in Oak Brook, Illinois, congratulating him on being selected to represent the East Central Region as the National Youth Representative for Cub Scouting.

This region consists of West Virginia, Ohio, Michigan, Illinois, Indiana, Wisconsin and part of Kentucky.

Dr. Stark went on to say that this selection was based on his outstanding record of achievement in the Cub Scout program and in school and community which indicates that he was leading the way and setting a good example for the pack to follow.

This selection made Jimmy one of six finalists selected for the national

See SCOUT - Page 11

Cubbing gets a boy off to a good start on the upward trail of scouting.

Pack 95 used "Westward Ho" as a theme for a scout fair in 1974.

Cub Scout Packs To Collect Books

Cub Scout packs of the Long Rifle District, Boy Scouts of America, will collect books as a "good turn" project from 9 a. m. until noon Sept. 28.

Ed Beaver, chairman of the camping and activities committee, said the books will be collected in an effort to start libraries at the Dunbar and Davis Child Shelters.

Magazines, newspapers and comic books will not be picked up. Persons not reached by Cubs are asked to take their books to the shelters or to get in touch with Cub Scout packs in their neighborhood, Beaver added.

Governor John D. Rockefeller, IV, signed a proclamation declaring 1980 the 50th anniversary of cub scouting. Shown with the governor are (left to right) Virginia Thompson of Rainelle, Michael Moore of Scott Depot, Sam Walker of Hillsboro, Jamie Sullivan of Charleston, Troy George III of Lievsay, and Todd Morrison of Clendenin.

This 1960s era photo shows cub scouts of Pack 93 at Simpson Memorial Church in Charleston. Benjamin Tolliver (Scoutmaster of Troop 93) is at right.

These Pack 71 Cubs are dressed as "Knights of the Round Table." The picture was snapped by Den Mother Nancy Crouser in March 1962. Shown are Kenton Dilly (at left), Rick Crouser (at right), Rob Crouser (front) and Junior Westfall (center, rear). The sponsoring institution is Wesley United Methodist Church.

Cub Pack Plans Blue-Gold Event

Cub Pack 37 of the Swannie district, St. Agnes School in Kanawha City, will hold its annual blue and gold banquet, Thursday at 6:30 p. m. in the school cafeteria.

The four den mothers sponsoring the dinner are Mrs. J. L. Burns, Mrs. Jules Wazelle, Mrs. C. Grecco and Mrs. Joe Pauling.

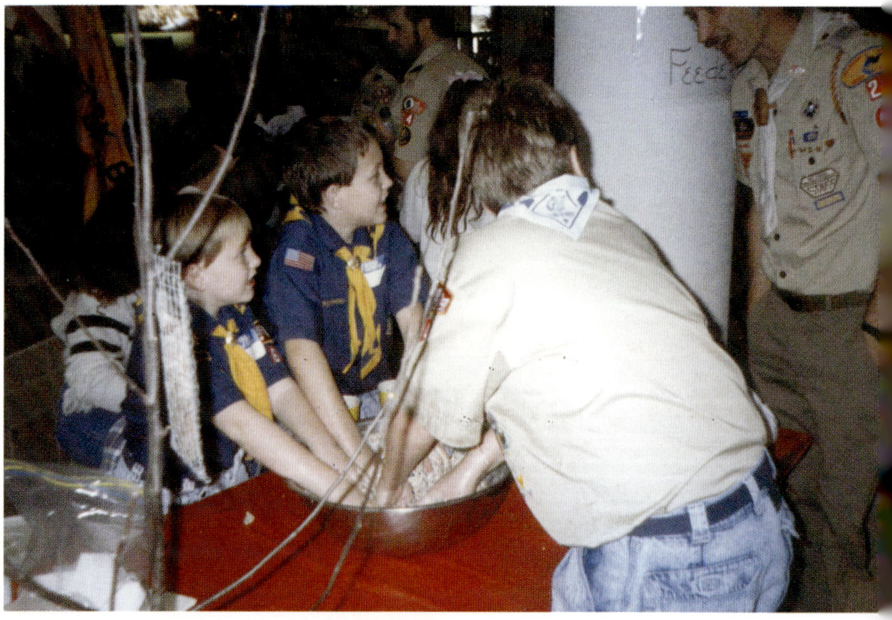

The Chief Cornstalk District's Pack 64 of Taplin, West Virginia, was led by Edgar Johnson. Shown here making bird feeders with white lard and bird seed mixed together are (left to right): Cubs Josh Wingler and Justin Spense. Obscured is Tony Dean.

The Wilderness District's Pack 122 of Lewisburg has fun at a 1982 scout fair.

A Pack 64 Pinewood Derby brought out many cubs in 1990.

The Cubs of Pack 286 in Hurricane, West Virginia, show off their Pinewood Derby trophies in this 1981 photo.

Pack 286 Cubs and leaders are shown here in their sponsoring agency, St. Timothy's Church. Among the leaders are Joan Whipkey (extreme left) and Janice Aliff (white blouse).

Bill Wyatt and his grandson Dan Wyatt, son of this book's author, are seen here at the February 1985 Blue & Gold Dinner of Pack 236 of Hurricane. This pack is sponsored by Forest Burdette United Methodst Church.

1978

Camera Corner

Eight-year-old Robby Jacobs teeters across a swinging rope bridge Saturday at the district scout fair held at the FMC park in South Charleston. Robby, a member of Den 1, Pack 75 in St. Albans, is a third grader at the Bevil Elementary School. He is the son of Mr. and Mrs. Robert Jacobs of 542 Drew St., St. Albans.

There is always a new adventure on tap for Cub Scouts, as these newspaper photos from 1978 and 1981 (right) show.

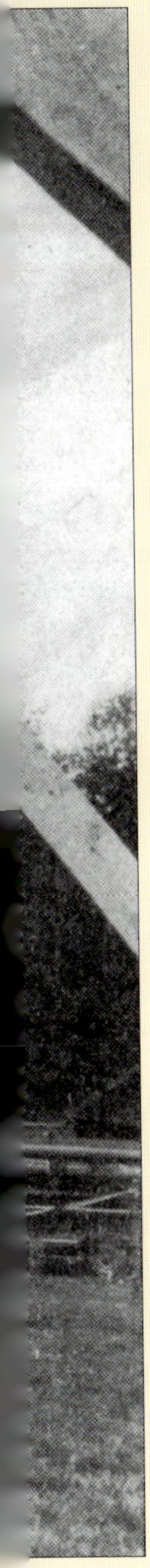

Staff photos by LAWRENCE PIERCE

Challenge

Boy Scouts and Cub Scouts from throughout the Kanawha Valley displayed their outdoor skills Saturday during Scout Expo '81 at Coonskin Park. An obstacle course tested the endurance of Shawn Cottrell of Hurricane (left photo) while above, John David Martin (left) and his brother Harold of Culloden test their bronco-busting talents on a mustang oil drum.

Brothers' toy keeps Scouts on right track

By Sandy Wells
STAFF WRITER

"They say the only difference between a boy and a man is the price of his toys," said Bill Jones. "I guess you'd say this is our toy."

Bill and Lyle Jones can't put a price on their race track, but they say the money doesn't matter. "The look on a winner's face, or the look on his face when his buddy wins, that's the thing," said Bill Jones. "That's what we look for."

Their toy is an elevated, electronic 32-foot track used by hundreds of Cub Scouts during an annual model car race known as the Pine Wood Derby.

For years, the Jones brothers, owners of Cash Auto Parts, have been donating their track, as well as their time, to perpetuate the derby tradition. From 10 a.m. to 5 p.m. every other Saturday from January through May, they are at the South Charleston Recreation Center to conduct races for various Cub packs. During the months preceding the race season, they are busy building test cars and improving the track.

A computer on the track controls the starting sequence, releases the cars, times the race and determines the winner. Another computer, purchased by the brothers this year and programmed by Ralph Burchett, a volunteer from Union Carbide, determines who races when and on which lane. "We type in the pack number and the names and the computer does the rest," Lyle explained. "I don't think anybody in the country has a track quite like this one."

The project started nine years ago when Bill's son, Casey, was a Cub participating in his first derby. "He finished 17th. We knew we could do better than that," Bill said. "First we built a test track. We bought a couple of boards, measured off 32 feet and propped the boards on stilts. Then we practiced. When Casey raced with his pack on derby day, he came in second."

The pack was reorganized the following year, he said, and the new sponsor, the First Methodist Church, didn't have a track. "We modified our practice track until it was suitable for the derby. We thought it was a shame to use it only once a year, so we called the Scout office and offered it to other packs. Every year we got more requests and every year we made improvements."

Twenty packs are using the track this year, he said.

"It's hard to say how much money we've got tied up in this thing," said Bill, "but we spent close to $1,100 on it just this year."

When the Jones brothers talk about racing, they sound like computers themselves. "Some people say a wedge-shaped car will have less drag," said Bill. "But a car that's going a maximum of 7 mph travels one inch in one one-hundredth of a second if it makes the run in 3.75 seconds and that doesn't create much drag."

Used to be, he said, parents standing at the end of the track called the winners. But at 7 mph, you can't see a difference of a quarter of an inch or even a half inch. Our electronic equipment can pick up differences in hundredths of seconds." The record time on their track is 3.60 seconds.

Lyle's son, Lyle II, raced for the first time this year. He won the den competition but lost the runoff with the pack.

But Lyle Jones Sr. says the derby teaches Cubs how to be losers, too. "A race is competition. Life is competition. The hardest thing to do in life is lose, but everyone loses at one time or another. Building the car teaches them responsibility. We teach them how to compete, how to win and how to lose. That's how society is constructed."

Bill Jones holds the coveted shirt.

A winner, perhaps?

Gazette photos by RANDY OLSON

Derby expert Lyle Jones (center) mans the controls.

THE PINE WOOD DERBY IS A HIGHLIGHT FOR MANY CUBS.

HERALD, BECKLEY, W. VA., THURSDAY MORNING, MAY 17,1973

Fair, Camporee Held In Rainelle

RAINELLE (RNS) — Seneca District Scout Fair and Camporee was held Saturday at the Rainelle Armory. The fair began with a camporee Friday night at the Greenbrier Archery Range in Rainelle. Participating in the camporee were scouts from the following troops: Pack 95, Rainelle; Pack 261, Quinwood; Pack 118, Oak Hill; Pack 170, Danese and Meadow Bridge; Pack 82, Rupert; Pack 51, White Sulphur Springs; Pack 56, Winona; Pack 16, Gatewood; Pack 179, Fayetteville; Pack 143, Page, and Pack 110, Oak Hill.

A campfire program was held with each troop presenting skits following a song fest. Cub Pack 95 presented an Indian dance for the group. The campfire was directed by David Hall scoutmaster from Rupert.

From 11 a.m. to 7 p.m. Saturday each troop and pack in the Seneca District that participated set up an exhibit booth at the armory and the scouts presented live demonstrations all-day for the public. During the day the exhibits were judged and the close of the day ribbons were presented to the troop.

Exhibits of scouts were Pack 110, outdoor cookery; Pack 82, model camp site; Pack 170, camp gadgets; Pack 179, monkey Bridge; Pack 95, first aid; Pack 261, shotgun-rifle; Pack 51, rope making, pack exhibits, Pack 95, Indian Teepee; Pack 261 and 122 display of crafts; and Pack 70, circus items and crafts, explorers, entertainment rodeo trophy exhibits.

Ribbons were awarded by Fred Pack, former scoutmaster of 95; B ratings went to Troop 51, 71, 261, Explorer, 95, Pack 170 and 261. A ratings went to Troop, 82, 95, 110, 170, 179, Pack 51, 95 and 122.

Presidents ribbons picked out of A rating, overall exhibits went to Troop 82 and 170 and Pack 51 and 95.

A number of Cub Scout Packs participated in this 1975 fair.

Summersville Pack 70 finished first in Class B. Some of the boys are included in the picture above.

Craigsville Pack 109, pictured above made a fine showing in finishing second overall in the Cub Scout division.

Cub Scout Pack 122 Ceremony

Cub Scout Pack 122 held its November meeting Tuesday evening at the Lewisburg United Methodist Church Fellowship Hall. Den 3 conducted the opening ceremony with a welcome skit and the pledge to the flag.

Cub Scouts Alan DeOlloqui and Marvin Grier were transferred to Boy Scout Troop 70. The ceremony was conducted by Wesley Elmore and Tom Elmore, Life Scouts; Mitch Arbaugh, and Dan Chase, Eagle Scout from Troop 70.

Wesley Elmore presented participation awards to Lee Hinkle, Ronald Shafer, Mike Dodd and John Yates for their part in the Olympics held recently.

Lee Hinkle and George Deitz were presented their Bobcat Awards. Jerry Yates and Michael Seldomridge received their Wolf Awards.

Awards presented to Webelos Den 2 were Alan DeOlloqui and John Yates, outdoorsmen. Webelos Den 1 awards were presented to William Synder, 2 year attendance, aquanaut, athlete, engineer, naturalist, outdoorsman, scientist; Jeffery Rodgers, engineer, forester, athlete, outdoorsman; Steven Montgomery, aquanaut, engineer, forester, geologist, athlete.

Denner and assistant denner cords were presented to Den 1, Gregg Roemke, denner; Brian Morrison, assistant; Den 3, James Killian, denner; James Scarborough, assistant; Den 4, Mark Gragg, denner; Ronald Shafer, assistant.

The cub scouts enjoyed a farm tour on November 6. Seventy three scouts, parents and other smaller children toured Morlunda Farm, Wilson Turkey Farm and 5-J Farm. A hot dog dinner at the Fellowship Hall of Old Stone Church followed the tour. The Ronceverte Baptist Church provided their bus for transportation. The Gospel Bible Class at the church helps sponsor the Den from Ronceverte. A special thanks was extended to all who helped make this event a success.

The scout sales campaign was a success with a profit of about $1300.

Orders will be delivered soon. Prizes will be awarded at the December Pack Meeting on December 21.

Den 1 presented a skit with Thanksgiving as their theme.

A "Cow Milking" contest was held with all scouts participating. Prizes for this will be distributed next month.

Den 3 won the Attendance Award.

The closing ceremony was conducted by Den 4.

Heavily involved as a leader for Pack 122 was Judy Cooper of Lewisburg. This 1976 Cub Scout Fair shows the pack's demonstration. Pictured at left (rear) is Jo Ann Yates.

A pinewood derby win is satisfying in 1999. Pack 61 is located in Richlands, Virginia.

Cub Scout Day Camp 2001, Poca, West Virginia.

Debbie Dean and Kim Gibson supervise Pack 162's "Raingutter Regatta."

Pack 61 of the Mountain Dominion District does a good turn.

Day Camp, 1994. Pack 162 cooks lunch.

Chapter Twelve

Ramp Patrol

This January 1999 photo shows most of the 16 members who were involved at that time. The Ramp Patrol was named for the onion-like plant that blooms in the spring. This photo was taken at the Wyatt Scout Museum in Charleston. Members shown are (kneeling, left to right): Ed Lewis, Kurt Shultz, Harry Mills, Bill Murray, Vic Sands. Standing (left to right) are: Bill Wyatt, Bob Skinner, Don Ellis (behind Skinner), Leonard Taylor, Joel Patton, Roger Rasmussen, Buck Rogers, John Howell, Harold Cook, and Jan Hacker.

Within the Buckskin Council the Ramp Patrol is comprised of a group of adult scouters formed to do special projects in the scout council. These projects are designed to be over and above their regular scouting jobs such as scoutmaster.

The Ramp Patrol originated in 1946 when a number of men were taking a scoutmaster's basic training course and, as in most such courses, they had to have a name. It was spring, the season of the onion-like plant that grows wild in the mountains. Thus, they chose the name Ramp Patrol.

After the training course the scouters decided to meet together to establish a club-like group. They invited eight more scouters, making a double patrol of 16 members.

The Ramp Patrol has met monthly since that time. Most of the meetings have been in the homes of the members. The original founding members of the group were W. W. "Buck" Rogers, Don Cathers, Milton Goodholm, John Hover, Bruce Leech, and Bob Riggall.

The Ramp Patrol has been responsible for many projects and events through the years. Some of them include Buckskin Scout Reservation projects such as painting camp cabins, painting the camp chapel, building a challenge course at the camp, painting the interior of the health lodge, putting a new roof on the same health lodge and developing an archery range equipment storage area. The Patrol has done programs for council camporees and repair work on the scout service center. It established and built the scout museum, conducts numerous training courses, and many other activities.

The Ramp Patrol also has an annual dinner for members and their wives, and a summer picnic for their families.

The Ramp Patrol is limited to 16 members at any time. When an opening occurs through death of a member or other circumstances, such as when a member moves to another state, new members are selected. Election to membership is by the unanimous vote of the active members. At the publication of this book the patrol's members were:

2004 RAMP PATROL MEMBERS

Harold Cook
Donald Ellis, Chef
Jan Hacker, Photographer
Steve Hardman
Newton Harman
John Howell, Scribe
David Kelly
Ed Lewis, Quartermaster and Project Manager
Harry Mills
Bill Murray
Joel Patten
Roger Rasmussen
Vic Sands, Patrol Leader
Bob Sharp, Assistant Patrol Leader
Bob Skinner, Assistant Quartermaster
Leonard Taylor

This April 1965 trip by the Ramp Patrol shows the members cooking ramp stew. Pictured are (left to right): M.S. "Goodie" Goodholm, John Oxley, John Hover, Bill Wyatt, Larry Schmidt, John Howel, and S.J. "Si" Broadwater.

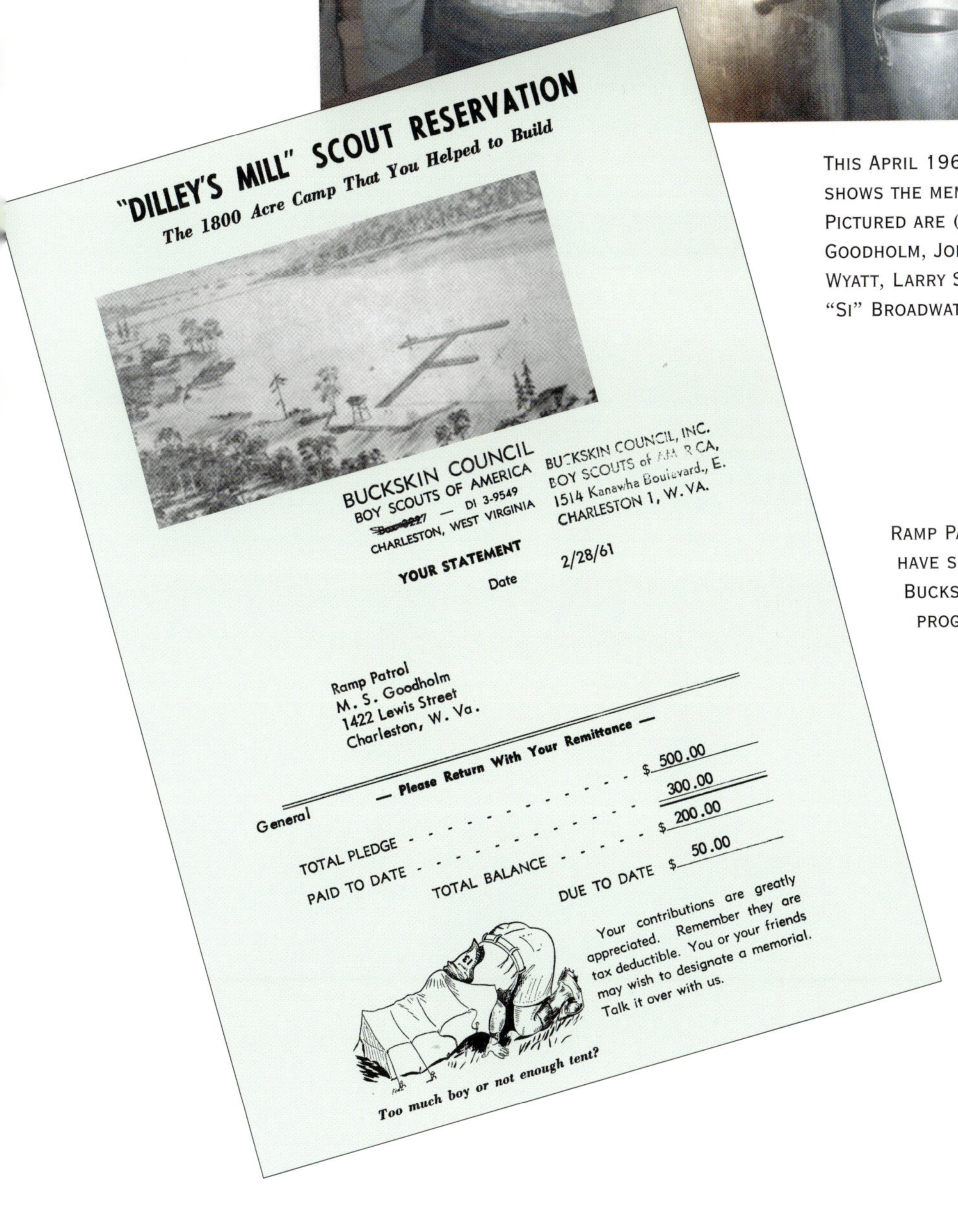

"DILLEY'S MILL" SCOUT RESERVATION

The 1800 Acre Camp That You Helped to Build

BUCKSKIN COUNCIL
BOY SCOUTS OF AMERICA
~~Box 2227~~ — DI 3-9549
CHARLESTON, WEST VIRGINIA

BUCKSKIN COUNCIL, INC.
BOY SCOUTS of AMERICA
1514 Kanawha Boulevard, E.
CHARLESTON 1, W. VA.

YOUR STATEMENT

Date 2/28/61

Ramp Patrol
M. S. Goodholm
1422 Lewis Street
Charleston, W. Va.

— Please Return With Your Remittance —

General

TOTAL PLEDGE	$ 500.00
PAID TO DATE	300.00
TOTAL BALANCE	$ 200.00
DUE TO DATE	$ 50.00

Your contributions are greatly appreciated. Remember they are tax deductible. You or your friends may wish to designate a memorial. Talk it over with us.

Too much boy or not enough tent?

Ramp Patrol members have supported the Buckskin Council's programs in many ways.

Shown in this Ramp Patrol camping trip at Cranberry Glades in April 1977 are Donald Ellis (foreground with catch) and Bill Mason.

In 1965 members Charles Davisson and S.J. "Si" Broadwater celebrate their catch.

Chapter Thirteen

Silver Beaver Award

The Silver Beaver Award is the highest award that can be given to a volunteer by the local scout council. The Buckskin Council has awarded numerous Silver Beavers over the years.

The first recipient was Charles P. Guice, in 1932. Guice was a St. Albans area educator who took a great interest in scouting. He became a scoutmaster and engaged his troop in numerous activities for many years. See pages 1–4 for more on the career of Charles Guice.

The selection is done by reviewing the scout-related activities of anyone who is nominated. The review is generally done by a committee made up of scouters who already hold the Silver Beaver Award, one from each district within the council. The review is done "blind" so that the committee does not know the names of the candidates whose credentials they are reviewing. Only the record of service is known to the committee.

Silver Beaver Recipients

1932	Charles P. Guice
1933	George S. Laidley
1934	Wentworth Williams
1938	George H. Belches
1939	William O. Abney
1940	Dr. B. H. Swint
1941	Dr. H. A. Duncan
1942	Hereford Eggleton
	E. C. Richardson
1943	E. McHardesty
1944	Charles E. Kreb
1945	Maurice A. Mendel
1946	Dewey E. S. Kuhn
1947	Charles McCabe, Sr.
	Dr. C. F. McClintic
1948	M. B. Goldman
	A. K. Bailey
1949	Joseph W. Londeree
	E. C. Colcord
	Mason Bell
1950	R. O. Raine
	Francis Roller
	R. H. Morris
1951	Ellsworth Curtin
	William Woodroe
	J. D. Treanor
	Sebert Brown
1952	Charles H. Gilmore
	W. W. "Buck" Rogers
	Dr. Leroy Montague
1953	L. B. White
	Fred Bloomberg
	Thomas Fields
	Charles Sullivan
	Fred Waters
	William H. Wyatt
1954	L. N. Thomas
	G. J. Cottrell, Sr.
	Sam C. Hill
	G. Fred Ours
	Fred Pack

Charles P. Guice was the first person to receive the Buckskin Council Silver Beaver. That was in 1932. Guice is pictured here in 1951. He had been active in scouting in the council area starting in about 1912.

FORD

WELLS

M. TAYLOR

L. TAYLOR

Four Receive Silver Beaver Scout Award

Buckskin Council, Boy Scouts of America, has honored four with the Silver Beaver award, highest council award.

For the first time in the history of Buckskin Council Boy Scouts, a man and wife have won the Silver Beaver recognition award at the same time.

They are Leonard E. and Mary Frances Taylor of St. Albans, both Scouters of many years in the area.

The council also conferred the highest council award on John M. "Slim" Wells Sr., of Charleston and John Othor Ford of Lewisburg.

At the annual awards dinner recently when the Beavers were announced, the Taylors' two sons, Cub Scout Thomas Taylor and Scout Charlie Taylor, were honor-bearers for the awards.

The Silver Beaver is given to Scouters who "by their exemplary participation in community, church and Scouting endeavor, best personify the principles set forth in the Scout Oath and Law."

1955 Ernest J. Mondron
W. A. Coffey
William J. Graham
Robert M. Thomas
W. R. Trimble

1956 Col. W. C. Phillips
Dr. George T. Hoylman
Fred Otto
Robert D. Morris
Ralph W. Moore

1957 Ronald C. Shonk
Charles L. Donnally
Arthur B. Bower
M. H. Patterson
Rev. Carl Doddrill
Ralph A. Moore
Carl Withrow
E. A. Bartels
William Lee
C. I. Adkins

1958 Charles McCabe, Jr.
Dr. James Thornbury
Bishop W. C. Campbell
Ward Eister

1959 John Oxley
William G. Bowling
W. A. Boone
J. Curtis Legg
William N. Westlund

1960 Homer A. Holt
Dr. Robert D. Ketchum
Paul Moore, Sr.
Richard C. Cronmiller
Dr. Ivan B. Stafford

1961 Carroll Barker
T. W. Bartram
J. Alex Gettman
William Keely

1963 Eugene L. Peninger
Lance Powers
Merl A. Aitken

1964 Kenneth F. Robbins
E. W. Poinier, Jr.
Arthur R. Pierce
Lowell C. West
L. W. Deitz
John W. Ayers, Jr
Howard B. Miller
W. L. O'Neal
E. V. Wickline

1965 T.B.H. Anderson
A. Herchiel Sims
Earl Vickers
Myron Renick
A. Rosser Long
M. S. Goodholm
Jennings Straley
Robert Riggall
Edward Stemple
Jordan S. Hugart

1967 Charles C. Albert
Clarence Flesher
J. B. Harmon
R.V. Knicley
Grady K. Moore
Bernard L. Murray
Denzil Skinner
James R. Thomas, II

1968 Sylvester Childers
C. Paul Cleek
John W. Eakin
K. Kermit Groves
J. P. Hager

4 Adults To Receive Top Scouting Honor

Silver Beaver Awards will be presented to four adult Scouts by the Buckskin Council for the Boy Scouts of America. The award recognizes distinguished service to youth and is the highest honor bestowed by the Council to adults in Scouting.

Receiving awards at the council's annual recognition dinner at 6:15 p.m. Saturday at Beni Kedem Temple will be Allen S. Pack of Charleston, Arlene Kuryla of St. Albans, Warren Dubee of Falls View and Billy Carr of Gassaway.

Other scouting awards will be presented at the dinner. Reservations can be made by contacting the Buckskin Council headquarters, 2829 Kanawha Blvd., E.

Charleston Daily Mail, 1981

The Silver Beaver

The National Court of Honor, Boy Scouts of America, in recognition of exceptional and noteworthy service to youth, and in grateful acknowledgement of the good that will ensue therefrom, is both pleased and honored to confer upon these distinguished citizens the Award of the Silver Beaver; and it cherishes the lively and enduring hope that this honored emblem and the certificate of commendation accompanying these presentments bearing the signature of the President of the United States of America will serve as enduring evidences of a grateful people.

The nature of their several services to youth and the wide range of their professional and civic responsibilities is indicative of Scouting's universality in bringing all youth everywhere into companionship with people of good character. They have served at great personal sacrifice creating opportunities for increasing numbers of youth to have happy, constructive and purposeful formative years and the promise of a useful life.

Five Receive Scouting Awards

Five persons received the Silver Beaver award at the Buckskin Council's annual recognition dinner Saturday.

Okey Lee Groves, Jr., Phillip P. Joseph and James A. Stogden, all of Charleston, Zela Young of Mount Nebo and Ronald B. Hensley of White Sulphur Springs were honored for exemplary participation in the scouting endeavor.

GAZETTE-MAIL, FEBRUARY 26, 1977

Paul Hinkle
W. C. Kuryla, Ph.D.
William R. Newman
Fred Parrish
L. G. Schmidt

1969 Ken Anderson
B. W. John
Robert K. Kelly
Charles McClain
Dan Toney

1970 James F. Cox, Jr.
Jack Gannon
John C. "Jack" Horton
Oliver C. Lloyd
John P. Swint
F. E. Weinheimer

1971 Nannie Chambers
Frank N. Clark
Donald L. Ellis
Franklin W. Kern
John R. Moore
Margaret Mullins
Andrew C. Overpeck, Jr.
Doyle L. Parkins

1972 Marshall Buckalew
Paul J. Gilmer
Ray C. Hamon
W. W. Harrington
John H. Howell
Dorothy James
John W. James, Jr.
Ruby O'Neal

1973 Charles L. Evans, Jr.
Austin C. Palmer
Glen K. Parsons
Delbert D. Pauley
Nettie Rayburn
L. Newton Thomas, Jr.

1974 Robert F. Baronner
Dr. K. G. McDonald, Sr.
Norman D. Perkins
Bane Shafer
John A. Shanklin
Virginia P. Thompson

1975 Harold L. Cook
George W. Mason
Alva W. Deardorff
Albert I. Pennington

1977 Okey L. Groves
Ronald B. Hensley
Zela Young

Shown here are individuals who received the Silver Beaver Award in the early 1960s. From left to right they are Carl Withrow, C.I. Adkins, J. William Lee, Ernest Bartells, and Ralph Moore.

Those receiving the Silver Beaver in 1965 were (front row, left to right) Edward Stemple, T.B.H. Anderson, Myron Renick, Rosser Long, Jordan S. Hugart. Back row (left to right): Bob Riggall, Herschel Simms, Earl Vickers, Jennings Straley, and M.S. Goodholm.

Philip P. Joseph
James A. Stogdon
1978 John O. Ford
Mary F. Taylor
Leonard E. Taylor
John M. Wells, Sr.
1979 Colene Heim
William C. Miller
Patrick O'Neal
John M. Wells, Jr.
1980 John A. Hopkins
Edward O. Lewis
Carl Osborne
Roger J. Rasmussen
1981 Billy H. Carr
Warren T. Dubee
Arlene B. Kuryla
Allen S. Pack
1982 Judith A. Cooper
Richard R. Gibson
Robert G. Sweazy
George C. Westerfeld
1983 Veda T. Anderson
Clifford S. Bell
1984 Dennis D. Butcher
Edward G. Deitz
Jack E. Robertson
Lorene Thompson

In 1963 these individuals were awarded the Silver Beaver. They are (left to right, front row) S.J. Broadwater, Eugene L. Pleninger, Lowell C. West, W.L. "Pat" O'Neal. Back row (left to right) Kenneth F. Robbins, E.V. Wickline, Merl A. Aitken, Howard B. Miller, Lance Powers, E.W. Poineer, Jr., and Arthur R. Pierce.

IN 1969 THE SILVER BEAVER WAS AWARDED TO (LEFT TO RIGHT) KEN ANDERSON, B.W. JOHN, BOB KELLY, CHARLIE MCCLAIN, AND DAN TONEY.

1985 Paul D. Black
Eula M. Cole
Richard S. Master
James M. Poindexter
1986 Edwin C. Anderson, Jr.
Phillip L. Gainer
Donald J. Good
Lawson W. Hamilton, Jr.
Raymond F. Thomasson
John D. Thompson, Sr.
Charles L. Vance
1987 Arthur L. Altman
Alfred J. Atkins
Charles J. Filbin
Larry L. Jones
Cindy Worlledge
1988 Clifford W. Baker
G. H. Cunningham
Shelby J. Osborne
Carl E. Johnson
1989 Ruth A. Blake
Paul D. Marshall
Robert Vandall
1990 George T. Lanham
Olin J. McClanahan
Robert G. Skinner, Jr.
Glen O. Wade
1991 Paul M. Blake, Jr.
Jan D. Hacker

ALSO IN 1969 EPISCOPAL BISHOP W.C. CAMPBELL (RIGHT), WHO WAS COUNCIL PRESIDENT, WAS AWARDED THE SILVER ANTELOPE AT A CEREMONY IN LOUISVILLE, KENTUCKY. PRESENTING THE AWARD IS L.N. THOMAS. IN THE BACK ROW (LEFT TO RIGHT) ARE ALDEN BARBER, WHO WAS CHIEF SCOUT EXECUTIVE, REGIONAL CHAIRMAN ROGER FRIMAN, AS WELL AS W.B. HUBBELL WHO WAS REGIONAL SCOUT EXECUTIVE.

EST 'SILVER BEAVER' TURNOUT — The largest crowd witness such a ceremony last night gathered in the Arena of Charleston's Civic Center to salute outstanding scouters. The program's highlight was presentation of Beaver awards to five men in recognition for their to the youth movement in the Buckskin Council. The winners, pictured at left, are William A. Boone of Ronceverte, John Oxley of Charleston, J. Curtis Legg of Fola, Clay County, William N. Westlund of Nitro and William C. Bowling of Dunbar. The center picture shows some of the 853 persons registered for the dinner and program. In the picture at the right, Samuel C. Hill (center) won the coveted buckskin jacket as the council's "Man of the Year." At the left is Richard Lebetsamer, who came here only three days ago to take up duties as scout executive within the council. The other man in the group is Maurice A. Mendel, whose 45-year career as a scoutmaster is considered the longest within the nine-county area the council embraces. Despite death in the family — his father-in-law, Frank M. Shirey of Spout Spring, Va., having died only a few hours before the dinner at the age of 92 — Mendel remained here to accept his new honor. He left this morning for Virginia, where funeral services for Mr. Shirey will be conducted tomorrow.

	Cheryl A. Ingraham
	Harry S. Mills
	Isabel "Bonnie" Starling
	Paul Cooper, Jr.
	Clark G. Lamp
1992	Steven M. Adkins
	Phillip L. Arrington
	Jessie L. Boyd
	Mildred K. Gwin
	Patricia A. Hartley
	Dana H. McCorkle
1993	Dreama K. Bolen
	Robert B. Basham
	Franklin D. Ferrell
	Gordon L. Hensley
	John Patterson
	Patricia H. Sheets
1994	Donald M. Atkison
	T. Howard Butcher
	Glenn A. Harrison
	Joel H. Patten
	Russell W. Taylor
	Charles W. Troup
	Robert L. Wilson
1995	Thomas B. Boggess
	Edward E. Evans
	Gary R. Freeman
	Thomas V. Hall
	Stephen J. Hardman
	Robert S. Sharp
	Robert L. Wheeler
1996	Sue Akers
	Millard P. Cook
	Ginger Hensley
	Roger J. LaFleur
	J. Michael Reynolds
	Burton Vic Sands
1997	William H. Barnard
	Albert A. Duff, Sr.
	Thurman D. Haywood
	Elliott E. Maynard
	William E. Murray
	O. Kurt Schultz
	Danny White
	Steven P. McGowan
	Betty Y. Montgomery
1998	Christine M. Blankenship
	Duane H. Zobrist, II
	James D. Wells
	Katrina L. Newberry
	Clifford Gateless
	Patricia L. Walczak
	Thomas E. Moses

★ WED., FEB. 17, 1982 Charleston Daily Mail 5A

WESTERFELD COOPER GIBSON SWEAZY

Four State Residents Get Boy Scout Award

Four West Virginians have been awarded the Silver Beaver, a recognition by the Boy Scouts of America for volunteer service to youth.

Award recipients include Judith A. Cooper, a Lewisburg homemaker; Richard R. Gibson of Sutton, involved in church and volunteer work, Robert G. Sweazy, vice president of Poole Associates, and George C. Westerfeld, general superintendent of the DuPont plant at Belle. Both Sweazy and Westerfeld are Charleston residents.

HONORED BY THE BUCKSKIN COUNCIL scouts for over 20 years of volunteer service to scouting was Bill Miller of Institute. Bill was awarded the prestigious Silver Beaver at the recent Council Recognition Dinner. He is shown with his wife, Joy a member of the Engineering Department. Bill, who was a Sea Scout as a boy, has been a cub-master, District Commissioner, and Trainer and is presently on the Pioneer District Committee in St. Albans. He is a 30 year Carbider and has been working at the Goff Mountain Landfill area for the past 15 years.

CARBIDER, APRIL 12, 1979

Thomas I. Birch
Charles R. Lewis, II
1999 Jim Walsh
Mary Beth Murphy
Donald J. Greene
Mary M. Midkiff
Eldon R. Larson
Grace Ann Tolbert
Judith E. Polak
Sam Olive
Christopher A. Parsley
2000 Jeffrey K. Burt
Joseph W. Gero
Harry S. Kammer
David M. Kelly
Stephen R. Niday
Paul R. Ritchie
Hardy G. Shaffer, III
Robert D. West
Walter M. Winant
2001 Rosann E. Brooks
Dana L. Burns
Ruth A. Craigo
Robert E. Farley
John P. Kiriluk
Richard E. Koontz, Jr.
Henry J. R. Nichols
2002 James H. Belcher
Timothy R. Bowles
William B. Eades
Paul D. Reed
Kermit F. Tolbert
Richard Vanaman
2003 Solomon S. Sowers
Michelle L. Shumate
Stephen L. Wellons
Faith N. Bragg
John F. Whiteley
Timothy P. Cox
Kelli D. Barton
John N. Harman, IV
Ronald L. Shumate
2004 Stephen A. Caldwell
Juanita B. Duff
James C. Phares, III
Rita G. Ramey
David Ritter
Colleen Sergent
Marie M. Sharp
Gary Shifflett
George M. Soltis

Chapter Fourteen

The Council

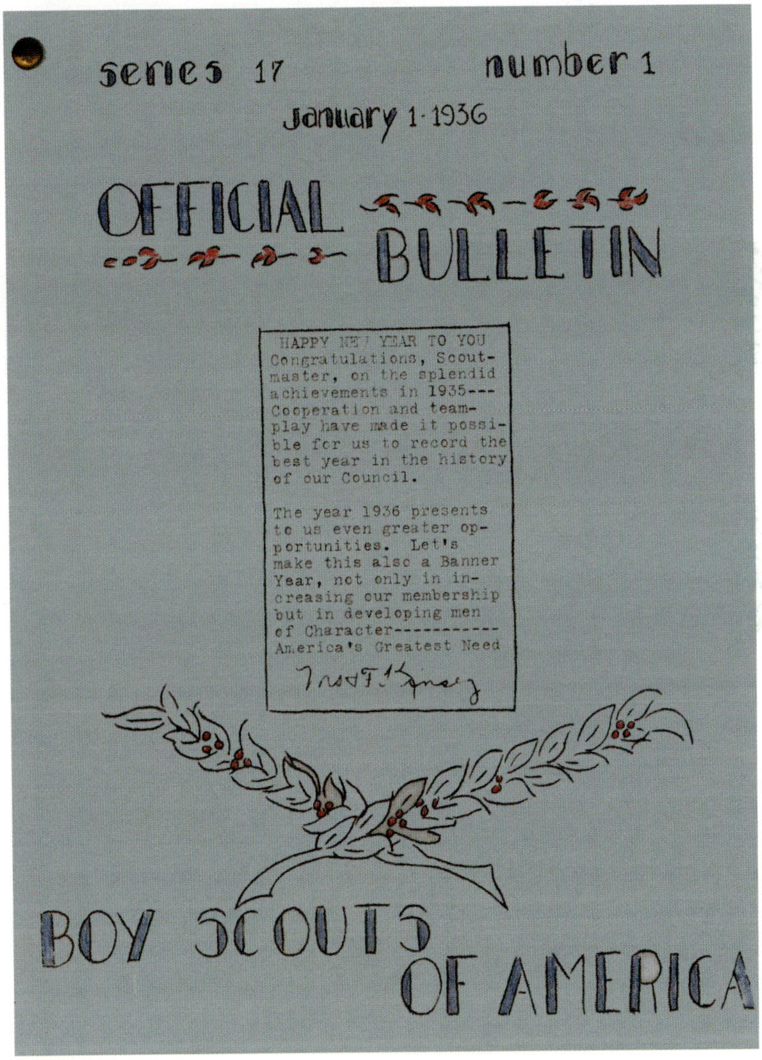

series 17 number 1

January 1-1936

OFFICIAL BULLETIN

HAPPY NEW YEAR TO YOU
Congratulations, Scoutmaster, on the splendid achievements in 1935---Cooperation and teamplay have made it possible for us to record the best year in the history of our Council.

The year 1936 presents to us even greater opportunities. Let's make this also a Banner Year, not only in increasing our membership but in developing men of Character-----------America's Greatest Need

BOY SCOUTS OF AMERICA

THIS WAS THE COVER OF THE COUNCIL NEWSLETTER, JANUARY 1936.

News of the Council

Getting the message of scout activities out to the various scout units has been an important part of the Buckskin Council. Several papers and newsletters have been used to inform the scouts about what is going on in the council. News includes such important information as upcoming council activities, awards, and more.

Perhaps the earliest of these was a magazine called *The Charleston Scout*. It contained news of troop activities, awards, short stories and inspirational messages. It also had a nature department, a serialized story written by the first Scout Executive, M.H.F. Kinsey, and numerous advertisements. A 1922 edition listed Isadore Lebow as Editor in Chief and Paul High as Assistant Editor. By the early 1930s and '40s the magazine was replaced by the *Official Bulletin of the Charleston Area Council*. It differed from *The Charleston Scout* in that it did not have features. Rather, it was oriented only toward providing basic news.

Still later, the council news bulletin became known as the *Buckskin Courier*. The *Courier* remains the council newsletter at present. In the 1990s the *Courier* had to be collated by hand each month and this was done by volunteers including such people as Bob Skinner, George Lanham, Harry Mills, Harold Cook, Ed Deitz, Barbara Mitchell, Bonnie Starling, John Howell, Juanita Duff, Ruth Craigo, Roger Rasmussen, Grace Tolbert, Leonard Taylor, and Bill Wyatt.

OFFICAL BULLETIN
BOY SCOUTS OF AMERICA
CHARLESTON AREA COUNCIL

Series 19 February 1, 1938 Number 3

HEAR!!!
THOMAS J. KEANE
At The
ANNUAL MEETING
FEBRUARY 8, 1938
To Be Held At The
DANIEL BOONE
HOTEL

THOMAS J. KEANE

If You Have An
Older Boy Problem
In Your Troop
Hear What Keane Has
To Say About It.
It Will Be The Best
$1.00 Investment
You Ever Made

ANNIVERSARY NUMBER

Official Outfitter Since 1916
FRANKENBERGER'S
CHARLESTON, WEST VIRGINIA
Uniforms and Accessories For Scouts, Cubs, and Sea Scouts

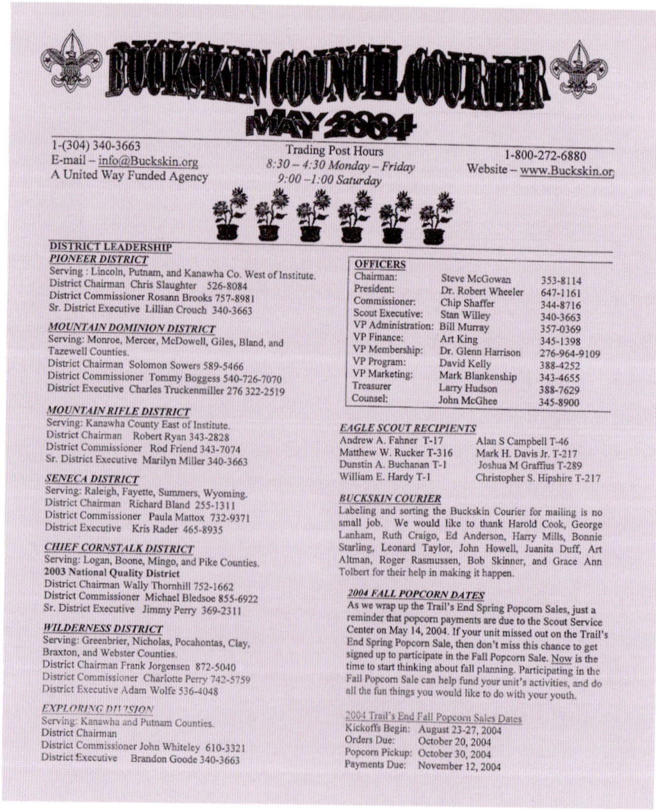

BUCKSKIN COUNCIL COURIER
MAY 2004

1-(304) 340-3663
E-mail – info@Buckskin.org
A United Way Funded Agency

Trading Post Hours
8:30 – 4:30 Monday – Friday
9:00 –1:00 Saturday

1-800-272-6880
Website – www.Buckskin.or

DISTRICT LEADERSHIP

PIONEER DISTRICT
Serving : Lincoln, Putnam, and Kanawha Co. West of Institute.
District Chairman Chris Slaughter 526-8084
District Commissioner Rosann Brooks 757-8981
Sr. District Executive Lillian Crouch 340-3663

MOUNTAIN DOMINION DISTRICT
Serving: Monroe, Mercer, McDowell, Giles, Bland, and Tazewell Counties.
District Chairman Solomon Sowers 589-5466
District Commissioner Tommy Boggess 540-726-7070
District Executive Charles Truckenmiller 276 322-2519

MOUNTAIN RIFLE DISTRICT
Serving: Kanawha County East of Institute.
District Chairman Robert Ryan 343-2828
District Commissioner Rod Friend 343-7074
Sr. District Executive Marilyn Miller 340-3663

SENECA DISTRICT
Serving: Raleigh, Fayette, Summers, Wyoming.
District Chairman Richard Bland 255-1311
District Commissioner Paula Mattox 732-9371
District Executive Kris Rader 465-8935

CHIEF CORNSTALK DISTRICT
Serving: Logan, Boone, Mingo, and Pike Counties.
2003 National Quality District
District Chairman Wally Thornhill 752-1662
District Commissioner Michael Bledsoe 855-6922
Sr. District Executive Jimmy Perry 369-2311

WILDERNESS DISTRICT
Serving: Greenbrier, Nicholas, Pocahontas, Clay, Braxton, and Webster Counties.
District Chairman Frank Jorgensen 872-5040
District Commissioner Charlotte Perry 742-5759
District Executive Adam Wolfe 536-4048

EXPLORING DIVISION
Serving: Kanawha and Putnam Counties.
District Chairman
District Commissioner John Whiteley 610-3321
District Executive Brandon Goode 340-3663

OFFICERS

Chairman:	Steve McGowan	353-8114
President:	Dr. Robert Wheeler	647-1161
Commissioner:	Chip Shaffer	344-8716
Scout Executive:	Stan Willey	340-3663
VP Administration:	Bill Murray	357-0369
VP Finance:	Art King	345-1398
VP Membership:	Dr. Glenn Harrison	276-964-9109
VP Program:	David Kelly	388-4252
VP Marketing:	Mark Blankenship	343-4655
Treasurer	Larry Hudson	388-7629
Counsel:	John McGhee	345-8900

EAGLE SCOUT RECIPIENTS

Andrew A. Fahner T-17	Alan S Campbell T-46
Matthew W. Rucker T-316	Mark H. Davis Jr. T-217
Dunstin A. Buchanan T-1	Joshua M Graffius T-289
William E. Hardy T-1	Christopher S. Hipshire T-217

BUCKSKIN COURIER
Labeling and sorting the Buckskin Courier for mailing is no small job. We would like to thank Harold Cook, George Lanham, Ruth Craigo, Ed Anderson, Harry Mills, Bonnie Starling, Leonard Taylor, John Howell, Juanita Duff, Art Altman, Roger Rasmussen, Bob Skinner, and Grace Ann Tolbert for their help in making it happen.

2004 FALL POPCORN DATES
As we wrap up the Trail's End Spring Popcorn Sales, just a reminder that popcorn payments are due to the Scout Service Center on May 14, 2004. If your unit missed out on the Trail's End Spring Popcorn Sale, then don't miss this chance to get signed up to participate in the Fall Popcorn Sale. Now is the time to start thinking about fall planning. Participating in the Fall Popcorn Sale can help fund your unit's activities, and do all the fun things you would like to do with your youth.

2004 Trail's End Fall Popcorn Sales Dates

Kickoffs Begin:	August 23-27, 2004
Orders Due:	October 20, 2004
Popcorn Pickup:	October 30, 2004
Payments Due:	November 12, 2004

COUNCIL NEWSLETTERS FROM 1938, 1939, 1940 AND 2004.

COUNCIL PRESIDENTS

EACH BOY SCOUT COUNCIL has a Council Executive Board made up of volunteers who are responsible for the operation of the organization. The Council President presides over meetings of the Council Executive Board as it oversees operation of the organization. The President works closely with the professionals involved, especially with the Council Executive.

From 1919 to the present many outstanding individuals have served as Council President. Beginning in 1992 the position of Council Chairman was established to co-lead the council with the President.

COUNCIL PRESIDENTS AND (SINCE 1992) CHAIRMEN:

1919	George S. Laidley
1920	John L. Dickinson
1921	Robert E. L. Ruffner
1922	Okey B. Johnson
1923	W. E. R. Byrne
1924	Alfred H. Lea
1925	J. D. Woodroe
1926	Walter E. Clark
1927	Dr. B. H. Swint
1928	Charles E. Krebs
1929	Rev. Frank C. Brown D.D.
1930	W. E. R. Byrne
1931	Dr. B. H. Swint
1932	R. E. O'Connor
1933	R. H. Morris
1934	Dr. J. Ross Hunter
1935	A. W. Laing
1936	Arthur B. Hodges
1937	Stanley C. Morris
1938	C. C. Dickinson
1939	Ray W. Hitchman
1940	Fred A. Bloomberg
1941	Dewey E. S. Kuhns
1942	Charles P. McCabe Sr.
1943	Dr. Daniel Barber
1944	J. W. Londeree
1945	E. K. McHardesty
1946	Charles P. McCabe, Sr.
1947	William Woodroe
1948	Francis O. Roller
1949	Francis O. Roller
1950	J. R. B. Crigler, first half Francis O. Roller, last half
1951	L. N. Thomas
1952	L. N. Thomas
1953	L. N. Thomas
1954	Col. Walter C. Phillips
1955	Col. Walter C. Phillips
1956	Donald C. Shonk
1957	Donald C. Shonk
1958	Donald C. Shonk
1959	William A. Boone
1960	J. Alex Gettman
1961	J. Alex Gettman
1962	J. Alex Gettman
1963	J. Alex Gettman
1964	J. Alex Gettman
1965	Bishop W. C. Campbell
1966	Bishop W. C. Campbell
1967	Bishop W. C. Campbell
1968	Rosser Long
1969	Robert K. Kelly
1970	Robert K. Kelly
1971	Robert K. Kelly
1972	Robert F. Baronner
1973	Robert F. Baronner
1974	Eugene Perchak
1975	D. Frederick Wertz
1976	D. Frederick Wertz
1977	John A. Hopkins
1978	John A. Hopkins
1979	Allen S. Pack
1980	Allen S. Pack
1981	James M. Poindexter
1982	James M. Poindexter
1983	James M. Poindexter

1984	James M. Poindexter
1985	John M. Wells, Jr.
1986	John M. Wells, Jr.
1987	L. Newton Thomas, Jr.
1988	L. Newton Thomas, Jr.
1989	David B. Frost
1990	David B. Frost
1991	David W. Lanham
1992	James R. Thomas II – Chairman
1992	Michael T. Webb – President
1993	James R. Thomas II – Chairman
1993	Michael T. Webb – President
1994	Allen S. Pack – Chairman
1994	Michael T. Webb – President
1995	Allen S. Pack – Chairman
1995	Glenn H. Harrison – President
1996	Allen S. Pack – Chairman
1996	Glenn H. Harrison – President
1997	Samuel M. Bowling – Chairman
1997	Glenn H. Harrison – President
1998	Samuel M. Bowling – Chairman
1998	Glenn H. Harrison – President
1999	Samuel M. Bowling – Chairman
1999	Harry "Chip" Shaffer – President
2000	Rick Morgan – Chairman
2000	Harry "Chip" Shaffer – President
2001	Rick Morgan – Chairman
2001	Dr. Robert Wheeler – President
2002	Rick Morgan – Chairman
2002	Dr. Robert Wheeler – President
2003	Steve McGowan – Chairman
2003	Dr. Robert Wheeler – President
2004	Steve McGowan – Chairman
2004	Dr. Robert Wheeler – President

Council Executives

Many fine men have served as Buckskin Council Executive, starting with M.H.F. Kinsey in 1919. We pay tribute to them here.

M.H.F. Kinsey was the first scout executive of the council. He served the longest, from 1919 to 1947.

Charleston Daily Mail, January 25, 1960

M. L. JOHNSON DIES

Scout Executive Taken By Illness

The scout executive of the Buckskin Council died Monday morning in a Charleston hospital after a long illness. Melvin L. Johnson, 56, of 699 Gordon Dr. had been chief executive for six years.

He began his scouting career in St. Joseph, Mo., more than 20 years ago. Before coming to the Buckskin Council he held positions in Kansas City, Kan., Casper, Wyo., served in rural services for the National Council and as deputy regional executive with headquarters in Cincinnati. He was a native of Humboldt, Kan.

Mr. Johnson was a member of Christ Church Methodist, the Rotary Club, Masonic Lodge, Royal Arch Mason Chapter and Knights Templar. He served as a Sunday school teacher and on various church boards in the towns in which he worked.

Survivors include his wife, Virginia; a son, Melvin D. of Louisville, Ky.; his mother, Mrs. C.E. of Chanute, Kan.; a sister, Mrs. Carl Mull of Carney, Kan.; two brothers, E. E. of Wichita, Kan., and Maurice V. of Houston, Tex., and three grandchildren.

Services will be held Tuesday at 2:30 p. m. in the Barlow-Bonsall Funeral Home by the Revs. Harry Light and Dr. George H. Vick. Burial will be in Chanute, Kan., later in the week.

The body is at the funeral home. The family requests any memorials be in the form of donations to the Boy Scout camp construction fund or the cancer fund.

MELVIN JOHNSON

Melvin Johnson served as scout executive from 1953–60.

Buckskin Council Committeemen Make Final Plans For Scout Jamboree

Camping and activity committeemen of Buckskin council Boy Scouts of America, are shown planning the council Camporee to be held at Coonskin park June 6 to 8. Some 1,600 scouts from the council are expected to participate.

Seated, left to right, are Council Commissioner Charles Gilmour; Charles McCabe, Sr., camping and activities chairmen; Dr. LeRoy S. Montogue, Daniel Boone district chairman; William Woodroe and Scout Executive Henry G. Shires.

Standing, left to right: Jack L. Lewis, assistant scout executive; Byron McNeely, field scout executive; Clark Kendall, Jr., field scout executive; John Harzo, field scout executive; W. S. Hall, camping and activites chairman; Ernest Bartels, camping and activities chairman for Daniel Boone district; Charlie Sullivan, Burning Springs district commissioner; W. R. Trimble, commissioner for the St. Albans-Nitro-Putnam district; and Jim R Locke, district chairman.

The second exeuctive was Henry Shiers, who served from 1947 to 1953. He is shown here, seated, on the right.

9A—Jan. 31, 1960 *Sunday Gazette-Mail* —Charleston, West Virginia—

TO BE AT DINNER

New Scouting Leader Named

Buckskin Council's new chief executive, Richard Lebetsamer, will make his first appearance here next Thursday at the council's Annual Scouter Recognition Dinner.

The dinner will begin at 6:30 p. m. in the grand arena of the Civic Center.

Lebetsamer will assume on Feb. 15 the duties of the late M. L. Johnson. Johnson died last Monday at the age of 56. He had been chief executive of the Buckskin Boy Scout Council for six years.

The new executive's last post was chief executive of the Saginaw, Mich., council. Still in his 30's, Lebetsamer has successfully managed important official assignments in the Midwest, including the post of chief executive at Champlain, Ill.

* * *

GOV. UNDERWOOD will be the principal speaker at the dinner Thursday. As vice president of Salem College, he was closely associated with the Humanics Foundation, a training program in professional work in social agencies, including the Boy Scouts. The governor has actively participated in Scouting activities before and since taking office.

Gov. Underwood and Vice President Nixon were both speakers at the opening of the Fourth National Boy Scout Jamboree at Valley Forge, Pa., in 1957.

An annual Recognition Dinner event is the awarding of the Silver Beaver, the council's highest award for exceptional service to boyhood. The Silver Beavers will be presented Thursday by Rt. Rev. Wilburn C. Campbell, Episcopal bishop of West Virginia, and Fred Otto, general manager of the duPont plant at Belle.

Dr. George H. Vick, pastor of the First Presbyterian Church, will be master of ceremonies at the dinner.

Other events will include presentation of a 50-star flag to the council from the American Legion, a memorial service for Scouters who died during the past year and a songfest.

RICHARD LEBETSAMER
New Scout Executive

Richard Lebetsamer was the council's executive from 1960–62.

Kenneth Eakin served from 1962–66.

Art Greiner was executive from 1966–71.

12A The Charleston Gazette *Sat., June 22, 1974*

DISPLAYING FLAG of Denmark is Henrick B. Michelsen, 19, (right) a Scout from Copenhagen, who is on the staff of the Buckskin Scout Reservation for the summer camp session. Looking on are B. Robin Meadows (standing), Scout executive, and Charles R. Gardner, chairman of the Charleston Rotary Club youth committee, Michelsen's sponsor.
(Gazette Photo by Leo Chabot)

B. Robin Meadows was the Buckskin Scout Executive from 1972–75.

From 1975–82 the Scout Executive was Elbert W. Aspinall, shown here on the right. Pictured with him are District Executive Ken Shanes along with Jim Carver and Kurt Schultz.

Glen Johnson served as Scout Executive from 1982–88 (no photo available).

James D. Stone was the executive between 1988–92.

Donald R. McChesney was the Council Executive from 1992–97.

From 1997 to the publication of this book the council has been ably served by Executive Stanley C. Willey.

Chapter Fifteen

Bill Wyatt and the Wyatt Museum

Wyatt Museum

The late William H. "Bill" Wyatt, the author's father, was a longtime scouter who amassed a large collection of scout memorabilia. It was his wish to have a place to display his collection, perhaps as a way to inspire others to the benefits and love of scouting.

As it turned out, there was a space beneath the council office in Charleston. The council office is located in Daniel Boone Park on the eastern end of Kanawha Boulevard, a mile or so east of the State Capitol Building.

The lower section of the council office faces the Kanawha River and originally was constructed as an open patio and a garage. The front of the office building faces away from the river and toward Kanawha Boulevard. Thus the open area underneath the Scout Office building became the location for the museum.

Under the guidance of the Council President, David Frost, the Executive Board approved the enclosing of the open area for the museum. A group of scouters, mostly from the Ramp Patrol, had a small fund drive. Construction of the museum began

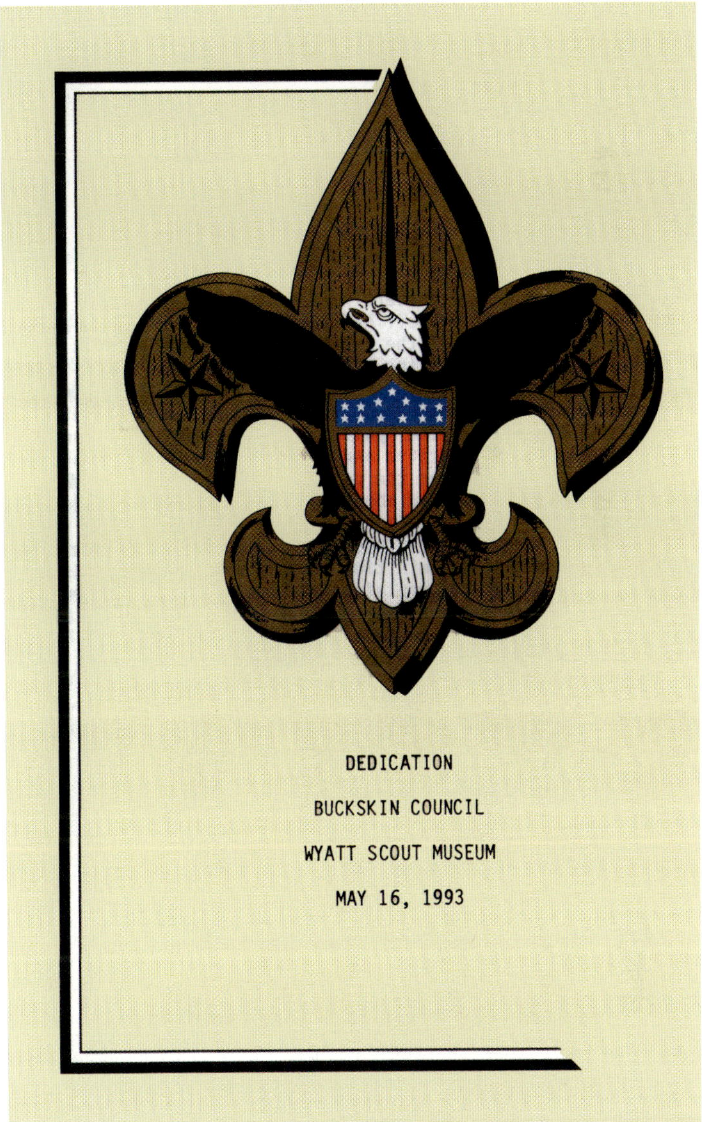

The museum was dedicated on May 16, 1993.

Shown at the museum are two of its original organizers and board members, William Wyatt, for whom it is named, and Larry Schmidt. The museum is located at the Scout Service Center at Daniel Boone Park on Route 60, one mile east of the State Capitol.

in October, 1989. The open sides were blocked in to form a large room, approximately 65×30 feet.

As the project progressed some of the more active individuals who took part in construction and development of the museum were Bob Skinner, Larry Schmidt, John Howell, Harold Cook, Ed Lewis and Roger Rasmussen.

Skinner and Schmidt along with Elden Goldsmith, Robert L. Wilson, William Murray, Curt Schultz, James M. Poindexter, and Bill Wyatt formed the initial museum committee. Wyatt became the Committee Chairperson.

The museum has about two dozen showcases, and the walls are filled with displays of scouting memorabilia as well. Patches, neckerchiefs, axes and knives abound. One bookcase contains scouting literature and includes a copy of every scout handbook ever published. Photos of various scouting events, old and new, are mounted on the walls.

Many people have visited the museum since its dedication on May 16, 1993. They often tell museum committee members that the job has been well done, especially for a group of "amateurs," who up to that point had not been involved in museum activities.

Known today as the Buckskin Wyatt Museum, it is operated by the museum committee, a group of volunteers chaired by Vic Sands. Other committee members are Joe Wyatt, Bob Skinner, John Howell, Roger Rasmussen and Russell Bennett.

William H. Wyatt

Here Bill Wyatt demonstrates rope spinning at Camp McClintic in 1952.

William H. "Bill" Wyatt was born on August 21, 1918, in Charleston, West Virginia. He was the oldest of six children. In 1930 at the age of 12 he joined the Boy Scouts and formed a special bond with M.H.F. Kinsey, the Council Executive. Kinsey became a second father to Bill, who became an active member of Troop 71 sponsored by Wesley Methodist Church on the west side of Charleston. He loved the hiking and camping that went with Kinsey's version of scouting. He was the first to receive the 1,000 mile hiking award that had been established by Kinsey, as part of the Appalachian Trail Blazers Hiking Group. When he became too old to be a registered Boy Scout, Bill continued at Troop 71 as an Assistant Scoutmaster for another four years.

In time he had married the former Geraldine Pettit and was living in St. Albans. He was employed at Union Carbide and was not actively involved with scouting, as he soon had a daughter and then was called to military service in World War II. After serving in the Army Air Corps from 1944 to 1946, he found himself back in St. Albans, West Virginia, his wife's hometown, and soon had a son as well. It was around that time that the Scouting Committee at St. Andrew United Methodist Church asked Bill to consider becoming the new Scoutmaster of Troop 146. He accepted the position and remained Scoutmaster for 21 years. After stepping down as Scoutmaster he remained as an Assistant Scoutmaster, Institutional Representative and Committeeman of Troop 146 until his death at the age of 81 in 2000.

Shown in this photo, from about 1935, are three of M.H.F. Kinsey's "Trail Blazers" on a hike to the "Big Tree." Bill Wyatt is shown on the left, the others are unidentified.

Bill did many other things involving scouting. He served as a member of the Buckskin Council Executive Board for a number of years until his death. He earned the Woodbadge Award, which is the highest training award given to volunteer scouters.

WYATT AT ABOUT AGE 16. THE INSIGNIA ON HIS SWEATER IS ONE OF SCOUT EXECUTIVE M.H.F. KINSEY'S MILESTONE PATCHES GIVEN TO MEMBERS OF THE APPALACHIAN TRAIL BLAZER HIKING GROUP.

Like Charles P. Guice, Bill earned the Eagle award long after he had ceased being a Boy Scout and had become a leader. This was in the late 1940s.

In 1953, Bill became the youngest council volunteer to receive the Silver Beaver Award, the highest award at the local level for a volunteer. That award came on the heels of several years of service in building Troop 146 into one of the outstanding units in the area. It also came soon after he had served as Scoutmaster for a local jamboree troop at the 1953 National Jamboree in California. He would later serve as Scoutmaster for a troop at the

Bill was awarded the Silver Beaver at the council dinner on January 21, 1953. Presenting the award is Sebert H. Brown, Wyatt's former scoutmaster from Troop 71 in Charleston. At the left is Joseph Londeree.

1960 National Jamboree in Colorado Springs, Colorado, as well. Additionally, Bill served as an Assistant Scoutmaster at several other National and World Jamborees, and on the regional support staff at various National Jamborees on four occasions.

The National Jamborees were an important part of his life, starting with the first one in 1935. Then 16 years old, he had done odd jobs for Kinsey in the scout office in order to earn money to pay the registration fee during the Depression. However, about two weeks prior to the opening of the 1935 National Jamboree, which was to have been held on the National Mall in Washington, D.C., the Jamboree was cancelled due to a polio epidemic. By the time another Jamboree was held at the same location two years later, Bill was working and unable to attend.

Another of his interests was in the Brownsea training course for junior scout leaders. He founded the course in the Buckskin Council area and led it for a number of years.

Many people will recall his interests in speed knot tying. He taught a number of scouts to tie eight standard knots in 20 second or less. It was not unusual for the scouts of Troop 146 to sweep the speed knot tying competition wherever they went.

BILL CONTINUED TO BE ACTIVE IN SCOUTS AS THIS 1970S PHOTO SHOWS.

Bill served as District Scout Camporee Chief on many occasions. He could be seen leading campfires and competitions and it is fair to say that, aside from his family, the Boy Scout movement was the central focus of his life.

In his retirement (he had worked for 26 years as an agent for the Prudential Insurance Company, and earlier for 17 years at Union Carbide) he worked with a number of people to establish the Wyatt Scout Museum which is now located in the basement of the Scout Service Center at Daniel Boone Park on Kanawha Boulevard East. The museum is open to any who wish to tour it on a by-appointment basis.The previous section of this book features more on the museum.

In addition to his scouting activities, Bill was involved in other kinds of community service and efforts. He was a Sunday School teacher at St. Andrew United Methodist Church for more than 20 years. He coached the boys' basketball team in church league games there for several years as well. He was a member of the St. Albans Civitan Club for more than 25 years. In 1950, he was chosen Young Man of the Year by the St. Albans Jaycees.

Bill was the team photographer for St. Albans High School football and basketball games for 31 years. He frequently recounted standing in the rain and snowstorms on the tops of press boxes as he took movies of football games.

Bill and his wife, Gerry, became interested in the foreign exchange student movement in the 1960s and twice hosted students, one from Japan and the other from Austria, for one year each while they attended high school in St. Albans. Additionally, his home was frequently a stop-over location for exchange students for short periods as they traveled throughout the United States.

In December, 1999, in ill health a month before he died, Bill was visited by a contingent of local scout leaders and the Scout Executive, Stan Willey, at his home in St. Albans. They informed Bill that the Scout Service Center would be rededicated in his honor. The rededication ceremony was held about six months later, July 5, 2000.

Bill passed away on January 14, 2000, and was buried in his scout uniform. His graveside service at Cunningham Memorial Park in St. Albans was true to form. There stood an honor guard of scouts in uniform, and local scout leader David Kelly played taps on the same bugle that Bill had played so often during his days as a Boy Scout.

AT A PIONEER DISTRICT WINTER CAMPOREE IN JANUARY 1977, BILL WAS HELPING SET UP A TENT AT KANAWHA STATE FOREST.

Chapter Sixteen

They Were Prepared

"Be Prepared"—Boy Scout Motto

William "Uncle Bill" Graham was long devoted to scouting in the Buckskin Council.

CHARLES THOM, THE AREA'S OLDEST BOY SCOUT, DISPLAYS A PICTURE OF HIS SCOUT TROOP TAKEN IN THE 1920s

Daily Mail Photo by Craig Cunningham

Boy Scout Code Guides Man's Entire Life

By JACK DEUTSCH
Of The Daily Mail Staff

Sitting casually on his sofa in his West Side home, Charles Thom Jr. doesn't look all that prepared.

But for the past 60 years, Thom has followed the Boy Scouts' motto, "Be Prepared," with such devotion that he has become the dean of area Boy Scouts.

At 72 he is the oldest Boy Scout in the Buckskin Council, scouting officials in the nine-county organization say.

Thom proudly ticks off the qualities the Boy Scouts imbued him with — independence, pride, and leadership. He believes the Scouts have as much to teach youths today as they did when he joined in 1924, he said.

"They have as much to offer today, probably more," he said. "You might find your life's work in the Scout program. You learn to play and work together and learn to give and take. You learn many skills you won't learn in school . . . It lets you live a better life."

Thom was 12 when he joined a troop at the Calvary Baptist Church. His brother, long-time Charleston sports figure Rat Thom, encouraged him to play sports and join the neighborhood troop.

"You didn't have all the activities you do now. Boy Scouts was the only thing," he said.

The Scouts gave Thom a sense of camaraderie in a childhood fraught with more than the normal quota of fears and uncertainty.

"I was shy. I was born with a double harelip and a cleft palate. As a result I was withdrawn. My brother Rat encouraged me in sports and scouting and the other kids were more likely to accept me. It helped me along in my early years."

Competition between the troops in the city inspired the Scouts to outperform their rivals, and Thom said he quickly became his troop's champion at semaphore.

He boasts of a medal proclaiming him the world national record holder, having sent 50 letters in just under 23 seconds. While no plaque exists to commemorate the event, the record was set in the gymnasium of Lincoln Junior High.

After several years as a scout and finally Eagle Scout, Thom became a leader of the Calvary Baptist Church troop. He said he tried to pass on the lessons he had learned from his scoutmaster.

"He [his scout leader] taught us to meet things on your own and to have the ability to get things done on your own . . . Many, many times I'm reminded by things he taught. Young people should have somebody to trust and have a positive influence on your life."

Thom had to give up his scoutmaster position when he went back to school to get a teaching degree.

Since then, Thom has helped scouts in earning merit badges and sits on a council that determines the budget and programs for the troops.

Through the years, his Calvary Baptist Church troop has dwindled from the 40 members who belonged when he was a child to the nine boys who now make up the troop.

"In the early '40s, they eliminated the competitive angle. That one thing hurt scouting. It eliminated jamborees and rallies. Scouts in Kanawha County went down, down, down and never came back," he said.

Thom predicts glumly that the scouts won't enjoy a revival soon, but says youths can be convinced to join "if you can get their interest."

Still Thom helps out the few boys with merit badges, particularly those dealing with swimming and canoeing. He said he first enjoyed these activities as a Scout and takes pride in showing them to a new generation.

Thom brags of weighing the same now as he did as a high school football player, and owes the debt of fitness to the Boy Scouts. He said today's Scouts are are learning the same lesson he learned: "How to learn to take care of yourself."

CHARLESTON DAILY MAIL, NOVEMBER 5, 1984

Maurice Mendel: He's Still Grand Old Man Of Scouting

By ADRIAN GWIN
Of The Daily Mail Staff

When Lindbergh flew the Atlantic Ocean alone 51 years ago, Maurice Mendel had already been a Boy Scout for 13 years.

Today, at 76, Maurice Mendel is still scouting, the oldest active consecutivley registered scout and scouter in the Buckskin Council — and one of the oldest in the nation.

Ill but indomitable, Mendel reiterated the philosophy which has kept him in Boy Scouting for 64 years:

"If I have helped one boy, my life has been worthwhile!"

One boy?

Hundreds. Thousands!

He has helped thousands by his work as a volunteer leader on the council level in every capacity but one. "I've never been council president," he said.

He has helped hundreds in a personal way on the troop level — a Scoutmaster gets to know the boys, and they turn to him for aid and comfort when they wouldn't turn to their own fathers.

He has helped boys solve their Scouting problems and their personal problems; he has been a counselor of faith and of morals as well as a counselor of work and integrity.

He has lived and taught the Boy Scout Law throughout his 64 Scouting years, firmly believing that boys who adhere to the Scout Law will become better men in maturity — using the principles of trustworthiness, loyalty, helpfulness, friendliness, courtesy, kindness, obedience, cheerfulness, thrift, bravery, cleanliness and reverence.

"I've done every job a man could do in Boy Scouting," he said, not boasting, simply recounting.

When he joined the Boy Scouts in 1914 as a 12-year-old, he lived in Ohio, and his first Scoutmaster was a man named M.H.F. Kinsey. Kinsey came to the Charleston Council about the same time that Mendel did, in 1937, and became one of the most highly regarded Scout executives the council ever had.

MAURICE MENDEL
In Scouting Since 1914

Remembering, Mendel said, "For a man who stood barely five-foot-three, Mr. Kinsey was 10 feet tall in the eyes of every boy who knew him!"

And today, in Charleston and throughout the Buckskin Council, there are old men who remember Maurice Mendel — a little taller than five-three, but a small man — as taller than 10 feet and still growing as a leader of boys and men.

Awarded the Silver Beaver in 1945 for his outstanding work with the council's boys, he has continued for the ensuing 33 years to be a beaver in Scouting, always striving for continuity in the Scout program, from 12 to manhood.

"We've lost our drive, our leadership, somehow, in the Scouting movement," he said. "Cubbing has become too much an entity, is not related in an overlapping way with Scouting, and Scouting is not overlapped with Exploring. We lost the continuity of the whole program," he said.

In "civilian" life, Mendel was with the old State Road Commission for 35 years, in charge of landscape work along the berms of the roads and at roadside parks.

He helped develop the system of seeding high banks through cuts on state roads, and pioneered the system on the West Virginia Turnpike.

He has been a member of Temple Israel since coming to Charleston 41 years ago. He is the father of two girls and a devoted family man, a grandfather twice over and a devoted husband to his wife, Louise.

And with 64 years of Boy Scouting behind him, he only looks forward to more years working with the boys, as the Grand Old Man of the Buckskin Council.

Charleston Daily Mail
July 7, 1978

LEONARD AND MARY FRANCES TAYLOR ... Super Scouters

—Daily Mail Photo by Adrian Gwin

A Dynamic Duo

St. Albans Family Puts Togetherness To Work

By ADRIAN GWIN
Of The Daily Mail Staff

Beavers? They make the beaver look like Rip Van Winkle!

Leonard and Mary Frances Taylor do more in a week than most people do in a month.

Raising seven children.

Fostering dozens of others over the years in Boy Scouting and Girl Scouting.

Doing six people's work in the operation of their church.

Taking part in various community affairs including their volunteer fire department.

For years they've churned like windmills in a gale, and like the windmill, every turn produces something worthwhile.

Recently the Buckskin Council, Boy Scouts of America, presented both of them with the Silver Beaver Award, highest honor for Scouters in the council.

It was the first time that a man-wife combination had won the recognition together.

The overworked phrase "togetherness" seems to be the key to their incredible energy and creativeness. They're "in step" with each other all the time.

And while their children have developed as individuals, they've been right in step with the family on every beat of the tempo: one is grown and teaching in Florida; one is a senior at Fairmont State College; another is a junior (and a Merit Scholar) there; one is a freshman engineering student at VPI; three are at home and as active as their parents in the daily business of giving and getting in the game of living.

Through the years they've all done things together like the dam had just burst. And that's just their normal pace.

Leonard and Mary Frances met at Concord College and were married in 1955. She had been raised in Wyoming County and he mostly in Mercer. She taught school for several years in Wyoming and Greenbrier counties and he taught for a year and a half in Greenbrier.

He wanted to become a physician, but financial circumstances and a car wreck obviated that. When things looked bleakest, he got on at Carbide's Institute plant as a chemist, and for 22 years he's been there, now senior chemist at the Institute plant.

Leonard Taylor was never a Boy Scout when he was growing up, but he always liked the outdoors, and always liked young people.

"It's great being married to a woman who has an interest in working with young people!" he said, keynoting their beaver-like activities which would virtually paralyze anyone else.

In 1961 he was invited to sit in on a committee meeting for Scout Troop 250 at Riverlawn Presbyterian Church, "and came from that meeting as chairman of the troop committee," he said.

After five years at that, with the troop going like a house afire, he became Assistant Scoutmaster so he could participate more actively in the program.

Five years ago, still maintaining his leadership in the troop, he became Cubmaster for Pack 250, the Scouting program for younger boys, and he's still both Cubmaster and Assistant Scoutmaster. Sons George and Robert are both Eagle Scouts. Son Charlie, 13 and a 7th-grader at Hayes Junior High School, is a Star Scout. Son Thomas, 10, is a Webelos Cub in Pack 250.

Meanwhile, Mary Frances got into the act. She's been a Den Mother in the Cubs for 13 years. (Most Den Mothers do well to last three years!)

And she wasn't neglecting the girls. Barbara, the eldest who now teaches, was a Senior Girl Scout. Frances Lynn the Merit Scholar, was a Senior Girl Scout. Susan, a sophomore at St. Albans High, is a Senior Girl Scout.

Mary Frances is Cadette Girl Scout Leader of Troop 2375 at Riverlawn Presbyterian.

Whenever the family took vacations — they've been to Florida, New Mexico and many places closer by — they've gone as a unit, and they've camped.

With a 9x9 tent and a station wagon, they cut the costs, made a luxury of roughing it, and developed into as tight a family unit as ever was. Each member functions as a perfectly-meshed cog in the precision-gears of their lifestyle.

Aside from Scouting, the Taylors are a church family.

Leonard is an elder and clerk of the session of Covenant Presbyterian Church. They both teach Sunday School classes. On Wednesday nights she teaches a primary group called "The Whirleybirds." She works in the bus ministry and the puppet program and is a member of the Women of the Church. And she's attending training sessions in Charleston to better equip her to work in the Vacation Bible School this summer.

Leonard has for several years been on the staff of the "Brownsea 22" training program for youth leaders among Buckskin's scouts. He was a Philmont leader in 1971 and is Scoutmaster for the 1978 Philmont contingent which goes to New Mexico in July.

He's an organizer and charter member of the Lakewood Volunteer Fire Department, and is a seven-year advisory member of the Kanawha Valley Junior Achievement program for high schoolers.

On top of all that, he dug and built the basement recreation room of their home at 210 Sun Valley Drive and has maintained an excellent standing in his job at Carbide.

The doors of their home and the doors of their hearts are open to every young person in the neighborhood. Their energy and their concern for youth shines in their smiles.

They're unbelievably believable.

CHARLESTON DAILY MAIL, MAY 5, 1978

LONG-TIME RANGER — Dewey Sharp of Pocahontas County is shown with the plaque which honors him and his dog Bridget.

Boy Scouts To Honor Now-Retired Ranger

The Charleston-area Buckskin Council tonight will honor Dewey Sharp, the long-time ranger of the Boy Scout Camp in Pocahontas County.

Sharp retired Jan. 1 after working for the Scouts for 24 years. A reception for Sharp is scheduled tonight following the annual dinner honoring volunteers at Christ Church United Methodist. Also honored at the dinner will be Silver Beaver recipients. The awards are given to Boy Scout volunteers.

Sharp was well known to many area Scouts who spent time at the camp. As ranger, Sharp was responsible for upkeep of the camp, a job that including everything from mending fences to fixing roads. Sharp was known for taking pride in keeping the grounds and the facilities in top shape.

Sharp, 72, had a lifelong interest in conservation and farming. A Pocahontas County native, Sharp served in World War I and worked in Baltimore. But he said he wanted to return to West Virginia, and bought a farm in West Union, Pocahontas County.

He was a soil conservation district supervisor for 27 years. He also worked with youth and was a 4-H leader in the community for years.

In 1963, he went to work for the Buckskin Council as ranger at the scout reservation in an area known as Old Dilleys Mill. His great-grandfather, Josiah Dilley, is buried on the reservation.

Charleston Daily Mail, April 11, 1987

Dewey Sharp is shown with longtime scouter Vic Sands in a photo taken at the Buckskin Scout Reservation in 2000.

Freeland Ferrell is shown here on an "Eskimo Camporee" in 1967.

Harold Cook

John Hover

Good Scout

Scouting Pioneer Paved The Way

By ADRIAN GWIN
Of The Daily Mail Staff

When Bane Shafer was 12 years old he joined the Boy Scouts — and he was nine years older than the Boy Scouts of America. (He still is!)

He's a Silver Beaver and a Wood Badger, which means he holds the Silver Beaver award to Scouters, and wears the two "Wood Badge" beads of Lord Baden-Powell's Troop 1, Boy Scouts of Gilwell, England.

Bane Shafer at 77 is one of the active Scouters who help boys be Boy Scouts in St. Albans and vicinity — the Pioneer District of Buckskin Council. He's an assistant district commissioner, is chairman of the committee of Troop 146 at St. Andrews Methodist Church, and he was on the staff of the national jamboree in 1973.

BANE SHAFER

Reminiscing about his early days as a Boy Scout, Bane grinned and said,

"I made second-class Scout. I think that was about as high a rank as anybody got in those days, because nobody knew much about the advancement program then, it was too new.

"But we did a lot of Boy Scouting. Oh, my! We went places and did things.

"I remember that once I was in charge of the whole group. I was supposed to be a patrol leader, but I was the leader for the troop on this trip.

"It was in Richlands, Virginia, where I grew up. We got our stuff together for a week-long trip, and we caught a logging train to Durand and then went on out on the Dismal River and camped for a week, and fished and had a real good time!"

Born in Coeburn, Va. near Richlands, he stayed in the Scouts there for "two or three years" he reckoned, and then went to work, and Scouting was a thing of the past for a few years.

He graduated from the University of Virginia, and taught school for severla years, after having worked as a soda-jerk, store clerk and a lot of selling jobs to help pay his way along.

Bane got back in Scouting in 1928 for a year or two when he served as Scoutmaster of a troop in Coeburn, but business transferred him so he dropped out again.

He was married in 1933 to a Coeburn schoolteacher, Ruth Trevorrow, and they have a son and a daughter, Philip of Indiana and Carolyn Shafer of Michigan. Both are graudates of St. Albans High School.

He worked "in and around coal mines" for 25 years, 10 of them underground, he said. He came to West Virginia in 1940 as an engineering expediter at the old Carnegie Steel Co. at the Naval Ordnance plant.

In 1947 he was supervisor of Mingo County Trade School, and in his lifetime he's had a lot of jobs in selling, and some in building materials.

In 1950 when "Uncle Bill" Graham moved to New Jersey, Troop 146 was left without a troop committeeman, and the Scoutmaster, Bill Wyatt, asked Bane to fill in.

Since then he's put in a lot of hours as a Scouter, and still does. In 1975 he and Ruth went to the World Jamboree, 'Nordjam" in Norway — but that's not the extend of their traveling.

Together they've toured Europe several times, have been to Egypt and the Holy Land, England and Scandinavia.

He's one of the grand old men of Scouting, one of those who paved the way for today's boys to enjoy the things he did, when scouting was so new that nobody knew much about it.

Gassaway Doctor Finds Scouting Good Medicine for Young People

By Skip Johnson
Staff Writer

GASSAWAY – Dr. George Hoylman, a Gassaway physician, will be leading a group of Braxton County Boy Scouts on a wilderness canoe trip this summer for the 13th straight year.

The party of 16, including 12 Scouts and four adult leaders, will canoe, camp and fish for nine days and nights in the Boundary Waters Canoe Area in Minnesota and Ontario.

The trip is considered a reward for youths who have done well in Scout work in their own troops and in county camporees. Among the attractions of the Boundary Waters is its excellent fishing for northerns, walleyes and bass. Last year, one of the Scouts caught a 34-pound northern that flopped back into the water after it was weighed on a small pair of fisherman's scales.

DR. HOYLMAN, district Scout chairman for Braxton County, originated the trip after a family outing to the same area. Some of the Scouts who have made the canoe outing have gone back a second time as adult leaders.

The journey starts and ends at Ely, Minn., and includes 50 miles of paddling and 30 miles of portaging.

Over the years, 240 boys and leaders have taken the trip.

"I believe in Scouting and its principles," said Dr. Hoylman, who became a Scout at age 11 and has remained active in scouting. "I believe in the Scout law and oath. I think it's one of the most important things a person can do outside of home, church and school.

"Somebody in the community has to promote Scouting, and it happens to be me here."

He has received most of the adult awards available, including the Silver Beaver in 1956 for outstanding contribution to boyhood.

"Dr. Hoylman has put a lot of time and money into Scouting," said Jimmie Albright of Frametown, a scoutmaster. "He's there at every camporee. Kids like him and show a lot of respect for him."

In addition to the wilderness canoe trip, Dr. Hoylman hosts a winter camp for Braxton County Scouts each year at his camp on Birch River, and makes his camp available to individual troops for outings.

He originated a week-long county-wide Scout camp last year at the Braxton County 4-H Camp, and will head it again this year.

Dr. Hoylman also served as director of the first Christian Youth Retreat held at the 4-H Camp last weekend.

A NATIVE of Coalton, Randolph County, Dr. Hoylman is a graduate of West Virginia Wesleyan College, West Virginia University Medical School and the Medical College of Virginia at Richmond.

He taught school in Logan County for five years while waiting to get into medical school, and during that time became a scoutmaster.

After serving his medical internship at Charleston General Hospital, he came to Gassaway in 1950 and has been here ever since.

His wife, Alta, is a former president of the West Virginia Federation of Women's Clubs. The Hoylmans have two daughters, including Mrs. William Cunningham of Midland, Mich., and Mrs. M.B. Ayoubi of Charleston. Mrs. Ayoubi and her husband are both doctors.

The Charleston Gazette
June 14, 1978

BOB WILSON

ALICE AND JIM POINDEXTER ARE SHOWN IN THIS PHOTO FROM 1998.

CHARLES C. ALBERT

BLAIR MCNEEL WAS THE FIRST CARETAKER AT BUCKSKIN SCOUT RESERVATION. HE IS SHOWN HERE IN JULY 1979.

'Young' Legend Aiding Scouts

By LYNN WITHROW
Of The Daily Mail Staff

DILLEY'S MILL—Blair McNeel stood by the Trading Post at the Buckskin Council Boy Scout Camp and looked over the grassy slopes and Sam Hill Lake to the woods beyond.

"Sixteen years ago, this was dust and dirt and rocks and weeds and crabapple sprouts," he said. "It looked like an Indian reservation."

McNeel has watched—and helped—the 2,800-acre Pocahontas County site grow from a wilderness to a well-cared for Boy Scout camp.

Around the camp, he's something of a legend. Everyone—even the campers—call him by his first name and know stories of his exploits.

McNeel will tell you he'll be 80 years old on Oct. 24.

"He was 72 about 12 years ago," camp program director J. Brabban laughed. "We figure he's somewhere between 79 and 85."

"Don't tell," McNeel said of his age. "I might get me a wife yet." He is a bachelor.

A native of the Hillsboro area, McNeel started working at the camp when it opened 16 years ago.

"I do all I can to help the scouts," he said. "I cut bush where the water (line) is at."

An "oldster" in age, McNeel is a youngster when it comes to being a Boy Scout. He's only been a Scout for 10 years, though he's worked longer at the camp. He wouldn't have joined then, McNeel said, but he was talked into it.

Some of the land for the camp was donated by individuals while other acreage was purchased by the Scouts from the Thorny Creek Sportsmen's Assn. There was an unofficial understanding that McNeel would always be cared for. He lives with the camp ranger and during the summer eats with the Scouts in the dining hall.

"I believe he helped put the water system in," Brabban said. "He's amazing. He'll go out in the woods, come up to a tree, take 10 steps to the right, a few more in another direction and pick up a rock. Under it is one of the water valves. He knows where they all are."

Area man looks back on decades of Scouting

Sandy On Sunday
Sandy Wells

IN 1919, Boy Scout Troop 5 at First Presbyterian Church gave the Buckskin Council its first Eagle Scouts — Joe Hill and Dudley Morrison. The troop committee included 55-year-old John L. Dickinson of the Kanawha Valley Bank.

Troop 5 formed in 1914. The original roster of 24 boys included some familiar names — Lewis Cablish, Frank Field, Joseph Gainer, William Britt, Cabell Davis.

Ninety years and 192 Eagle Scouts later, First Presby's inveterate Troop 5 is still going strong. "The Scouts started in Charleston with Troop 1, but we're the only troop that's been continuously active for 90 years," said Scoutmaster Bob Skinner. "It's a fabulous record."

Skinner has racked up a commendable record himself. The troop's Scoutmaster for 20 years, its assistant Scoutmaster for 10 years before that, and Scoutmaster for Troop 13 at Bream Church for nearly 10 years before that, he still meets with the troop on Wednesday evenings in the church recreation building.

He shrugs off his continued involvement. "I've got a bunch of young fathers down here now, and they're carrying the ball," he said in a booming voice that belies his age. "I'm ex-officio. They let me come to the meetings on Wednesday nights."

Speaking of age, don't ask. "That's not pertinent," he said. "Let's just say I'll be too crippled to walk if I'm around when they celebrate their 100th."

He started with Troop 13 in 1952 and started assisting with Troop 5 in 1974. "I wasn't a Scout myself," he said, "but I always enjoyed outdoor activities, and I thought everybody ought to devote some time to civic endeavors."

Fifty-one Scouts earned their Eagle badges in his 20-year tenure as Scoutmaster. The list includes his two sons. "I made sure of that, sometimes with a stick or a baseball bat."

In a small, crowded Scout office in the basement of the church activities building, a large wood plaque preserves the names of every Eagle from Troop 5. You'd recognize the names. Ellsworth Clark in '35, Sam Flournoy in '39, Otis and Robert O'Connor in '51, Frank Taylor in '53, Herchiel Sims in '54, Bill Marshall in '57, Robert Smallridge in '59, Chris Smith in '63, John Mitchell in '71.

Scouting stuff covers the walls — framed merit badges, rope knots, scads of plaques, the 1914 charter, a paddle commemorating first place in a 1977 water carnival, a mounted ski pole signifying a certain Scout's klutzy performance on the slopes and, Skinner's favorite, a commode seat award.

"That was an award for the boys who had the dirtiest tent. You can see by the picture that it looks like a hurricane hit it. They were really sloppy boys, so someone gave them the commode bowl award."

CHIP ELLIS/Sunday Gazette-Mail

Still strong in Scouting like the 90-year-old Troop 5 he leads at First Presbyterian Church, venerable Scoutmaster Bob Skinner reminisces in an office brimming with Boy Scout memorabilia.

A gallery of troop photos dominates one wall. A picture taken on Valentine's Day 1955 included Andy Alexander, Bill Marshall, Richie Ireland, Jack Blair, Lyle Sattes, Lang Palmer, Doug McMillan and John Cook. Pictured in 1946 are Echols Hansbarger, Sam Hill, Jim Valentine, Eugene Stump and Charlie Love. Anybody know those guys?

Starting in the late 1950s, Skinner said, membership swelled to more than 100 boys, then gradually dropped into the 40s, 30s and 20s. Today, he leads a class of 28, down from his high of 51 in 1989.

"You've probably heard of Jim Thomas. He was a Scoutmaster when we had the big troops. The troops got so big and unruly that they had to split them into two groups and they met on different nights.

"Now there are so many other things for them to do. Even little kids play soccer. When I first started, the only thing that was a conflict was baseball."

He discovered just how busy his boys were when he tried to change the meeting night. "The church wanted us to change our Scout night and it was a disaster. A lot of the boys in this troop are plugged into something every night. They have Wednesday plugged in for Scouting."

The boys are too busy to remember to wear their uniform shirts to meetings, he said. That explains the rack of Scout shirts in the middle of the office. "One of the parents suggested leaving the shirts here."

"Now there are so many other things for them to do. Even little kids play soccer. When I first started, the only thing that was a conflict was baseball."

Bob Skinner

Ever the recruiter, Skinner asked to include the requirements for Scouting: "They have to be 11 or finish the fifth grade and be 10. And they can be a Boy Scout until they're 18."

Calling himself "more of an administrator now than anything else," Skinner said he leaves the outings to younger helpers.

"There's Charlie Wright's picture in 1962," he said, pointing out the Charleston dentist. "He was senior patrol leader. That means he was the top boy in the troop. He's an adult leader now. He's in charge of the canoe troop every summer and usually helps with the ski trip."

Wright started working with Skinner and the First Presby troop in 1983. He appreciates the venerable Scoutmaster's commitment. "I think Bob is an ideal example of the spirit of Boy Scouting," Wright said. "I admire and respect him as much as any man I know."

To contact staff writer Sandy Wells, call 348-5173 or e-mail sandyw@wvgazette.com.

October 3, 2004, Sunday Gazette-Mail

Buckskin Council office staff at publication of this book, left to right, Becky Hustead, Debbie Slack, Angie Moses, Melissa Darnell and Kelly Thaxton.